Business Theft and Fraud

Detection and Prevention

Business Theft and Fraud

Detection and Prevention

James R. Youngblood

CRC Press
Taylor & Francis Group
Boca Raton London New York

CRC Press is an imprint of the
Taylor & Francis Group, an **informa** business

CRC Press
Taylor & Francis Group
6000 Broken Sound Parkway NW, Suite 300
Boca Raton, FL 33487-2742

Printed on acid-free paper
Version Date: 20160226

International Standard Book Number-13: 978-1-4987-4243-6 (Paperback)

Library of Congress Cataloging-in-Publication Data

Names: Youngblood, James, 1960- author.
Title: Business theft and fraud : detection and prevention / James R. Youngblood.
Description: Boca Raton : Taylor & Francis, 2016. | Includes bibliographical references and index.
Identifiers: LCCN 2016005420 | ISBN 9781498742436 (alk. paper)
Subjects: LCSH: Employee theft. | Employee crimes--Prevention. | Fraud. | Fraud--Prevention. | Identity theft. | Computer crimes.
Classification: LCC HF5549.5.E43 Y68 2016 | DDC 658.4/73--dc23
LC record available at http://lccn.loc.gov/2016005420

Visit the Taylor & Francis Web site at
http://www.taylorandfrancis.com

and the CRC Press Web site at
http://www.crcpress.com

This book is dedicated to my mother,
Joan Kathryn Youngblood,
July 22, 1940–September 2, 2009

I owe everything I have ever achieved to this wonderful woman.

Contents

Foreword

Fraud occurs in every business. It does not discriminate by size, industry, geography, or any other factor. Since recorded time, people and money have always been a combustible mixture. Some people have a true need of some kind and believe that money will solve their problems, so they turn to fraud as a means of relief. Others are just greedy—whatever they have is not enough, and they will do anything to obtain wealth. If they cannot earn it honestly, they will steal it from those who did.

I've been in the fraud business for over 30 years. My first job out of law school was with a small firm that handled consumer fraud and deceptive trade practices claims. I absolutely loved it. I did not love the hassles of navigating the legal system and fighting with the opposing attorneys, but I loved the fact that we were fighting against businesses and individuals who sought to enrich themselves at the expense of others. That desire led me to take a position with the Association of Certified Fraud Examiners (ACFE) in 1995. It was at that point that my fraud horizon expanded, and the view was not pretty.

As I began writing, researching, and talking to our members about fraud, it became abundantly clear just how big the problem is. In fact, the ACFE's research suggests that organizations lose 5% of revenues each year to fraud. If applied to the estimated gross world product, this means that in excess of $3.5 trillion is lost to fraud each year. The bottom line is that if organizations are not fighting fraud, they are definitely losing money.

The problem with fighting fraud is that there are so many different types: internal frauds, external frauds, cyber attacks … and the list goes on. Indeed, you will see the list in the table of contents.

Although it seems grim, it is not. Every business has to make a choice: either accept the losses and plan for them in the budget or fight back.

The ACFE and members like Rick Youngblood are fighting back. I have known Rick for more than 15 years. He was an early member of the ACFE, and he understood immediately that you have to fight fraud with both barrels. First, you have to design controls to prevent fraud as much as possible on the front end. And, second, you have to be constantly on the alert. Potential fraudsters have to know that if they try to steal, they will be caught and brought to justice. Controls are necessary, but they alone cannot do the job. Fraudsters look at controls as something to get around. Someone has to be on patrol looking for signs of fraud.

John D. Gill, CFE
Vice President—Education
Association of Certified Fraud Examiners
Austin, Texas

Author

James "Rick" Youngblood, CPP, CFE, has extensive experience in the fields of loss prevention, security investigations, law enforcement, and fraud investigation. Rick has authored numerous articles on the topics of fraud/security/loss prevention for many national publications. He has also provided fraud/security/loss prevention presentations for many national and international organizations, including ASIS International (formerly the American Society for Industrial Security), the Association of Certified Fraud Examiners, the Institute for International Research, etc. Rick is a current and long-time member of the ASIS Crime and Loss Prevention Council and is also a member of the ASIS Investigations Council.

Rick is the author of the book, *A Comprehensive Look at Fraud Identification and Prevention*, published by CRC Press in April 2015 (ISBN 978-1-4987-0032-0). He is coauthor of the book, *Security for Colleges and Universities*, published in 2014 by ASIS International (ISBN 978-1-934904-57-2), to which he contributed the chapter, "Risk Management for Campus Administrators." Rick also coauthored a book to be published by ASIS International in 2016: *Security in 2025*.

Rick currently holds a master's degree in financial management and a bachelor's degree in criminal justice/business management. He is a retired chief warrant officer from the US Army and spent over 21 years on active duty and in the National Guard as a CID special agent. Rick currently resides in Phoenix, Arizona, with his wife, Rosanne.

1

INTERNAL EMPLOYEE THEFT AND FRAUD (NONRETAIL ORGANIZATIONS)

Fraud and theft can strike an unsuspecting organization through all avenues. The perpetrator can

- Enter through the front door as a visitor, employee, vendor, customer, etc.
- Enter through the back door, after hours and uninvited
- Gain access to the business computer system and networks through some type of deception
- Access the legitimate company website for the purpose of committing various types of fraud

No matter what avenue is used to gain access to the business, the intent of the perpetrator is to commit various types of theft and fraud. The end goal of those committing business-related theft and fraud is to

- Perpetrate employee theft
- Embezzle
- Commit vendor-related fraud
- Engage in cyber fraud
- Underreport sales

- Conduct new account bank fraud
- Engage in employee sweethearting (when the employee is working with a customer, accomplice, or friend to provide merchandise at a lower than advertised price)

These types of business-related theft and fraud activities start a discussion on the many avenues used to victimize an organization.

The purpose of this text is to provide a detailed discussion on the numerous types of theft and fraud that organizations face, both internally and externally.

Chapter 1

What Type of Business Is More Susceptible to Internal Theft/Fraud?

Introduction

According to the 2015 Hiscox Embezzlement Watchlist:

- Of employee theft cases, 72% took place in a small business operation.
- The organizations victimized had fewer than 500 employees.
- Four out of every five victimized organizations had fewer than 100 employees.
- More than half of the victimized businesses had fewer than 25 employees.
- Over 40% of the losses took place in the finance/accounting section of the business operation.
- Women accounted for 78% of the incidents.
- Men accounted for 22% of the incidents.
- Businesses offering financial services, such as banks, credit unions, insurance companies, etc., are at a higher risk for internal theft/fraud.
- Other affected business entities are unions, municipal offices, nonprofit organizations, etc. [1].

Based on the study information referenced, small businesses bear the brunt of overall theft/fraud losses. These theft/fraud losses pertain to incidents that take place from an internal perspective.

For varying reasons, business employees and retail store associates choose to commit their theft and fraud activities in small business operations.

Based on these statistics, the following questions can be asked:

- Do small business operations decide not to prosecute internal theft offenders?
- Is an employee who steals from a large organization more likely to be prosecuted?
- Are security and loss prevention procedures more lax in small business operations?
- Is a majority of a large business's operating budget devoted to preventing internal employee theft and fraud?
- Do small business activities have to rely on individual employees performing multiple job functions?
- Do large business activities have the operating budget necessary to prevent employees from performing cross-functional job duties?
- Is it easier to get hired by a small versus a large business operation?
- Why do many small business employees not go through a detailed new-hire background check?
- Do most employees who steal from their employer commit the act immediately after being hired?
- Who created the opportunity for the theft/fraud—the employer or the employee?

In order to provide a more detailed understanding on the issues related to employee theft/fraud, answers to these questions are discussed in the following sections.

Do Small Business Operations Decide Not to Prosecute Internal Theft Offenders?

Employees who have been caught stealing from their small business employer have been successfully prosecuted for their crimes. On the other hand some small business employees who committed internal theft/fraud and were simply terminated for their offenses.

The rationale behind prosecuting or not prosecuting employees who steal is up to the individual business, the offense committed by the employee, the type and amount of the loss, and the available evidence.

In order to prosecute a case of theft/fraud, the victimized organization has to gather the available evidence and present the case to law enforcement. It is then up to the law enforcement agency and the prosecutor to determine if sufficient evidence exists to bring a case to trial.

Restitution also comes into play for business operations that suffer a monetary loss due to employee theft/fraud. Many businesses are satisfied with the responsible employee making full restitution and resigning. The business is made whole, the victimized organization learns a valuable lesson, and the offending employee is no longer employed.

In addition to accepting restitution being paid by the offender to avoid prosecution, community embarrassment could be another reason for a business choosing not to prosecute. The victimized business could be a single-owner operation that is very active and popular within the local community. The offender could be a long term employee with the organization, who is also well known and respected within the local community. In order to save face for one or both parties, a business decision could be made to simply forget the incident took place. The business accepts the loss and continues about its daily operations, while the offender agrees to retire or pursue other career opportunities.

Is an Employee Who Steals from a Large Organization More Likely to Be Prosecuted?

It is possible for an employee of a large organization to be prosecuted for a theft/fraud violation by his or her employer. As previously discussed with small business losses, a decision to prosecute comes down to the available evidence, the type and amount of the monetary loss, and the willingness of law enforcement and the prosecutor to accept the case. Large organizations could also be satisfied with receiving full restitution from the offending employee.

From an evidentiary standpoint, many large business operations could be in a better position to have stronger evidence in the case of prosecuting the offender. Due to budgetary constrictions, a small mom and pop retail operation might have one or two additional employees who work the location. Based on customer flow and daily sales amounts, only one employee works per each eight-hour shift. Many small businesses choose to hire associates on a part-time basis and their staffing requirements have one employee working the morning shift and another for the evening shift.

In addition to having a budget that only covers one associate per working shift, the small business might not have installed proper surveillance cameras within the retail location. Knowing that day-to-day activities are not monitored by the store owners, a dishonest associate could choose to remove items from the store without making proper payment.

A smart owner, with proper inventory control procedures, could recognize items being removed from the store inventory without proper payment being recorded. The owner could also deduce that the specific item losses are occurring during a certain employee's shift. What he or she cannot prove is that the employee in question was the person who removed the items from the store without paying. This leaves a crime, a suspect, and no physical evidence.

At best the owner can question the associate in hopes of a confession. If no confession is provided, the option exists to terminate the questionable associate.

An area of caution the store owner needs to consider is that the items were removed due to customer shoplifting. Based on the state of operation, varying laws exist on proper termination and the related causes. Even though the merchandise losses can be attributed to the shifts worked by a certain employee, there is also a need for compelling evidence. Without witness or video verification, the owner is left with a strong case of suspicion. The employee is a strong suspect for internal theft or one that is lax in monitoring customer activity. The suspect employee could also be involved in a "sweethearting" operation with one or more friends [2].

Looking at the previously discussed scenario, a much larger business operation would not be in the position of having a single associate work an entire retail shift alone. The business would most likely employ the most up-to-date video monitoring and point-of-sale equipment. In the case of an internally created inventory shrink, the business would be more likely to develop sufficient evidence to prove a certain associate was removing merchandise from the retail location.

Another area that requires consideration as a reason not to prosecute dishonest associates falls under the category of intelligence gathering. For certain theft/fraud losses that took place as the result of a complex internal operation, a business might consider allowing the offender to avoid prosecution if he or she agreed to provide a detailed analysis as to how he or she was successful.

In order to provide a more detailed understanding as to why an organization that suffered a large monetary theft/fraud loss could forgive the loss for the purpose of intelligence gathering, it is important to understand the concept of opportunity.

Theft/fraud losses take place through what is referred to as opportunity. The question to be asked is who creates the opportunity—the employee or the business?

1. Due to internal operating procedures within an organization, an opportunity for theft/fraud could be created on the part of the business. A simple example could be a loading dock associate who is charged with receiving merchandise. This sole employee meets the delivery truck, unloads the product, conducts an individual count of the items delivered, and updates the internal inventory system. A simple inventory control system like the one discussed creates an open opportunity for theft. An associate hired to work this position could enter the job with good intentions. Over time and recognizing there is no oversight of what is being delivered, item delivery verification, or the number of items entered into the inventory system, this associate could recognize an opportunity to commit theft. A loading dock associate with single control and no oversight could recognize the theft opportunity created

by the organization. These types of opportunities created by unsuspecting organizations could exist in perpetuity with no internal losses taking place. These types of opportunities also work to make somewhat honest employees consider the alternatives—basically creating an opportunity so great that it leads to theft/fraud losses.

2. From an employee perspective, the opportunity for theft/fraud could be created by the associate. These types of opportunities are work-related situations, where associates looking to commit theft/fraud capitalize on somewhat lax internal operating procedures. Another simple example could be an employee working in a retail operation who volunteers to take out the trash at closing time. Instead of using clear trash bags, the associate insists on using black trash bags and has no problem with taking the trash to the dumpster unaccompanied. With many associates viewing trash duty as a demeaning procedure, anyone volunteering for the duty is quickly awarded the job. Recognizing the opportunity to commit theft, the employee is able to place store items in the trash bags and remove these items undetected from the location. This employee has used weak store operating procedures and turned this practice into an opportunity for theft. The weak store operating procedures reside in management not requiring all trash bags to be clear and the need to rotate employees tasked with removing trash from the location.

No matter how the theft/fraud loss took place, it is important for a business operation to develop an understanding of opportunity. Answer the question of who created the opportunity. Did the business develop operating procedures that allowed a somewhat honest associate to steal or did a newly hired person use lax operating procedures to create an opportunity to commit theft/fraud?

In order to create a working environment that is less susceptible to theft/fraud losses, an organization could choose to forgive an employee's transgressions for information. The information desired from the employee is the factor related to the decision to commit the crime. The questions to be asked are as follows:

- Did the individual seek employment in order to commit acts of theft/fraud? If so, the organization needs to conduct a complete analysis of its new-hire verification process.
- Did the employee act on an opportunity to commit theft/fraud based on internal staffing and operating procedures?
- If the opportunity was not created by the organization, would the employee have even considered looking into committing acts of theft/fraud?
- Did the employee manipulate systems or operating procedures in order to commit the act?

- Did the employee work with accomplices inside or outside the organization?
- Has the employee had previous success over a number of years? If so, obtain an explanation of the incidents, procedures used to commit the acts, monetary gain, etc.
- Ask the offending employee to provide an analysis of the organization's operating procedures and where he or she sees an opportunity for theft/fraud.

These questions are provided to give a starting point in the intelligence-gathering process. The purpose of trading nonprosecution for intelligence is based on gathering quality information in an effort to create stronger barriers in the fight against theft/fraud.

Another reason to consider the offer of freedom for information revolves around the idea that the offending individual was caught on this one occasion. If the individual has been working for the organization for a number of years, he or she could have been committing acts of theft/fraud on more than one occasion. If this is the case, the employee was successful in committing various acts of theft/fraud and was able to cover up the crimes. In order to create a strong theft/fraud prevention policy, the organization needs to gather as much intelligence as possible.

Are Security and Loss Prevention Procedures More Lax in Small Business Operations?

One of the main issues affecting small business operations in the theft/fraud prevention arena comes down to budgeting, staffing, technology, employing a professional security/loss prevention staff, etc. As discussed in the 2015 Hiscox Embezzlement Watchlist, over half of the victimized businesses had fewer than 25 employees.

Based on the business type and cash flow, it is quite possible business decisions are made on how best management and the owners think assets should be allocated. With many small business operations, expenditures are based on tight margins. Many small business owners and managers do not have the luxury of operating with large cash reserve accounts and a somewhat guaranteed weekly/monthly cash flow. As a result of operating within tighter margins, the following business decisions have to be made:

- Should assets be focused on growth and expansion?
- Should assets be focused on maintaining a competitive inventory?
- Can our administrative functions be accomplished with the minimal number of employees?

- Instead of hiring new associates, is it acceptable to increase administrative duties with the staff on hand?
- Why expend the costs associated with an increased security posture that does not produce an immediate and noticeable benefit?

Countless small business operations answer the aforementioned questions and make decisions based on growth, looking at the assets on hand and making decisions based on what is referred to as a "cost/benefit analysis."

In simple terms, a cost/benefit analysis answers the question, "What is the expected benefit versus the initial expenditure?" To answer the question, many small businesses look at their operation through the lens of noticeable benefit:

- In order to increase sales, a smart decision would be to divert more assets into marketing and advertising. (When orchestrated properly, the business will see a noticeable benefit.)
- In order to divert more assets toward marketing and advertising, should we hold off on hiring a new associate to work on accounts payable? Why not have employee A, who currently works in Accounts Receivable, handle the additional accounts payable duties? (As long as the employee assuming dual duties operates above board, the decision to divert the saved assets toward marketing and advertising will show a noticeable benefit.)
- Should the business make a large capital expenditure on an in-house video monitoring and surveillance system, hire one or more security/loss prevention personnel, and begin an access control program? (A sound decision, but one that does not show a noticeable benefit.)

The previously discussed question-and-answer game can be used to discuss numerous business-related scenarios. With many of these scenarios, a business decision is made that benefits the organization in the short and hopefully the long term. Unfortunately, many of these business-related decisions also work to increase the risk factor:

- As long as employee A assumes the additional duties and works in a professional manner, the risk pays off.
- As long as the small business is not struck with a large loss due to an internal or external theft/fraud incident, the risk of not beefing up the security/loss prevention program pays off.

With many small business operations, the owners and managers place a minimal effort on individual and financial assets targeted toward a security/loss prevention program. Hopefully, the minimal effort generated works to keep losses under control, while the business grows. Unfortunately, many small business operations go under by basing their security/loss prevention program on hope.

Is a Majority of a Large Business's Operating Budget Devoted to Preventing Internal Employee Theft and Fraud?

With many large organizations, they have the cash flow necessary in order to staff a professional security/loss prevention department. They also have the assets necessary for

- Implementing and operating location access control systems
- Installing and operating a video surveillance system
- Developing and operating an employee theft/fraud training program
- Installing and operating detailed antishoplifting programs
- Conducting detailed new-hire screening programs
- Initiating employee-based theft/fraud prevention reward programs
- Ensuring staffing is available to avoid one associate being responsible for dual functions (A risky type of dual function is having one employee conducting accounts receivable and accounts payable duties.)
- Ensuring that security/loss prevention staff join professional (security/fraud) organizations (Membership in these professional organizations ensures they are educated on the most up-to-date trends and employ cutting-edge security/surveillance programs.)

Large business operations have the luxury of being able to operate professional security/loss prevention departments, without having to make critical budgeting decisions. For many business operations, the critical budgeting decisions come down to a yes or no decision: yes to create a security/loss prevention department, or no in order to focus on growth. Successful larger businesses conduct a proper budget analysis and devote necessary department funding where needed. This is to include initiating and maintaining a security/loss prevention department.

Even though these large business operations have professional security/loss prevention departments, they are not immune to becoming a theft/fraud victim.

Do Small Business Activities Have to Rely on Individual Employees Performing Multiple Job Functions?

For many small business operations, the answer is yes. These employee staffing decisions are based on budgeting restrictions, ignorance of the potential ramifications, and a trust based on longevity:

- With many small business operations, employees are required to wear many hats as part of their daily job functions. One day the operations manager could be tasked with an additional duty of overseeing the security/loss prevention functions of the business. With an operation focused on growth, a large percentage of this individual's time will be concentrated on the business operations aspect. Along with management wearing many hats in a small business, many employees are also tasked with assuming multiple job functions. A classic example where many small businesses create a theft/fraud opportunity is in the receiving end of the operation. One employee is responsible for receiving all new merchandise deliveries, conducting the item counts, and updating the inventory control system. Without a separation of duties and a second set of eyes ensuring the integrity of product deliveries and item counts, the organization has laid the groundwork for fraud-related losses.

- Many small business operations allow associates to wear many "hats" as part of their daily activities. They also allow associates to perform dual accounting type duties. With a large majority of these decisions, they are made in good faith. The decision makers are looking out for the long-term growth of the business, by saving additional assets on employee staffing. Although the intentions are good, they are also based on a level of ignorance as to the potential for theft/fraud to take place.
- With many small business operations, they are staffed with associates with a long record of tenure. The associates enjoy working for the small business and the owners develop a level of trust in these long-term employees. Over time some of these devoted associates are trusted with performing multiple job functions. With a majority of these decisions, the employees perform their duties without incident. As discussed previously with opportunity, the small business is creating a potential opportunity for theft/fraud. Print and televised news stories from across the country tell the tale of a small business or local nonprofit organization that was a victim of employee embezzlement. With a majority of these stories the perpetrator was a long-term and trusted employee.

Do Large Business Activities Have the Operating Budget Necessary to Prevent Employees from Performing Cross-Functional Job Duties?

The answer to this question is yes. Many large business operations establish oversight as part of their daily functions. Staffing and verification policies are created in an effort to prevent theft-/fraud-related losses:

- These operations establish a two-person rule policy for all accounts payable decisions. Prior to payments being made, the decision has to be approved by more than one associate. Once approved, a third employee makes the payment.
- These operations also establish job rotation policies. With a job rotation policy, employees move from one position to another. Employee A could work six months in accounts payable, then move for six months to vendor

relationships, etc. The purpose is that, with a job rotation policy, associates are not allowed to get comfortable in any one position where they can work to develop opportunities for theft/fraud.

- These operations also establish mandatory vacation policies. Associates are required to take a mandatory two week vacation every year. In order to keep a current theft/fraud scam afloat, it requires the offending associate to oversee the operation on a daily basis. The theory is that, with the associate being out of the position for two weeks, the theft/fraud scheme will be discovered.

Is It Easier to Get Hired by a Small versus a Large Business Operation?

Each and every business operation has its own specific hiring standards. The benefit for larger business operations is the budget availability for new-employee background verifications. The smaller business operations are constricted by the amount of assets that can be allocated to conducting new-hire verifications.

Additionally, larger business operations have the luxury of using industry-specific headhunters during their candidate searches. By using a headhunter operation, their new-hire pool of applicants come somewhat vetted—vetting as it relates to who knows whom in a specific industry. The actual headhunter might not have an initial personal relationship with the referred candidate, but somewhere along the way one or more referrals took place. These referrals speak to the candidate's qualifications, as confirmed by one or more trusted sources.

A major issue with the hiring of new associates in this day and age is the inability of former employers to provide a detailed account as to why the applicant left their organization. Due to litigation concerns, prior employers typically confirm the position held, dates of employment, and eligibility for rehire. What they do not provide is the down and dirty details of the applicants work history and the reason for separation, basically creating a window of uncertainty on the applicant's time with the previous employer. With this level of uncertainty, it becomes necessary to conduct detailed new-hire background verifications. (Chapter 2 provides a more detailed discussion on the new-hire verification process.)

Why Do Many Small Business Employees Not Go through a Detailed New-Hire Background Check?

As previously discussed with small business operations, many decisions are based on budgetary restrictions. With the smaller business operations, the budget is not available to conduct national candidate searches or employ the use of headhunters.

With the larger businesses they employ numerous associates that can be used to cover the duties of open positions, while an extended candidate search is conducted.

On the other hand, small businesses usually have to make hiring decisions much faster. With a need to immediately fill an open position, the small business managers might choose to conduct a basic new-hire candidate verification.

Additionally, many small business operations do not have the budget allocations to fully advertise their open positions. Many small businesses advertise open positions in their local community newspapers and by using "Help Wanted" window signs. Many times they are at the mercy of anyone who walks in off the street and applies for the open position.

Do Most Employees Who Steal from Their Employer Commit the Act Immediately after Being Hired?

There are individuals who look for positions for the purpose of committing theft/fraud. Their only goal is to use the position to collect the first paycheck or to conduct other types of illegal activity. (Individuals getting hired in order to steal is discussed in detail in Chapter 19.)

There are other individuals who accept a new position with good intentions and can work for years without incident. As previously discussed, many seasoned employees who eventually commit theft/fraud act on an opportunity created by the employer. These opportunities vary per the employer, but work to create a thought process in the mind of the employee. The thought process is, "I can use this opportunity to conceal my theft-/fraud-related activities."

An ideal example would be a long-term bookkeeper with a nonprofit organization. For years this associate was responsible for processing incoming payments to the business. Based on longevity and commitment to the organization, the associate is given the additional responsibility of the bank account reconciliation. Now the employee oversees the incoming payments to the business and reporting the financial status to the powers that be. This creates an opportunity for theft/fraud.

Some business operations still provide their employees with an actual paycheck. This check in the hands of a person looking to commit fraud is a golden ticket. The check can be used to make other counterfeit checks on the account of the business in question. All the counterfeiter needs is the business account and routing numbers at the bottom of the check. After creating a number of counterfeit checks, these items are then cashed leaving the targeted business with a depleted bank account.

Who Created the Opportunity for the Theft/Fraud—The Employer or the Employee?

The answer to the question can be both. Based on the incident and type of loss, the opportunity could have been created by the employer or a situation acted upon by the employee. In order to create an operation (small business or large) that places barriers in place for theft/fraud, it is necessary to conduct an overall operational analysis that looks for opportunities. This analysis is based on, but not limited to, the following sections.

Developing Intelligence from Talking with Past Offenders

Previous discussion took place on the rationale behind decisions made as it pertains to the prosecution of employees that commit theft/fraud crimes against an organization. Organizations have had success with allowing the offender to walk away from the crime by providing intelligence on the crime committed.

With many individuals who commit acts of theft/fraud against an organization, they are not caught on their first attempt. Many crimes take place over a few months and some successful criminals operate for over a year. As long as they are successful and no one within the organization is aware of their illegal activities, the incidents of theft/fraud will continue.

It is the hope of any sized organization to prevent all theft/fraud activities from taking place. If they cannot prevent all theft/fraud incidents, the goal shifts to detecting the activity early. This will hopefully allow the security/loss prevention personnel to shut down the theft/fraud activity without suffering large losses.

No matter the length of time the organization suffered theft-/fraud-related losses from an offender, it is important to speak with the individual after detection. Hopefully, the offender will provide information on where the opportunity was created so the gaps in operation can be closed. In addition to speaking with the offender about the specific crime, it is also important to ask the individual if he or she has observed other gaps or opportunities within the overall process. Even though the employee acted on opportunity A, he or she could have been contemplating opportunity B.

Based on the amount of the loss to an organization, it might be a tough sell to the owners or management trading freedom for information. Many business owners and managers might be reluctant to forgive a six- or seven-figure loss in trade for theft-/fraud-related intelligence. What all parties need to keep in mind is industry-related theft/fraud loss recovery levels. The offender might have stolen more than $500,000 over an extended period. The point to keep in mind is that, even though the courts order restitution, the offender most likely does not have the means to repay the court-ordered amount. This is especially true if the offender is ordered to serve a prison sentence. Upon release, his or her job prospects are minimal.

If an organization is considering the prospect of trading forgiveness for intelligence, all outcomes need to be considered. Yes there is satisfaction in seeing a stealing former employee receiving a stiff prison sentence. The question to ask is, "Is this satisfaction greater than the information that could be provided that can be used to prevent future and possibly larger losses?"

It all comes down to a cost/benefit analysis.

Develop Intelligence from Current Employees as to How They Would Carry Out Theft-/Fraud-Related Activities

The longer an employee works for a particular business, the greater is his or her understanding of the overall operation. Employees develop an understanding of how departments interact, individual responsibilities, overall procedures, and weaknesses within the system.

While not accusing each and every employee working for an organization of being deceptive, it is quite possible at one time or another they have considered how they could pull off a successful theft/fraud act. For a large majority of business employees, the consideration stays at just that.

As previously discussed there are those employees who look for windows of opportunity and act. Their actions can lead to successful incidents of theft/fraud, which could cause the organization to suffer large monetary losses.

In order to develop the intelligence necessary to prevent future theft/fraud losses, security/loss prevention personnel need to get into the habit of discussing opportunity windows with associates.

In order to have success with this type of intelligence-gathering program, there has to be groundwork constructed. Within many organizations the security/loss prevention departments are viewed in a negative light and the only interaction between them and employees is negative. Just like community policing [3] being successful, security/loss prevention personnel need to devote time creating quality relationships within the organization.

Once the security/loss prevention department is viewed by organizational associates as being part of the team, discussions can take place on secret thoughts. The purpose of having theft-/fraud-related discussions with organizational associates is for them to provide information on where they see opportunities—both opportunities where operating procedures create open windows and opportunities that can be created by employees.

Create Organizational Working Groups That Meet for the Purpose of Discussing Theft-/Fraud-Related Opportunities

In addition to speaking individually with associates within an organization, success has been realized with the creation of theft/fraud working groups. The purpose of these working groups is to bring employees together from all departments within the organization. The goal should also be to have the various departments represented by associates at all levels. This is to include department managers down to the entry-level positions.

Individuals representing their departments should also be rotated. New ideas and information cannot be generated by having the same associate from each department attending the meetings.

Facilitated by one or more members of the security/loss prevention department, the goal of the working groups is to initiate discussion on observed windows of opportunity. Basically encourage associates to discuss ideas on the theory of "if I were a thief." Because they know the inner workings of their individual departments, valuable information can be obtained from associates in order to close windows of opportunity.

Consider Using Fraud Tip Hotlines

Presently there are several loss prevention organizations that offer to set up fraud tip hotlines for a business. The purpose is to offer associates the ability to provide fraud-related information to a third-party resource.

These third party organizations establish individual accounts for their clients and offer the following services:

- Create media for registered organizations to provide to their employees. These media detail the services provided by the fraud tip hotline provider.
- Provide employees the ability to submit an anonymous report either online or telephonically.
- Allow employees the opportunity to provide anonymous tips on fraud issues or incidents of unethical behavior.
- Provide reports to designated members of the client organization.

Instead of using an outside source to provide a fraud tip hotline, an organization can establish one in house. This could be done as a cost saving measure, but caution has to be taken on the results. It is the opinion of this writer that employees would be more open to providing information to a third-party source versus submitting a report in house. Even though the in-house hotline allows the employee to submit reports anonymously, there will always be doubt in the back of many associates' minds.

Business owners and managers have to look at the big picture of theft/fraud prevention when it comes to establishing a fraud tip hotline. The goal has to be based on maximum participation from all associates. This creates a question of, "Will employees be more open to provide information to a third-party vendor versus an in-house hotline?"

As discussed previously, many theft/fraud prevention programs require a detailed cost/benefit analysis. With a fraud tip hotline, will the upfront cost of using a third-party vendor provide a cost savings benefit? To answer this question, decision makers need to ask another question, "What could be the long-term costs of a theft/fraud incident that was not reported, due to employee suspicion of using an in-house hotline?" [4].

Develop Intelligence by Using Security/Loss Prevention Personnel to Conduct Departmental Threat Analyses

In addition to using internal working groups, hotlines, and discussion with associates, security/loss prevention should also conduct its own individual departmental threat analyses by basically spending time in the various company departments to develop a detailed understanding of their operation. The goal is to develop relationships with associates within the various departments and to look for windows of opportunity.

Security/loss prevention personnel need to use the current departmental operating procedures to ensure policies are being followed. Additionally, the current policies need to be reviewed to ensure they are not creating windows of opportunity.

Participation in Professional Security/Loss Prevention Organizations (ASIS, ACFE)

Within the security/loss prevention industry there are several professional organizations on both the national and regional levels. In an effort to stay on top of industry trends it is necessary for security/loss prevention personnel to become active in one or more of these associations.

From a security perspective the most respected national (international) organization is ASIS International. Formerly named the American Society for Industrial Security, the name was simply changed to ASIS International once the organization achieved international status. ASIS International offers members industry-recognized certifications:

- Certified protection professional (CPP)
- Professional certified investigator (PCI)
- Physical security professional (PSP)

Additionally, ASIS International has numerous industry-respected councils ranging from security to financial institutions, education, investigations, loss prevention, etc. Members of the ASIS International councils provide services as subject matter experts for all association members.

ASIS International also provides members with a monthly newsletter. Members of ASIS International can also join a local chapter for interaction with security professionals in a specific city or geographical location.

From a fraud perspective the most respected national (international) organization is the Association of Certified Fraud Examiners (ACFE). ACFE members can receive an industry-recognized title as a certified fraud examiner (CFE).

The ACFE also provides members with numerous educational programs across the country on a yearly basis. ACFE members can also join a local chapter for interaction with fraud professionals in a specific city or geographical location.

Both ASIS and ACFE provide an opportunity for their members to attend annual national conferences. Both associations provide those in attendance with an opportunity to attend industry-related educational classes. Industry-related vendors can also be visited on large vendor floors during the annual conferences.

ASIS and ACFE also hold annual conferences on an international level at locations around the globe [5].

Participate in Tracking Security/Fraud Trends via Private and Government Organizations

In an effort to remain on top of security/loss prevention trends and information, it is necessary for security/loss prevention departments to make a point to visit industry-related websites of private and government organizations:

- The Internet Crime Complaint Center (IC3), in association with the Federal Bureau of Investigations (FBI) and the National White Collar Crime Center, offers periodic industry-specific alerts. Individuals can locate this alert information by visiting https://www.fbi.gov/scams-safety/e-scams
- The Better Business Bureau provides anyone who wishes to sign up with routine e-mail alerts of known and verified fraud trends. In order to receive these alerts individuals can sign up by visiting https://cbbb.wufoo.com/forms/email-sign-up/
- Individuals can visit the websites of the three major credit reporting agencies (Experian, TransUnion, and Equifax) and receive up-to-date information of fraud-related trends

In an effort to protect the assets of any size business, it is necessary for security/loss prevention personnel to remain on top of industry trends and to develop a detailed understanding of the entire business operation. In order to protect the assets of any size organization, it becomes necessary to be proactive rather than reactive. It is an easier process to keep the assets within the organization, rather than chasing them once they have gone out the front door.

Endnotes

1. "Small Businesses Get Hit Hardest by Employee Theft." http://www.securitymagazine.com/articles/86474-small-businesses-get-hit-hardest-by-employee-theft (accessed September 2, 2015).
2. "Sweethearting" takes place in retail establishments where an employee works with someone from outside the organization to steal from the business. A common example would be a bartender serving a friend at the bar. Throughout the night the customer consumes six beverages, but is only charged for a single beverage. To make the endeavor beneficial for both parties, the customer leaves the bartender a very large cash tip.

3. Community policing is a practice where local law enforcement interacts with residents in order to build relationships of trust.
4. Full disclosure: I have no affiliation with any organization offering fraud tip hotline services. The discussion I provided is based on information learned from speaking with industry professionals and everyday employees.
5. Full disclosure: I am a participating member of both ASIS and ACFE and hold the certifications of CPP and CFE. It is my opinion that both of these associations are industry leaders and industry professionals can benefit from membership.

Chapter 2

New-Hire Verification

As discussed in detail in Section III, one of the biggest threats to the retail industry is internal employee theft. In the United States, retailers suffer a higher dollar loss due to employee theft than through customer shoplifting [1].

From a theft/fraud standpoint, nonretail organizations also have a large threat issue that can be attributed to employees. Based on trends within the fraud arena and an increased reliance on technology, organizations are faced with threats that are employee based. All business operations need to be concerned with internal employee embezzlement and technology attacks targeted at all associates.

Cyber fraud is a growing threat to all industries, with a two-pronged focused attack:

- Employees are targeted through unsolicited phishing [2] e-mails for the purpose of gaining access to business-related computer systems. Once unauthorized access is gained to the internal business computer systems the goal of those committing the fraud is to obtain company-related financial information.
- The other goal of those committing the fraud is to gain access to employee and business owner information for the purpose of committing identity theft and business takeover fraud. (Both of these cyber-based threats are discussed in detail in Section V.)

In addition to the cyber threats targeted at various business organizations, companies also face an internal threat from employee theft/fraud. No matter what the employee's position is within the organization, history has shown incidents of theft/fraud at all levels. This includes entry-level associates, seasoned accounting personnel, customer service individuals, management and executives, etc. Based on the opportunities created by the organization or the associate, losses to employee theft/fraud is a multibillion dollar issue.

Along with the threat coming from all employee levels within the organization, no one particular type of business operation is immune. Successful theft/fraud cases have taken place within government operations, telecommunication companies, nonprofit groups, the financial service industry, labor unions, etc. If an operation employs workers and these individuals have access to anything of value, there is a potential for theft/fraud.

No matter the industry, size of the organization, or assets that can be targeted by a dishonest employee, theft/fraud prevention begins with the job applicant. The goal of any new-hire verification program is to make job offers to applicants that

- Possess the skills and expertise listed on resumes and job applications
- Are honest about positions held and the companies they worked for
- Actually hold college degrees that are listed on resumes and job applications
- Do not have a criminal history, other than incidents provided on job applications
- Have not been fired by a previous employer for theft-/fraud-related issues
- Are actually the person they claim to be

Based on the size of the organization and the professional level of applicants being hired, a portion of the verification process comes down to funding. How much of the total asset pie is allocated to new-hire verification?

Many small mom and pop operations with a handful of employees hire based on a personal recommendation from a known source. Others make hiring decisions based on the resume provided and a phone call or two to former employers.

As the size of the business operation increases, hiring managers have more assets at their disposal. They can go beyond making a few verification calls to former employers and use the services of trusted background screening organizations. These screening organizations offer a variety of options and can provide candidate reports based on the needs of the hiring employer. The reports requested are also based on

- Detail desired and cost
- Legal restrictions that vary from state to state

For companies that choose to use the services of one of the many applicant screening organizations, the services provided are many. Of the many services provided, perspective employers can select to

- Have a criminal records check on the federal, state, and local levels
- Have the actual identity of the applicant verified against the social security number provided
- Conduct an investigation into the applicant's work history
- Have the applicant's personal credit history accessed

- Have the applicant's driving records accessed
- Verify any educational information provided by the applicant
- Confirm any certifications the applicant claims to hold
- Have the applicant's references contacted
- Have a drug test administered to the applicant

Hiring operations that choose to use screening organizations can receive a wealth of information on potential new hires. One area that could be lacking from a new-hire screening process is receiving detailed information from former employers. Based on legal actions over the past years, former employers are reluctant to provide detailed information on their former associates. Most former employers simply choose to provide

- Position held
- Dates of employment
- Eligibility for rehire

One option those hiring new employees can use is to have candidates sign some type of employee release form [3]. Candidates signing these types of release forms are giving permission to their former employers to provide information on their detailed work history.

Prior to using an employee release form, organizations should check the legalities within their specific state and get a blessing from their own internal legal department.

Organizations can also choose to use the services of headhunters when conducting a candidate search. Instead of the company conducting the candidate search and initial interviewing process, the headhunting agency takes over this process. Headhunters rely on a known pool of industry professionals and can market open positions to those already working in the specific field.

Organizations using industry headhunters are assessed a fee for the services provided, but gain by having candidates referred that have a work history in the field desired. These candidates are also known directly by individuals working in the headhunter agency or have a known professional reputation in the specific industry.

Once the organization completes a detailed and thorough hiring process, it needs to create an environment of ethical expectations. These ethical expectation issues are discussed in detail in Chapter 3 and are used to close as many theft-/fraud-related windows of opportunity as possible.

Endnotes

1. "US retail Workers Are No. 1 … in Employee Theft." http://fortune.com/2015/01/26/us-retail-worker-theft/ (accessed September 6, 2015).

2. Phishing is to try to obtain financial or other confidential information from Internet users, typically by sending an e-mail that looks as if it is from a legitimate organization, usually a financial institution, but contains a link to a fake website that replicates the real one. http://dictionary.reference.com/browse/phishing?s=t (accessed September 6, 2015).
3. Employee release forms are used by some hiring organizations in order to obtain a detailed account from former employers. An Internet search reveals companies can create company-specific forms that are based on the laws of the state where the business operates.

Chapter 3

Establish Operating Procedures

Introduction

No matter the position held in an organization, there should be specific procedures that detail how associates carry out their duties. Beginning with the new-hire verification process, every company should have specific written details or operating procedures. These operating procedures should be written to detail the exact steps to be taken for hiring new employees. The procedures then carry over to new-employee orientation, which details the steps new associates proceed through prior to starting in their new position.

Included in the new-hire and orientation procedures, each individual should be required to read and acknowledge the following:

- The organization's mission statement
- Employee codes of conduct
- A conflict of interest statement
- The organization's acceptance statement on a whistleblower program
- A policy outlining the organization's fraud hotline program

Organizational Mission Statement

According to BusinessDictionary.com, a mission statement is defined as:

> A written declaration of an organization's core purpose and focus that normally remains unchanged over time. Properly crafted mission statements (1) serve as filters to separate what is important from what is not, (2) clearly state which markets will be served and how, and (3) communicate a sense of intended direction to the entire organization [1].

In order to start each new hire off on the right foot, the process begins with the organizational mission statement. The mission statement gives the business a sense of focus and direction, which hopefully bleeds over to all newly hired associates.

Employee Code of Conduct

Every employer needs to develop its own organizational and unique code of conduct that is acknowledged and signed by all newly hired associates. The code of conduct is one of the first steps in the theft/fraud identification and prevention process. It is also a policy that immediately sets the standards of what is expected by the organization as far as employee conduct and ethical and workplace behavior. Based on the type of organization, the code of conduct should discuss the legal and ethical guidelines between employees and other associates within the company. Additionally it should also lay out guidelines for relationships between employees and outside contacts, to include vendors, individual and business clients, service providers, etc. An effective code of conduct policy should include but not be limited to the following:

- The reputation of the organization is judged from within and by individuals outside the company based on the actions, conduct, and professionalism of the employees.
- The organization should detail expectations of acceptable employee behavior, to include the use of associate-based good judgment.
- The organization's internal value system and desire to maintain a professional reputation within the community and business world should be communicated.
- Employee compliance with all business regulations, statutes, state and local laws, etc. should be made clear.
- Prohibited employee actions and specific behavior types that are considered to be misconduct should be discussed. The code of conduct should provide some specific examples, but advise the reader and signer that the list is not

inclusive. It is a mere guideline. Based on the employer and its consultation with the legal department, the code of conduct could also provide the actions taken for violations.

- There should be a reference to the organization's policy on conflicts of interest [2].

Conflicts of Interest Policy

According to Business.Dictionary.com, a conflict of interest is defined as

1. A situation that has the potential to undermine the impartiality of a person because of the possibility of a clash between the person's self-interest and professional interest or public interest
2. A situation in which a party's responsibility to a second party limits its ability to discharge its responsibility to a third party [3]

In addition to newly hired employees' acknowledging and signing the company's code of conduct policy, it is also necessary to establish the same practice for the conflict of interest policy. The organization's conflict of interest policy is one that is industry and business specific. It is not a generic policy that can be downloaded with the organization's name typed across the top. An organizational conflict of interest policy for a financial institution will be different from one that pertains to a shipping business company.

For many, the question arises as to what is a specific conflict of interest. The answer is that what constitutes a conflict of interest at Company A might be acceptable at Company B. In order to provide some basic examples, the following information is provided:

- A very common conflict of interest comes from the military world. A male officer dating a female enlisted person in his direct chain of command constitutes a conflict of interest.
- The same scenario can apply to any organization. Can a department manager avoid providing special treatment to a subordinate boyfriend or girlfriend? This situation establishes an issue of fairness and equality for all employees in the department.
- A cafeteria manager contracts with a relative who owns a food supply company to provide vending services for the lunch room.
- A sales manager begins working part time for a competitor's organization.
- A department manager is offered free weekend use of a beach house owned by a major supplier.
- A married department manager has a secret relationship with a subordinate.

As discussed, conflicts of interest vary based on the business operation. Many people exercising common sense can quickly notice situations that could create a questionable operation or a conflict of interest. Avoiding workplace conflicts of interest is an important factor in the avoidance of potential integrity issues. These issues are those that can be called into question if one party of the conflict places pressure on the other.

A perfect example would be the sales manager working part time for a competitor's organization. What might be innocent at the inception could turn into a large issue if the sales manager is asked by the part-time employer to provide client information. On the other hand, the part-time sales manager may use current company information to help the part-time employer sway clients away from the manager's primary employer.

As previously referenced, a majority of conflict of interest issues border common sense. Even though these issues might appear as "no brainer" issues for many, it is still important to have them in writing. Once they are placed in writing, it is necessary to have all newly hired associates acknowledge and sign the policy.

In addition to having the organization's conflict of interest policy acknowledged by new associates, it is also important to have current employees reread and sign the policy on at least an annual basis. Employees' knowing and signing the organization's code of conduct and conflict of interest policies can work to close potential windows of theft/fraud opportunities.

The Organization's Acceptance Statement on a Whistleblower Program

An internal whistleblower program is another area for new-hire acknowledgment and acceptance. Like an organization's code of conduct and conflict of interest policies, the whistleblower program is one that is unique to the company. A well-crafted whistleblower program policy statement serves a dual purpose:

- It creates a program where organization can gain intelligence on potential ethical and fraud-related issues. The goal is to establish a program where the business creates an opportunity to identify potentially dangerous threat issues and shut them down.
- It also shows newly hired individuals that the organization is concerned about integrity issues and that those coming forward will not be treated unfairly.

As previously discussed with establishing a fraud hotline program, organizations need to consider using an outside vendor. Some employees might be somewhat reluctant to participate in the program if it is maintained in house. Many employees feel a degree of separation when reporting sensitive issues to an outside third party.

A Policy Outlining the Organization's Fraud Hotline Program

As discussed with the establishment of a whistleblower program, the same two benefits can be achieved with a fraud hotline program. Organizations can save money by thwarting potential theft/fraud attempts and show employees the company is committed to maintaining integrity within the business.

It is important that newly hired associates are made aware of the organization's fraud hotline program. As with all of the company policies, associates need to acknowledge and sign documentation discussing the fraud hotline program.

Business-Related Extortion

The purpose of establishing the operating procedures discussed so far in this chapter is to lay the groundwork for a solid theft/fraud prevention foundation. The foundation begins with making sure only quality associates are hired into the organization. Immediately upon the associate's entry into the operation, the company adds to the foundation with strong policies that are ethics related, thus ensuring all new associates are aware of the organization's policies pertaining to a code of conduct and conflict of interest. The foundation is then made solid by allowing the newly hired associates to be their own boss as far as taking the lead on reporting unethical behavior.

Constructing a strong foundation serves a twofold purpose:

- To immediately educate newly hired quality associates with the knowledge that the organization takes a serious stance on ethical behavior
- To bring the newly hired associates into the discussion of business-related extortion

Business-related extortion has to be part of the new-hire discussion. For a majority of newly hired associates, their belief is based on them personally not being in a position to fall under the pressure of extortion. As many go throughout their careers, the topic will never come up. Others might not be as lucky.

It would be easy for many individuals working for a business to think that they have nothing of value that would cause an outside party to bring pressure. Personally the individual might not, but his or her employer has plenty.

This is the important point to convey as part of the discussion on extortion. There are people in the working world who possess lower than average ethical standards. They might not wake up in the morning with the intent to bring pressure on the employee of Company A. However, their interactions with an employee of Company A could open a window of opportunity.

These windows of opportunity can be opened by a simple nonadherence to the agreed upon company code of conduct and conflict of interest policies—basically allowing their actions to violate the policies, while allowing an interested third party to bring the pressure of extortion. Some examples of possible situations are simple in nature, while others are more complicated:

- A married associate is having a relationship with a co-worker. As the relationship goes on it could possibly become water-cooler gossip within the office. So far it is harmless in nature, until someone outside the organization hears of it. This outside individual could be a vendor or contractor looking for an advantage in providing services to the company. The person having the so-called harmless affair can now be put under pressure in order to keep the relationship secret from his or her spouse. Based on his or her position within the organization, the associate could be put under pressure by the outside source to approve contracts. This could be especially harmful to the organization if the approval decisions violate the lowest bidder policy.
- An individual working in the purchasing department develops a friendly relationship with an outside supplier. The relationship starts out harmlessly, but grows into meetings after work over drinks, dinner, sporting events, etc. The associate believes he has struck a goldmine since the supplier always insists on paying. As time goes on the employee accepts a free getaway weekend at the supplier's beach house. Based on the company's code of conduct and conflicts of interest policies, the employee has eventually crossed the line. Once the line has been crossed, the supplier can now bring pressure to have the employee make larger and larger purchases. The pressure comes from the need to keep the free items provided by the supplier secret.
- A variation to the previously discussed purchaser/supplier relationship is the issue of rationalization. The employee could agree to work with the supplier and approve more contracts. In an effort to receive a benefit from the supplier, the employee could demand a percentage of the overall contract amount. Even though the employee broke the rules that lead to the unethical relationship, monetary payments from the supplier can help the associate rationalize the approval of additional contracts. His or her thought process would be that now the supplier is held "over a barrel" by providing kickbacks. This might be the case, but the employee keeps digging a deeper hole.

What makes the threat of extortion an issue for organizations are the assets available:

- The potential of the exposed affair of an employee working for a financial institution could result in a request to make questionable loan decisions, a need for the teller to cash known counterfeit checks, a request to provide commercial bank account information for a rival business, etc.
- For the organization where the employee keeps approving more and more of a specific supplier's contracts has the potential to receive subquality material.

Even though the supplier contracts call for certain quality standards, the employee might be pressured to overlook the issue.

- Extortion types of situations are going to be based on the assets of the targeted organization, along with the internal position of the employee. The higher up the ladder the associate being extorted is, the greater the threat for large losses will be.

As discussed, no matter the position of the associate within an organization, his or her individual actions could place the associate in position for extortion type pressure. This is why it is important for organizations to include a discussion on extortion as part of the new-hire process. As stated, the foundation is laid with an introduction to the code of conduct and conflict of interest policies. Now comes the discussion on individual actions and the potential ramifications for the associate and the employer.

Theft/Fraud Awareness Training

As part of the new-employee orientation process, it is important that the organization develop and deliver training on theft/fraud awareness. The training needs to be company specific and not just a discussion of industry-related fraud. Some organizations feel comfortable with providing a blanket discussion on theft/fraud, along with statistical information.

The billions of dollars lost each year as a result of internal theft/fraud is interesting, but it is not specific to a particular business—just like a computer technology company providing theft/fraud training on security procedures at the loading dock: interesting, but not valid.

However, if the organization is a wholesale supplier, the activities on the loading dock are important. Newly hired associates in this industry need to be made aware of current prevention procedures and the rationale:

- Why is there a dual control and associate rotation policy for trash disposal? The answer is that it helps prevent one employee from taking items out with the trash and coming back after hours to remove the stolen items. As far as rotating employees who take out the trash, it prevents collusion. By having the same two employees taking out the trash on a daily basis, the organization has created a window of opportunity. These two employees can develop a trust level together and conspire to create a product theft crime.
- Why do regulations require two employees to conduct an independent count of all delivered merchandise? (Individuals placed in these positions need to be rotated on a routine basis.) Why not accept what is listed on the delivery invoice and the word of the driver? This is the person who supervised the loading of the truck and was in charge of the items until they arrived at the

loading dock. If the company allowed the same individual to conduct all delivery inventories, it is creating a window of theft/fraud opportunity. This individual can quickly realize that whatever he or she reports is golden and begin to alter the actual delivery numbers. As far as having a rotation in the individuals conducting the delivery count, the company has taken away an opportunity of collusion. If the company takes the word of the delivery driver with each shipment, it is creating a theft/fraud window of opportunity. It will not take long before the driver realizes that whatever he or she reports is quickly accepted and that now there is an opportunity to remove items from the delivery pallets and boxes. Once the items are removed and bogus count numbers are accepted, the item shortage is the responsibility of the receiving organization.

- Why is it against company policy that one or both of the individuals conducting delivery count enter the numbers into the internal inventory system? If one person is allowed to take the agreed upon delivery numbers and enters them into the internal inventory system, the organization has created a theft/fraud window of opportunity. The same is true if policy also allows the same two associates to conduct the delivery count. This creates an opportunity for collusion. The organization can create a level of integrity into the process by having the dual control delivery count numbers presented to a disconnected third-party associate for entry into the inventory system.

In order to make the theft/fraud awareness training effective, it has to be realistic and company related. Additionally, it needs to be somewhat specific along the lines with the previously discussed scenarios. The purpose to provide company-related and specific discussion serves a dual purpose:

- It establishes policy as to how day-to-day operations are to be carried out by all associates in order to prevent theft/fraud.
- A detailed and specific discussion conveys a message to newly hired associates that the company is aware of the opportunity windows for theft/fraud.

By developing and delivering an informative theft/fraud awareness program, employees can gain an early understanding of where the organization stands as far as unethical behavior is concerned. Hopefully, the foundation built through early discussion of ethical issues and theft/fraud awareness training will carry the associates through their tenure with the company in an aboveboard manner. Additionally, the organization can rely on associates using the foundation of behavior in identifying and reporting newly developed opportunities through the whistleblower and fraud tip hotlines created.

Endnotes

1. Mission statement definition. http://www.businessdictionary.com/definition/mission-statement.html (accessed September 7, 2015).
2. HR policies and employment legislation. http://hrcouncil.ca/hr-toolkit/code-of-conduct.cfm (accessed September 7, 2015).
3. Conflict of interest. http://www.businessdictionary.com/definition/conflict-of-interest.html (accessed September 7, 2015).

Chapter 4

Main Components of Occupational Fraud

Introduction

According to a 2015 report to the nation from the Association of Certified Fraud Examiners (ACFE), the three main components of occupational fraud are

- Asset misappropriation
- Corruption
- Financial statement fraud [1]

Asset Misappropriation

Of the three referenced components, asset misappropriation is the most common type of fraud plaguing businesses across the country. Asset misappropriation can be defined as fraud that happens when people who are entrusted to manage the assets of an organization steal from it. Asset misappropriation fraud involves third parties or employees in an organization who abuse their position to steal from it through fraudulent activity. It can also be known as insider fraud [2].

Judging by the official definition of asset misappropriation, it can be described in a nutshell as stealing from the company. It can also be described as using an organizational asset for a purpose other than for its official use.

While in the US Army, I worked as a criminal investigator. For a year I was assigned in support of the 2nd Infantry Division in Camp Casey, Korea. (At the time Camp Casey was considered a hardship tour, where service members could not bring over family members or personal vehicles.)

As portrayed on the TV series M*A*S*H, the summers are extremely hot and the winters are extremely cold. A problem we had during the winter months on base was misappropriation of assets involving military vehicles. A typical scenario revolved around one or more service members walking back on the base from the village that was located outside the main gate. Due to the layout of the installation, a majority of the barracks buildings were at least a half-mile from the main gate. In a cold weather situation, it was common for those walking back to their barracks to look for a nice warm ride.

On all military installations, there is constant military vehicle activity driving around the roads on the base. Camp Casey was no different. Drivers of military vehicles would go from building to building as part of their official duties. In the winter months and due to the extremely cold weather, it was quite common for individuals on duty and driving military vehicles to park outside a building where they were making a delivery to leave the engine running to keep the inside of the vehicle warm.

Many times the walking and cold service members would come across the warm and running military vehicle. In an effort to get back to their barracks faster and in a much warmer position, they would borrow the vehicle and drive back to their barracks.

The service member who left the vehicle running outside a building would come back to where the vehicle had been parked and find it missing. He would immediately call the military police (MPs) and report the vehicle stolen.

Since the perceived value of the vehicle was over $1,000, the military police would call our Criminal Investigations Office to report the crime. Our stance was always to advise the MPs to drive around the base and look for the perceived stolen vehicle. On almost every occasion the vehicle would be located in good condition and parked outside one of the many barracks buildings on base. The keys to the vehicle were also left in the ignition.

Once the military vehicle was located by the MPs it became a crime not of theft, but one of misappropriation of assets. If the culprits could be located, they were charged with misappropriation of assets and not theft. All they wanted was a warm ride back to the barracks.

The same can hold true for the assets of an organization. Outside of stealing, various assets of an organization can be misappropriated by their employees. Some examples are as follows:

- From a government perspective, many employees are assigned company vehicles. Due to government regulations the use of these vehicles is restricted; they are to be used for official business only. Any government employee using a government vehicle to take the family on vacation or for personal use can be considered to be misappropriating assets.

- A simple and popular example from the corporate sector revolves around the office copy machine. An employee using the copy machine to make hundreds of copies of flyers a week for a child's school is misappropriating the asset.
- Another example that will most likely become an increasing factor in the future is the use of an office laptop. Many employees will, with permission, take the company laptop home to conduct official business. Using the company laptop, employees will also conduct personal business. Many employers overlook this practice and consider it a perk for their associates doing company business away from the office.

Looking down the road and as discussed in detail in Section V, "Cyber Security and Cyber Fraud," employees using office computers for personal use can open up their employer to becoming a victim of a data breach. No matter what type of laptop is used, personal or business, the user will most likely be targeted with phishing e-mails. An employee unknowingly responding to one of these e-mails while using a company laptop can expose the employer and network to a breach. The intent of those conducting the breach is to access the organization's financial database, customer database, and internal current and former employee files.

Many instances of asset misappropriation that are not outright stealing can also be a drain on the organization's financial standing. Employees, taking a carte blanche stance on the office copier, cost the business in the form of paper, toner, and increased maintenance expenses. Extended and unauthorized use of company vehicles also places an additional financial burden on the company due to increased maintenance fees and a shorter machine life span.

The previously mentioned and discussed nontheft asset misappropriation examples are just a few incidents among many. Based on the organization and how it conducts its daily operations, there are incidents of how employees can misuse property and material, producing an increased cost factor for the business. In an effort to lower the incidents of nontheft asset misappropriation, it is vital that businesses identify the areas of concern.

Along with the acknowledgment and signing of the organization's code of conduct and conflict of interest policies, newly hired associates need to be provided a detailed list of what are considered areas of concern for nontheft misappropriation of company assets.

Lack of Dual Control

For many jobs within an organization, it is necessary to establish policies of dual control. From the perspective of dual control, it basically states that no one employee should not be charged with seeing an account reconciliation, inventory, creation of financial statements, financial transaction process, etc. from beginning to end. Somewhere along the process there needs to be a second set of eyes on the activity. Leaving many of these work-related accounting/finance positions under a single layer of control only works to open a window of theft/fraud opportunity. A perfect example of a single layer of control that is an open invitation for theft/fraud is to have one employee individually in charge of the business's accounts receivable, accounts payable, check issuing, and bank account reconciliation processes, with no threat of a surprise or outside audit taking place.

The previous scenario might seem an extreme example to many, but there are still business operations that make similar work-related choices each and every day. The rationale behind allowing associates to operate with single control for finance and accounting functions comes down to a variety of business decisions:

- The choice could be monetarily based. Due to budgetary constrictions, there could be a limited number of employees to perform all of the business-related functions.
- The choice could be based on trust. Over time many smaller business operations allow one or more trusted and long-term employees the opportunity to take on additional duties. This decision could be made to save money from hiring additional employees and give additional job duties to longer term and trusted associates. Many times these decisions lead to the long-term associate opening the window of opportunity and committing what is referred to as embezzlement [3]. Cases of this nature are routinely reported on local news channels and in the newspaper, with the victim typically a nonprofit operation, a local church, a local municipal office, etc. The offending individual is usually a long-term, trusted associate, who no one in the operation ever believed would commit a crime.
- The choice could be based on employee trust that evolved as part of step level promotions. As the associate's pay grade rises within the company, so do responsibility levels. The rationale is that employees who are appreciated with merit and responsibility level increases would never steal from the organization.

Some notable areas within an organization where dual control is necessary to identify and prevent theft/fraud are discussed next.

Cash/check disbursements. Within many organizations, documentation comes through the office of the bookkeeper for payment. These payments could be arranged for disbursement via an electronic transfer or by a company check. Just like it is necessary for some type of dual control procedure to be in place for the payment information to reach the bookkeeper's desk, the person initiating the payment should not be the same person to authorize the electronic transfer or to sign the check. Based on the size of the business, a review and approval has to come from the head of the department, a designated representative, or a company owner. It is necessary to implement this layer of asset protection to ensure all money leaving the business is legitimate and not part of a theft/fraud operation because, once the assets leave the organization as part of a theft/fraud scheme, the likelihood of getting the money back is slim.

Unlike incidents of unauthorized account transactions or check forgeries, as discussed in detail in Section IV, Chapter 29 ("Financial Institution Fraud"), the company is on the hook for the loss. With a forged check, the organization is an actual victim and can make a claim with its bank in order to receive reimbursement. With an unauthorized check issued and signed by an authorized employee (bookkeeper) within the organization, the company is liable for the loss.

Most companies establish operations with their financial institution as to who within the organization is authorized to sign company checks. If the person signing the unauthorized check is an authorized signer on the account, the company is the victim and also takes the monetary loss.

It is necessary for organizations to ensure that individuals who generate payments for the company have no authority with the financial institution to initiate the transaction. This includes online money transfers from the business to outside parties. It is necessary that the business owner or the head of the accounting department retain tight control over the financial institution online bank account login information and passwords.

The same password protection policy needs to be established for businesses using the services of online payment companies. More and more business operations are using PayPal types payment processing services. In order to protect the integrity of these services, strict control of the account login and password information is necessary.

Additionally, business operations need to separate the bank account linked to the online payment service from the main depository account. The monetary balance of the account linked to the online payment system should be maintained at a low amount. Money transfers can be made into the online payment system account as necessary when known transactions are going to be processed.

This internal policy is necessary in case the online payment system account login and password information is compromised. The culprits will only have access to the low balance in the designated account versus access to the main business bank account balance.

Generation of an approved vendor list. Organizations work with companies outside the operation that provide products and/or services. These companies are normally referred to as approved vendors and have an established relationship with the organization. The approved vendors also have a preference as to the manner of payment (electronically or by check).

By establishing an internal policy of who is authorized to sign company checks and access the online bank accounts to make an electronic transfer, there also needs to be a procedure set up for the creation and monitoring of an approved vendor list.

Bookkeepers and other business employees have had success in stealing money from their employer through making payments to fictitious suppliers/vendors. Phony invoices are created as part of adding validation to the scam. In an effort to offset the phony invoice, a payment is made to settle the books. Unfortunately for the company, no services were provided or product received. In most instances the dishonest associate was working with an accomplice outside the organization or established a bank account in the name of the phony supplier/vendor. Either way, the organization is out the amount of the invoice.

In an effort to avoid this type of theft/fraud, businesses need to establish detailed procedures in order to create an approved vendor list. Once created, policy needs to dictate that no disbursements are approved prior to the invoice being compared with the approved vendor/supplier list.

Accounts receivable/accounts payable. Organizations need to ensure they do not allow any receivable/payable decisions to be made outside a dual control verification process. There needs to be complete separation between the Accounts Receivable Department, the Accounts Payable Department, and payment disbursement. Additionally, there need to be dual control policies established within the Accounts Receivable and Accounts Payable Departments.

No single employee should be in charge of ensuring the work or products provided through suppliers/vendors. More than one set of eyes need to verify that the products or services provided by suppliers/vendors are from those authorized to provide services to the organization. Additionally, more than one set of eyes need to be involved in the accounts payable process. Prior to any payments being approved for disbursal, verification needs to be made that the supplier/vendor is authorized to receive the generated payment.

Once validation has been made on the processes of accounts receivable through accounts payable, the parties approved for disbursement can now complete their independent duties.

The examples provided are based on incidents of embezzlement that have taken place in businesses for years. Additionally, the examples are common types of operating procedures that open up windows of opportunity for theft/fraud. As part of the theft/fraud identification and prevention process, organizations need to conduct an analysis of their entire operation. This analysis needs to look at all work-related operating procedures that, if left in control of a single employee, open windows of opportunity for theft/fraud. Each business has its own unique methods of operation and services provided. By this standard, there is no cookie-cutter blanket procedural policy that can be created to cover all types of business operations.

Corruption

According to Investopedia.com, corruption is defined as "dishonest behavior by those in positions of power, such as managers or government officials. Corruption can include giving or accepting bribes or inappropriate gifts, double dealing, under-the-table transactions, manipulating elections, diverting funds, laundering money and defrauding investors" [4].

A large majority of corruption cases taking place in the business world involve officials at the top of the organization participating in unethical behavior with the hope of benefiting their organization. Additionally, many of the corruption incidents involve the use of bribery [5]. Typically, the corporate or business leaders engage in bribes with government officials in order to receive special favors. These favors can include

- The awarding of government construction contracts
- The awarding of telecommunication contracts in emerging nations
- Companies looking to weed out the competition and have government officials promote the product or services of the organization initiating the bribe
- Being awarded company exclusive contracts for the shipping/transportation of products

Other areas of business-related corruption exist in the financial industry and on Wall Street. Numerous articles can be located on how the financial industry and investors use manipulation to gain favor and monetary gain.

Additional examples of corruption take place around the world on a daily basis. The purpose of this text is to provide a discussion on large areas of theft/fraud as they relate to businesses. These can be identified and prevented from occurring within the actual business operation. A majority of corruption incidents are identified, investigated, and prosecuted by outside agencies—typically, the US Department of Justice.

Financial Statement Fraud

No matter the size of the business operation, it is necessary to prepare some type of financial statement. Based on the business type (corporation, partnership, limited liability corporation), there are accounting requirements as to the financial statements to be completed. From a theft/fraud analysis perspective, the four financial statements that can be analyzed are the

- Balance sheet
- Cash flow statement
- Income statement
- Profit and loss statement

Balance Sheet

A balance sheet is a snapshot in time of the company's assets minus its liabilities plus shareholders' equity. According to Investopedia.com a balance sheet is "a

Balance Sheet Acme Industries Period Ending December 31, 2016 (in thousands of dollars)		
Assets		
Cash		$20,000.00
Accounts receivable		$9,000.00
Items in inventory		$54,000.00
Equipment		$2,500.00
Total assets		$85,500.00
Liabilities		
Accounts payable		$60,000.00
Total liabilities		$60,000.00
Shareholders' equity		$25,500.00
Total shareholders' equity		$25,500.00
Total liabilities and shareholders' equity		$85,500.00

Figure 4.1 Balance sheet example.

financial statement that summarizes a company's assets, liabilities and shareholders' equity at a specific point in time. These three balance sheet segments give investors an idea as to what the company owns and owes, as well as the amount invested by shareholders" [6].

Figure 4.1 shows a fictitious balance sheet for Acme Industries.

Cash Flow Statement

According to Investopedia.com a cash flow statement is defined as

> One of the quarterly financial reports any publicly traded company is required to disclose to the Securities and Exchange Commission [SEC] and the public. The document provides aggregate data regarding all cash inflows a company receives from both its ongoing operations and external investment sources, as well as all cash outflows that pay for business activities and investments during a given quarter [7].

Figure 4.2 shows a fictitious cash flow statement for Acme Industries.

Cash Flow Statement Acme Industries Period Ending December 31, 2016 (in thousands of dollars)			
Cash flow from operations			
Payments received			$10,000.00
Expenses for supplies and payroll			$4,000.00
Advertising expenses			$500.00
Interest paid			$350.00
Tax liabilities			$1,200.00
Net cash flow			$3,950.00
Capital expenses			
Equipment purchases			$2,500.00
Net capital expenses			$2,500.00
Additional income and payments			
Misc. income			$1,200.00
Net income and payments			$1,200.00
Cash at the beginning of the year			$1,100.00
Cash increase for the year			$2,650.00
Ending year cash balance			$3,750.00

Figure 4.2 Cash flow statement example.

Income Statement/Profit and Loss Statement

An income statement and a profit and loss statement can be classified as documentation reporting the same information. For both types of statements the equation is income minus expenses equals profit. Figures 4.3 and 4.4 show fictitious examples of an income statement and a profit and loss statement for Acme Industries, respectively.

Based on the specific business, one can choose to produce an income statement or a somewhat more detailed profit and loss statement. The purpose of both is to provide an analysis of the organization's income and expenses for the year.

Financial statement fraud can be defined as "...deliberate misrepresentation, misstatement or omission of financial statement data for the purpose of misleading the reader and creating a false impression of an organization's financial strength" [8].

Acme Industries Income Statement January 1, 2016 through July 31, 2016		
Income/revenues		
Sales income		$250,000.00
Investment income		$42,000.00
Misc. income		$12,000.00
Total income/revenues		$304,000.00
Expenses		
Material purchases		$145,000.00
Rental expenses		$12,500.00
Consulting services		$6,500.00
Travel expenses		$4,700.00
Payroll		$45,000.00
Marketing		$3,100.00
Capital expenses		$4,200.00
Accounting expenses		$1,200.00
Total expenses		$222,200.00
Net income		$81,800.00

Figure 4.3 Income statement example.

There are different reasons why individuals choose to manipulate the information on a financial statement:

- Individuals looking to purchase a business immediately want to look at the organization's financial statements. The potential buyers want to be able to develop an understanding of the financial stability of the business—basically answering the question, "Is this business worth purchasing?" An owner looking to sell his or her business could manipulate the financial information of a company in order to paint a positive picture of the operation.
- For the purpose of this text, associates working for a business could manipulate financial statement data in an effort to cover up theft/fraud activities.

In order to cover up theft/fraud activity within the business, dishonest employees could provide inaccurate departmental data. Areas of concern for any business where associates could manipulate financial statement data as a cover-up are

2016 Acme Industries P&L		
Income		
Sales		$180,000.00
Expenses		
Product purchases		$42,776.50
Rent		$28,795.33
Misc. expenses		$1,589.17
Insurance		$825.00
Utilities		$2,840.00
Phone		$560.00
Maintenance		$120.00
Trash		$350.00
Water		$200.00
Equipment		$418.00
Alarm monitoring		$403.32
Advertising		$4,200.00
Supplies		$5,412.00
Gifts		$400.00
Merchant fees		$3,052.71
Bank fees		$144.00
Employee expenses		$14,275.00
Theft		$300.00
FICA/medicare taxes		$2,135.00
Other taxes		$600.00
Professional fees		$700.00
Total		$110,096.03
Profit/loss		$69,903.97

Figure 4.4 Profit and loss statement example.

- Payroll fraud. An employee working in the payroll department could have created fictitious employee names. By creating fictitious employees the employee is allowing the business to provide payment to ghost employees. Records of the payroll department show the ghost employee names as receiving payment, but the actual funds are going into the pocket of the dishonest associate.
- Purchasing/inventory fraud. In order to cover up a theft of material or merchandise items, an employee could provide inaccurate expense numbers. Instead of the actual represented purchased items coming into the company, they are stolen by the employee and later resold. The dishonest employee could also be creating false invoices and providing payment to shell operations. Once the payment leaves the business, the money eventually winds up in the pockets of the dishonest employee.
- Cash theft. In an effort to pull off this crime, an employee will manipulate data within the financial statements. Expenses for purchasing, payroll,

miscellaneous expenses, etc. could be altered to validate the represented cash standing of the business. If the employee stole $5,000 from the business, he or she would create documentation for $5,000 in business-related expenses.

The previously discussed scenarios represent some of the schemes used by business employees to cover up theft/fraud. Based on the business type and the scams used, the types of financial statement fraud will vary. It is up to business owners and those charged with security/loss prevention functions to work to identify and prevent theft/fraud opportunities.

Theft/fraud identification and prevention measures for internal incidents are discussed in the following sections.

Accuracy in Purchasing

As with the previous discussion on dual control, this is a function that needs to be included to prevent theft/fraud for a business operation. This is especially true when looking at the purchasing aspect of a business operation.

In order to allow a business to function properly there is a need to make capital purchases such as vehicles, computers, printers, other office equipment, etc. Additional item purchases or operating expenses require the acquisition of office supplies.

Purchasing also includes the need to acquire inventory items for manufacturing purposes or for wholesale or retail sale.

In an effort to ensure the business assets are being used properly, there needs to be accountability in purchasing. The goal of this accountability project has to be centered on making sure all purchasing requests are legitimate and verified. The second part of the goal has to be to make sure all expenditures made are going to approved suppliers/vendors.

As previously discussed, each and every business operation has to develop a list of authorized and approved suppliers/vendors. It is up to individuals within the organization to properly vet the name, operation, and integrity of the suppliers/vendors. It is also up to the individuals within the business to establish procedures to ensure some type of dual control takes place on the development of an approved supplier/vendor list.

Organizations that develop a dual control approved supplier/vendor list and use this information prior to any purchases or request for services will work to lower the possibility of theft/fraud.

Accuracy in Invoice Payments

As discussed with the goals related to accountability in purchasing, the same practice holds true for the paying of invoices. These invoices can be from suppliers/vendors providing services or material to the business. Prior to any service- or merchandise-related invoices being approved for payment, it is necessary to verify that the supplier/vendor is listed on the dual-control-created approved list.

Many business operations face theft-/fraud-related threats from associates working within the walls of the organization. The employee can be a lone wolf or an individual working in cahoots with an outside supplier/vendor. In an effort to identity and prevent theft-/fraud-related incidents from taking place, the awareness measures are discussed in the following sections.

Phony Invoicing

A popular internal theft/fraud method targeted against a business operation is a phony invoicing scam. An employee working in the Accounts Payable section of a business can create an invoice for payment. The phony invoice can be for services provided to the business or for material/merchandise purchased. No matter what the actual rationale on the invoice for payment is, the goal is to have a payment made to offset the open document.

Payment instructions on the phony invoice could be to have a check made out to the business name of the supplier/vendor or to have an electronic payment sent to the bank account information provided.

Another payment option available—one that is a major red flag warning—is a payment request on the invoice to make a check payable to a named principal of the supplier/vendor operation.

Business policies should dictate that no invoices are ever paid by a check that is made out to an individual. This has to be the case even if a known and vetted supplier/vendor personally shows up at the business and makes a payment request for a check issued in his or her name. The same holds true for sending electronic payments from one business bank account to another. Efforts need to be made to ensure all electronic payments are made to an account with a business name.

As far as the phony invoice is concerned, there needs to be redundancy in the verification process prior to a payment being made. If the supplier/vendor name is not listed on the dual-control-created approved list, this could be a red flag warning sign. Without an approved supplier/vendor list, the phony invoice could be forwarded for payment.

Once the phony invoice is forwarded for disbursement and there is no approved supplier/vendor list for verification, it is quite possible payment will be made. In years gone by it was possible that someone in an organization could spot a crudely created supplier/vendor invoice. With the use of technology, it is a simple process to create professional looking documentation including professional wording and images.

Once the phony invoice payment is made by a check or by electronic means, the assets will eventually wind up in the hands of the dishonest associate. Some of the tactics used to ensure the payment amount is received by the dishonest associate are as follows:

- The employee could be working with an actual supplier/vendor, but one that has not been approved by the organization. The dishonest employee, working in concert with the unapproved supplier/vendor, could create the phony invoice to request payment be made via check or electronically. With either payment method, the assets will wind up in the account of the unapproved supplier/vendor. Once the assets have left the business, all or part of the money winds up in the pocket of the dishonest associate.
- The employee could be working alone and open up a business account at a financial institution in the name of a phony supplier/vendor. (See Section IV, Chapter 29, "Financial Institution Fraud," for discussion on how bogus business bank accounts are established.) Once the business account is established by the dishonest employee, he or she will have access to the phony invoice payment and can either deposit a check into the business account and later withdraw the funds, or remove the money once the electronic payment is received.
- As discussed in Section IV, Chapter 29, it is easier to open a personal bank account in the name of another versus opening a phony business account. This creates an issue with making invoice payments in the name of an individual. Once the check is received, the recipient can go to any bank branch where the check is drawn and cash it. All the person needs is the actual check and an easily created piece of identification.

Financial institutions will not directly cash checks made out to the name of a business, even if the account owner is presenting the check for payment.

Phony Purchasing Invoices

As previously discussed with phony invoices, the product or services were never received by the business making payment. Phony purchasing invoices are made with the intent of receiving some type of product or service. The goal of those creating the phony purchasing invoices is to have the business provide payment, while the product or service never benefits the organization. Or if it does provide some benefit, it is not for the original intent. Some incidents as to why employees would create phony purchasing invoices are as follows:

- Based on the business operation, there are certain quality standards that go along with product and/or material purchases. In the construction industry these standards could be in the quality of the raw material. Material that is below the industry-set standards could cause a safety hazard down the road. In the retail industry it also comes down to product quality and selling substandard material. Additionally, a purchasing agent could buy dresses that were made using forced labor in a Third World country and present them as coming from a well-known manufacturer.

- In order to cover the theft of cash from a business, a dishonest employee could present an invoice for payment for steel beams. The intent of the order was to purchase the product from Company A, which provides product that is in compliance with industry standards. For discussion purposes, the steel order was quoted as being $100,000. From the purchasing company, Employee A decided to purchase similar material from another vendor. The supplying vendor from Company B provided a similar product, but of cheaper quality and below industry standards. The cost of this material was $80,000. The invoice presented for payment was for $100,000 and payment was to be made to Company B. On face value the business received its material for the budgeted amount. After the payment was made to Company B, there was a kickback to Employee A in the neighborhood of $20,000.
- A dishonest employee creates a purchasing order/invoice to purchase a product from Company C. Company C receives the order and provides the requested items to the business. In order to settle the open invoice, it is forwarded for payment to Accounts Payable. Upon receipt of a valid invoice, Accounts Payable sends the product payment to Company C. On the surface Company C was compensated for providing a requested product to the business. The only issue is that the actual product never made it into the inventory system. The dishonest employee intercepted the product, ensured payment was made, and later sold the material through an Internet auction website or through other means.
- Company D has several vehicles in its inventory that are used as part of daily business operations. Over the life span of a vehicle, service needs to be performed. One day, Employee F takes a vehicle to the approved vehicle maintenance facility to service. The maintenance facility completes the requested services on the vehicle and sends the company an invoice for payment. Employee F, who is in charge of processing invoices for payment, receives the maintenance invoice and approves it for payment. The invoice is forwarded to Accounts Payable and paid. The maintenance facility receives payment for the services provided and Company D accepts the fact that its vehicles require routine upkeep. What sets this incident apart from other legitimate transactions is that maintenance was performed on Employee F's personal car. In order to make the transaction appear legitimate, Employee F will create and present an invoice that represents the work being performed on a company vehicle.
- Business-related suppliers/vendors have also been contracted to provide services by individuals working within Company D. Every quarter Company D contracts through a carpet cleaning vendor to have the office floors shampooed and polished. One quarter, in addition to conducting cleaning duties

at Company D, the vendor is also tasked with performing services at the residence of Employee F. Once the total job is completed, an invoice is presented for payment that shows all of the work being conducted at Company D.

The phony invoice scenarios discussed are a few of many reasons why employees will use the process to remove material from the company or obtain unauthorized services. Companies that erect the fewest theft/fraud prevention barriers for accounts receivable/accounts payable operations will most likely suffer monetary losses. It is vital that organizations establish internal verification and approval guidelines when creating an approved supplier/vendor list and the process of verifying invoices for processing and payment.

In an effort to avoid possible incidents of supplier/vendor collusion with dishonest employees, it is necessary that businesses contract only with operations they can trust.

Background Check for Suppliers/Vendors

Businesses looking to be successful begin their theft/fraud prevention program at the front door. This prevention practice pertains to establishing a detailed new-hire screening process of all job applicants. Prior to job offers being made, it is necessary that the hiring organization conduct a detailed background investigation. The goal is to ensure that only quality applicants are offered positions and there is no questionable activity in their work history.

With organizations looking to establish a strong barrier to theft/fraud, it should also be necessary that businesses conduct some type of background investigations on suppliers/vendors. If the intent of new-hire background investigations is to keep out undesirables, the same passion should also hold true for suppliers/vendors.

Steps that could be taken to ensure that supplier/vender organizations are credible and trustworthy are as follows:

- One of the best resources is the Better Business Bureau (BBB). The BBB operates on a national basis down to local offices across the country. Business operations can choose to apply for BBB accreditation. For business operations seeking BBB accreditation, there are eight standards organizations must adhere to. Accreditation standards require building trust, advertising honestly, telling the truth, being transparent, honoring promises, being responsive, safeguarding privacy, and embodying integrity [9]. Whether a business is accredited or not by the BBB, most receive some type of rating. These ratings range from A+ to F. The ratings are established on customer satisfaction and complaints made through the BBB. Complaints can be made on the business-related areas of advertising/sales issues, billing/collection issues, problems with products/services, delivery issues, and guarantee/warranty issues [9]. Additionally, customer experience reviews can be made on the categories of having a positive experience, a negative experience, or a neutral experience [9]. Prior to any organization approving a supplier/vendor to conduct business with, a quick history check with the BBB is necessary.

- It is also a good idea to make a check through the local Chamber of Commerce office/website. Numerous local and statewide business operations choose to join their local Chamber of Commerce for the many benefits provided. A quick check of a business name through a Chamber of Commerce office can reveal if the company is a member in good standing and when it joined the organization [10].
- Many business operations operate under some type of corporate umbrella. The types can range from a C-corporation, S-corporation, or a limited liability corporation (LLC). No matter what type of corporation the business elects to establish, all must be registered with one or more state corporation commission offices. Any individual looking to research a state-approved corporate entity can access the records through the various state corporation commission offices. Information can be obtained on the corporate officers, directors, members, date of incorporation, current status with the state, business address, business operating type, etc. With many states, information can also be obtained if the business has filed for bankruptcy protection. Any business pondering a decision to enter into a relationship with a corporate entity should conduct a public records check with the state's corporation commission office.
- Business operations looking to enter into an organizational relationship with contracting operation can access public records within the state where the contractor is licensed. States and cities have registered contractor offices, which establish the registration and testing procedures required for contractors to receive a license and a contractor number. Businesses looking to obtain information on a registered contractor can access the public records through the state or city office. Information can be obtained on the date of registration, license status, company officers, bond amount and status, business address and contact information, etc. Many offices also provide information on past customer complaints. Information can be obtained on previous customer complaints and the resolution of the incidents. To access the contractor records, all that is needed is the business name or registered contractor number.
- Prior to conducting any type of business with any individual or organization, it is necessary to conduct an Internet search. With many, this process is referred to as Googling a person or business. An Internet search can produce countless links to information on the business in question, including the company website (which needs to be looked at in detail), information provided by many customer tracking companies, industry complaints, customer satisfaction information, etc.
- As discussed with conducting perspective employee background verifications and the many companies that provide these services, the same avenue can be taken when looking into the history of a business operation. Companies can be contracted with for the purpose of conducting background checks on a

particular business. These services are fee based and can vary per the amount and type of information sought.

- In addition to conducting a background check on the actual supplier/vendor business, checks can also be conducted on the organization's principles. It is necessary to obtain integrity type information on those operating the supplier/vendor operation and, most importantly, any criminal related information. This type of detailed search of a supplier/vendor organization is necessary, especially for those operations that have been recently formed or those where little information can be located through the previously discussed search processes. This is especially true if little or no information can be located on the business operation via an Internet search.

Redundancy in the Accounts Payable/ Accounts Receivable Process

Business operating decisions should not be made on a cynical view of the world that most are out to deceive and get something for nothing. Operating procedures need to be developed around the view of opportunity and answering the question, "Do our operating procedures open a window of theft/fraud opportunity?"

For a small business operation where the owner conducts all of the bookkeeping and accounts receivable/accounts payable activities, the potential for theft/fraud loss is low. The owner is basically stealing from himself or herself. If the business owner has financially backed silent contributors or there is the presence of additional active partners, this practice could prove to be dangerous. With the addition of financially involved individuals in the overall business operation, there comes a need for operating scrutiny.

As the size of the business operation increases, those in charge have a responsibility to the employees and financially invested individuals to ensure that all operating procedures work to protect the organization from theft/fraud. Since the future of the operation can be in jeopardy from financially based theft/fraud incidents, the main areas to protect are where the money comes into the business and where the money goes out of the business.

Money coming in can pertain to actual cash types of transactions, services provided where payment is required and products or merchandise is later turned into monetary transactions as a result of the daily operation.

An example would be retail items received from a wholesaler that are placed into the organization's inventory. If the items never make it into the inventory system and onto the sales floor, no monetary transactions can be generated.

Money going out can pertain to payments made to keep the physical business building presentable and operating and for payments made to acquire the necessary business-related material and merchandise.

Principals in the money in/money out process involve suppliers/vendors that need to be vetted. This process begins with the supplier/vendor verification process that leads to the creation of an approved supplier/vendor list. Using this list as an operating requirement, the organization should never present an invoice to Accounts Payable for a supplier/vendor that is not listed. The same practice has to hold true for services, material, or merchandise required by the business for successful operation. No business-related expenditures should ever be approved for a supplier/vendor not on the approved list.

In order to ensure that the previously discussed approved supplier/vendor list verification procedures are followed, it is necessary to have redundancy in the process. Just like no one associate should be allowed to create the approved supplier/vendor list, no one associate should be allowed to approve purchasing or payment decisions.

Additionally, any associates involved in the organization's bookkeeping operation should not be allowed to participate in any purchasing or payment decisions.

Need for Job Rotation in Organizational Finance-Related Positions

As discussed, the smaller the business operation is, the fewer the number of associates that are available for conducting day-to-day activities. By having a limited number of associates, some are tasked with overseeing many functions. As the sizes of businesses increase in activity and personnel, there are more employees available. Based on this availability, employees can be tasked with having a more defined and limited job function. This also allows for a greater separation between departments.

A good practice all business entities need to use, as far as their theft-/fraud-related prevention procedures, is in the area of job rotation. Developing an organizational policy requiring employees to change job duties serves a two-pronged purpose:

- The organization is creating an associate base of highly diverse employees that will have the ability to complete many business-related job functions. The employees will most likely be happier by having the ability of learning new positions and not having to go to work each and every day to complete the same job-related function.
- The organization is benefiting by having a happier, more excited, and diverse workforce. What they are also doing is creating an atmosphere of theft/fraud awareness and prevention.

By establishing an internal policy of forced job rotation for finance-related positions (bookkeeping, accounts receivable, and accounts payable), the organization is achieving the following:

- Creating a deterrent to potential theft/fraud activity. With finance types of positions, associates will take some time to learn all of the duties of the position. During this learning process, an associate could locate a window of theft/fraud opportunity. If the associate has an understanding that he or she is going to remain in the same position for an extended period of time, he or she might act on the opportunity. However, associates who know that they are going to rotate positions understand that there is a potential for their theft/fraud activity to be discovered.

- As part of the organization's use of having its associate base involved in the previously discussed areas of **developing intelligence from current employees as to how they would carry out theft-/fraud-related activities and create organizational working groups that meet for the purpose of discussing theft-/fraud-related opportunities**, the current employee who is rotated into a new position could locate windows of possible theft/fraud opportunity. At times, a fresh set of eyes on a situation or work-related position can uncover potential that went unnoticed by others.

Mandatory Vacation Policies

In addition to an organizational job rotation program, it is necessary that policies also dictate that employees take an annual vacation. The mandatory vacation time should be at least one full business week and, if possible, two consecutive weeks. With many types of finance-related thefts/frauds, it becomes necessary that the offending associate come to work each and every day to keep the activity afloat and hidden. By forcing mandatory time away from the office, the associate is not present to keep the theft/fraud activity afloat.

As part of the newly hired associate orientation program, discussion needs to take place on the mandatory vacation policy. From the beginning of working for a business, associates understand they will be required to take an annual week-long vacation. This policy could act as a deterrent for associates working in a finance-related position who discover a theft/fraud window of opportunity. Knowing that he or she will have to be away from his or her position for an extended period of time could sway the associate away from acting on the opportunity.

Additionally, with the mandatory vacation policy, requirements need to be established on the time between vacations. An employee should not be allowed to take a week-long vacation during the first week of January for calendar year A and schedule the next week-long vacation during the last week of calendar year B (basically having a two-year gap between forced vacations).

The mandatory vacation policy needs to also reflect the allowed time gap between week-long vacations. Employers can establish their own internal policies, but should never allow over a year to go by between forced vacations.

Organization policies also need to address associate access to company systems while on mandatory vacation. For safety's sake, associates should not be allowed to check company e-mail. Also for safety's sake, associates should not be allowed to log in to company systems while on forced vacation. Based on the organization and business operation, it is possible that an associate could keep theft/fraud activity afloat remotely. By not being able to access company systems remotely, the ability for the offending employee to keep activity afloat is decreased.

When newly hired associates are informed of the organization's mandatory vacation policy during orientation, they should also be briefed on their inability to access company systems while away. Being provided with this information could keep an associate from acting on a discovered window of opportunity.

Employee Assistance Programs

On many occasions an associate could make a decision to commit theft/fraud against his or her employer due to an individual financial hardship. Within an associate's world there are numerous situations that could arise that place a person in a financial hardship:

- Spouse's loss of a job
- A personal vehicle accident
- A family incident with law enforcement (e.g., DUI)
- Extended personal debt
- Death in the family

There are numerous situations that could place an associate in financial hardship. Faced with a financial hardship, a desperate individual could rationalize many options to alleviate the pressure. One rationalized decision could revolve around stealing from an employer.

Working as a CID agent for the US Army in the Republic of Korea, a unit supply officer reported the loss of around 20 gas masks. The theft of the gas masks was reported early on a Monday morning.

Initial investigation revealed the gas masks were stolen from a supply hut, but there was no sign of an apparent break-in. The gas masks and other unit equipment were stored in a Quonset hut [11] (see Figure 4.5). Access to the unit supply Quonset hut was via a key that was maintained in the possession of the company charge-of-quarters (CQ). Any individual wishing to enter the supply hut had to sign out the key from the CQ.

Late on Sunday evening prior to the reported theft of the gas masks, Private Rationalize signed out the supply hut key from the CQ for a period of about 20 minutes. The key was returned to the CQ and placed back into the key box.

During the investigation it was established that the gas masks in question were in the supply hut prior to the key being signed out by Private Rationalize. On Monday morning they were discovered missing. Between the discovery of the missing gas masks and the last time they were observed as being present in the supply hut, Private Rationalize was the only person to sign out the supply hut key.

Private Rationalize was interviewed as part of the investigation process and eventually confessed to stealing the gas masks. The stolen items had been sold that

Figure 4.5 Example of a military Quonset hut.

Sunday evening to a pawn shop in the Korean town outside the base. (At the time pawn shops were paying between $50 and $80 per gas mask.)

The reason provided by Private Rationalize for stealing and selling the gas masks was so he could purchase a plane ticket back to the states to attend his grandmother's funeral. His grandmother had recently passed away and she was an integral part of raising him.

In his hastened desire to return to the states, Private Rationalize had his mind let him believe the fastest way to obtain the money needed was to pawn stolen gas masks.

Situations leading to Private Rationalize making a rash decision were that he was never briefed by his chain of command on the number of services provided by the US Army that help out soldiers in financial need. He could have easily obtained a quick hardship loan from the Army Family Services Center.

Many employers offer their associates some type of Employee Assistance Program that they can access during times of financial need. Programs of this nature can work to lower the theft/fraud threat level within an organization. Employees facing a financial hardship have an outlet to help relieve the related stress and pressure. Additionally, they will most likely make the choice to access the Employee Assistance Program versus attempting to steal the needed assets from their employer.

As part of the new-hire orientation process, discussion needs to take place with all new associates about employee assistance programs offered. Associates need to be made aware of all of the benefits of the program, as well as the fact that participation in the program is kept completely private. Many employees might choose to bypass the Employee Assistance Program if there is a belief that their co-workers will gain knowledge of their individual participation.

Endnotes

1. "Report to the Nations on Occupational Fraud and Abuse." http://www.acfe.com/rttn.aspx (accessed September 8, 2015).
2. "Asset Misappropriation." http://www.actionfraud.police.uk/fraud_protection/asset_misappropriation (accessed September 8, 2015).
3. "Theft or Misappropriation of Funds Placed in One's Trust or Belonging to One's Employer." https://www.google.com/search?q=embezzlement+definition&ie=utf-8&oe=utf-8 (accessed September 9, 2015).
4. "Corruption." http://www.investopedia.com/terms/c/corruption.asp (accessed September 10, 2015).
5. The offering, giving, receiving, or soliciting of something of value for the purpose of influencing the action of an official in the discharge of his or her public or legal duties. http://legal-dictionary.thefreedictionary.com/bribery (accessed September 10, 2015).
6. "Balance sheet." http://www.investopedia.com/terms/b/balancesheet.asp (accessed September 10, 2015).
7. "Cash flow statement." http://www.investopedia.com/terms/c/cashflowstatement.asp (accessed September 10, 2015).
8. "What Is Financial Statement Fraud?" http://smallbusiness.chron.com/financial-statement-fraud-57182.html (accessed September 10, 2015).
9. "BBB Code of Business Practices." http://www.bbb.org/tucson/for-businesses/about-bbb-accreditation/bbb-code-of-business-practices-bbb-accreditation-standards/ (accessed September 11, 2015).
10. Full disclosure: I have used the services of both the Better Business Bureau and the Chamber of Commerce. I have no personal stake with either organization. I am providing information where both operations can be used during the business verification process.
11. Quonset huts were used in the military as storage rooms and places to billet soldiers and Marines. https://www.google.com/search?q=quonset+hut&tbm=isch&imgil=MO-KYe0o8cynaM%253A%253B7nxJzKhfTThD1M%253Bhttp%25253A%25252F%25252Farchives.msu.edu%25252Fcollections%25252Fbuildings.php&source=iu&pf=m&fir=MO-KYe0o8cynaM%253A%252C7nxJzKhfTThD1M%252C_&biw=1366&bih=657&usg=__lFWs7xWWVLPS7YELw1DBUtZPmLc%3D&ved=0CFEQyjdqFQoTCNCm4aqc9ccCFccwiAodO-4Gmg&ei=aA72VdDSF8fhoAS73JvQCQ#imgrc=MO-KYe0o8cynaM%3A&usg=__lFWs7xWWVLPS7YELw1DBUtZPmLc%3D (accessed September 12, 2015).

Chapter 5

Additional Internal Theft/ Fraud Prevention and Awareness Guidelines

Analyzing Financial Statements

Dual control is needed in the creation of an approved supplier/vendor list, as well as with the approval process for paying invoices. Following these dual control standards, the same guidelines are necessary in the creation of financial statements. All information provided from the various departments within an organization that is necessary in the creation of the various business-related financial statements has to go through some type of dual control process.

For all of the reporting sections on the financial statements, each area needs to go through a verification process. As an example, an employee can collect and compile all of the information necessary for the organization's cost of goods sold. Prior to this information being placed on the specific financial statement, it needs to go through some type of an independent verification process. At least two sets of eyes need to review and approve the information provided.

Cost of goods sold is an important line on a financial statement; other important sections are

- Payroll expenses
- Advertising expenses
- Accounts receivable
- Accounts payable
- Items in inventory

- Tax liabilities
- Travel and entertainment expenses
- Miscellaneous expenses
- Capital expenses
- All expenses associated with the normal business operation

When conducting an analysis of a financial statement, there are many questions requiring answers. With the income statement or profit and loss statement, the question to be asked is, "Do the various expenses align with the profit or income?" For many businesses there are industry-related percentages for the various expenses. For the restaurant industry, payroll expenses should be in the range of 25% to 35% of sales or revenue [1]. This percentage will vary based on the exact type of restaurant operation, from full service to quick service, etc.

The same theory holds true for cost of goods sold percentages, as compared to overall sales. Raw material converted into a marketable product will yield a certain percentage amount. The more raw material purchased, the higher the amount of projected overall sales will be.

When conducting an analysis of production type financial statements, the industry should dictate line item percentages to overall sales or revenue. Large variations in the line item percentages are strong indicators of suspicious activity. A cost of goods percentage that is above the normal average as compared to sales revenue could be an indicator that all product sales were not accurately reported. Somewhere in the operation:

- Money from sales is being skimmed and underreported.
- Product is being provided to consumers as a result of "sweethearting."
- There is a tremendous amount of product waste.
- A larger than expected amount of product produced is flawed and not up to the standard for retail sale.
- Substandard raw material was initially purchased.

The same type of financial statement analysis can be relevant for almost any type of business operation. Individuals conducting the statement analysis need to view the financial data as part of a large puzzle answering the question, "Do the pieces fit together?"

Inventory Control

For many business operations, their inventory operations are vital for continued success—no matter if it is a retail operation, wholesale warehouse, distribution center, manufacturing business, etc. In order to keep a business operation afloat, it is necessary to purchase inventory that is turned into sales/revenue. What businesses need to be concerned with is what is referred to as the inventory turnover ratio. This ratio can be calculated by dividing sales over the inventory. A simple example is if the company has $1,000 in its average inventory and $10,000 in sales, the ratio is 10. This basically shows that the business was able to turn over its inventory 10 times during the reporting period.

Not wanting to turn this text into an accounting class, there are several variations of calculating inventory ratios. For business operations that deal in perishable items, they need to stay on top of the average days in inventory, recognizing how quickly the inventory items are being moved through the process.

For business operations that conduct manufacturing type operations, the items in their inventory will most likely remain in the business for a period longer than for a grocery store or other operation that works with perishable items.

One of the main reasons to track the inventory numbers for the business "bean counters" is to maintain a liquidity in assets. The higher the inventory numbers are and the longer these items stay in the system without generating assets, the greater the amount of capital that is remaining dormant. For most business operations, the inventory needs to be liquidated for growth and to have the assets available to make additional purchases. From a theft/fraud perspective, it is vital for the businesses bottom line to ensure the inventory purchasing numbers stay in line with the amount of items in the inventory:

- For Business A, it is a known factor that each $1,000 of material purchases equates to $3,000 in revenue.
- The $2,000 generated from turning the inventory into revenue is used to keep the business operating (rent, payroll, utilities, etc.) and for purchasing new product.

As long as Business A can continue to generate $2,000 in revenue for each $1,000 in material purchases, it can continue to remain solvent. If the expected revenue generation numbers change for the negative, additional solvent expectations are possible. For many business operations, changes in expected revenues can be related to some type of theft/fraud activity.

Business A makes the purchase of $1,000 for inventory items, knowing the continued operation is based on the $2,000 in projected revenue. If Business A becomes a victim of internal theft/fraud, the following scenario is provided:

- Business A spends the $1,000 for new product, but only receives $800 of inventory into its internal system. The negative difference of $200 in inventory is a result of employee theft. Internal records show the business received its typical order of $1,000 worth of product and the company inventory records reflect the same information. Prior to the total product order amount being actually placed into the storage area, it was skimmed by a dishonest employee.

- Based on the projected inventory to sales projections, Business A can only generate $1,600 in revenue. With a decreased revenue number, Business A is facing the following issues:
  - It needs to make a decision whether to maintain its $1,000 material inventory purchases.
  - If continuing with its normal purchase, what cuts need to be made due to a decrease in expected revenue?
  - If it lowers the inventory purchase amount to keep the business operating as normal, the business can expect decreased revenue amounts in the future.
  - It may be necessary to borrow money to make up for the decreased revenue in order to keep material purchases at $1,000.

Although simple in nature, the inventory theft/fraud discussion for Business A is provided as an example that can become an issue for many organizations. The goal for all business operations is to ensure the total amount of inventory material items purchased:

- Come in the back door and make it into the inventory system
- Go through the process of being turned into revenue-generating assets
- Go out the front door as the total projected revenue assets

In order to protect against inventory theft/fraud, the following detection and prevention measures are provided:

- Establish a dual control procedure for material delivery and verification.
- Never allow the same person to conduct the material delivery count and enter the numbers into the inventory system.
- Never accept the material numbers provided by the delivery driver.

Once the delivered material is accurately entered into the inventory system, it has to be protected against theft:

- All inventory storage areas need to be secured in access-controlled locations.
- Employee entry into secured inventory locations needs to be tracked through key card or biometric access.
- Only authorized employees should be allowed system access into the secured inventory location.
- Inventory storage areas need to be under constant video surveillance.
- All inventory tracking software programs need to be password protected.
- Random audits need to take place within the inventory control system.

- Employees using company inventory material should not be allowed to make the changes of the items used on the tracking software. Establish a separation of duties procedure.
- Develop procedures that establish material accountability throughout the inventory-to-revenue process.

Once the inventory material has been used for manufacturing purposes or is being shipped to another business, there also needs to be accountability in the packaging and shipping process. As with the need to have a dual control process for incoming inventory material, the same type of activity needs to take place for packaging and loading. No matter how the preshipping product numbers are generated, there needs to be a system in place where an independent verification occurs. The business needs to ensure the proper accountability for all items packaged and loaded for shipping.

Once the material/product post inventory numbers have been compiled and verified, a person who was separate from the process needs to update the company's internal computer system. The more redundancy used in the front door-to-back door inventory tracking process, the more secure the business can be in the accuracy of material counts.

As shown in the Business A example, employee theft/fraud-related inventory shortages can have a damaging effect on the entire operation. These damaging effects relate to

- Lower future revenues for continued operation
- Having a need to cut staff in order to maintain adequate revenue levels
- Acceptance of lower revenue expectations
- Insolvency

Auditing and Bank Statement Reconciliation

In order to ensure the integrity of the entire internal business operation, there is a need for two types of auditing. These two types of audits are to be used in addition to the traditional scheduled annual or semiannual audit:

- Surprise audits: A surprise or random audit is one that fits the name—an audit of a section of the business where those working in the specific department are unaware of the upcoming procedure.
- Independent audit: This type of audit can be scheduled or random, but is conducted by an outside third party.

There is a difference between the two types of necessary audits and each one serves a purpose. It is necessary that employers discuss the internal auditing processes with all newly hired associates as part of the orientation process. Employees need to know early on in their tenure that their operation could come under a surprise or independent audit. By not knowing where or when the audit can take place, employees will be reluctant to begin a theft/fraud scheme against the business. By having a random chance of an audit taking place, dishonest associates will not know when to begin the theft/fraud cover-up process.

A major point all employers and security/audit/loss prevention personnel need to understand is that whatever is promised needs to be delivered. No matter the type of business operation, employees talk. Water-cooler discussions take place on the internal business gossip, pending rumors, and other office-related activities. If a business briefs all new associates on the potential for the use of surprise or independent audits, it must deliver. Over time, one or more discussions will take place on the threat of surprise or independent audits never occurring. The same types of discussions will also occur as a result of departments going through a surprise or independent audit.

The same rationale holds true for the business conducting scheduled audits. If it is promised, it must be delivered.

The need for using all types of audits serves the following purposes:

- They act as a deterrent against theft/fraud.
- They can be used to uncover suspicious and illegal activity against the business.
- Surprise audits serve the purpose of working to prevent associates from beginning a theft/fraud scheme. Not knowing when an audit is going to take place, a dishonest associate will not know when to begin covering his or her tracks in order to keep the incident hidden.
- Independent audits work to prevent internal collusion. An employee could be successful in conspiring with one or two fellow associates to participate in a theft/fraud scheme. The internal participants could be in the positions necessary to keep the activity hidden. With the threat of an outside set of eyes looking into departmental practices, decisions could be made to abandon the proposed scheme.

In order to remove the temptation for theft/fraud, there needs to be redundancy in the bank statement/account reconciliation process. As with most business functions, there needs to be some type of dual control procedure. No single associate should be allowed to independently reconcile the businesses financial statements. Without some type of dual control in the reconciliation process, a single employee could continuously cover up unauthorized transactions. In order to prevent unauthorized financial transactions from taking place as a result of a single control policy, the following procedures need to be implemented as they pertain to the bank account reconciliation process:

- No matter when the business elects to have its financial accounts reconciled (daily, weekly, monthly), there needs to be an independent set of eyes to verify the results.
- All types of audits need to be included as part of the reconciliation process.

As discussed throughout this section, businesses need to look at their overall systems of operation and identify and close theft-/fraud-related windows of opportunity. The more windows that can be identified and closed, the greater the number of barriers in place for theft/fraud prevention.

Endnote

1. "What Percentage Should a Restaurant Spend on Payroll?" http://smallbusiness.chron.com/percentage-should-restaurant-spend-payroll-24851.html (accessed September 13, 2015).

UNDERSTANDING FRAUD/THEFT IN THE FRANCHISEE/ FRANCHISOR INDUSTRY

II

Anyone looking to purchase a product, reserve a hotel room, grab a quick oil change, etc. interacts with a business operation in the retail community. Based on how these retail establishments are structured, their operation can fall under one of the many following scenarios:

- A large, multiunit retail operation where all locations are company owned
- A regional multiunit retail operation where all locations are company owned
- A smaller, geographical-location-specific retail operation in which all of the retail locations in this smaller operation consist of company-owned units
- A large, multiunit retail operation where a percentage of the locations are company owned and the remaining are franchisee operated
- A regional multiunit retail operation where a percentage of the locations are company owned and the remaining are franchisee operated
- A large, multiunit retail operation where all of the locations are franchisee operated
- A large, multiunit retail operation where a large majority of the locations are franchisee operated, with a few company-owned locations
- A regional multiunit retail operation where all of the locations are franchisee operated

- A smaller geographical retail operation where all of the locations are franchisee operated
- Small mom and pop retail operations where the number of locations ranges from 10 to 20 locations
- A one-unit retail establishment with a single owner

No matter what the size and number of units of the overall retail operation are, all are faced with the potential of becoming fraud/theft victims. In an effort to develop fraud/theft awareness training programs, conduct loss investigations, investigate incidents of employee theft, etc., the breakdown of those responsibilities can fall into one or more of the following categories:

- The large, multiunit company-owned retail operation has an internal loss prevention/security staff. This staff has the responsibility of overseeing all of the aspects of the security/loss prevention operation, to include:
  - Establish security standards at the corporate headquarters.
  - Establish security standards at the regional offices.
  - Establish security standards for the individual retail locations.
  - Develop loss prevention standards for all of the individual retail locations.
  - Investigate incidents of loss and theft and internal employee theft, ensure actual unit sales are the reported sales, develop inventory control standards, etc.
- The regional multiunit company-owned retail operation has an internal loss prevention/security staff. This staff has the responsibility of overseeing all of the aspects of the security/loss prevention operation, to include:
  - Establish security standards at the corporate headquarters.
  - If there are enough units scattered over a large geographical area, there could be a need to have regional offices. If so, establish security standards at the regional offices.
  - Establish security standards for the individual retail locations.
  - Develop loss prevention standards for all of the individual retail locations.
  - Investigate incidents of loss and theft and internal employee theft, ensure actual unit sales are the reported sales, develop inventory control standards, etc.
- The smaller regional retail operation where all stores are company owned has an internal loss prevention/security staff. This staff has the responsibility of overseeing all of the aspects of the security/loss prevention operation, to include:
  - Establish security standards at the corporate headquarters.
  - Establish security standards for the individual retail locations.
  - Develop loss prevention standards for all of the individual retail locations.

- Investigate incidents of loss and theft and internal employee theft, ensure actual unit sales are the reported sales, develop inventory control standards, etc.

- The large, multiunit retail operation, where a percentage of the locations are company owned and the remaining are franchisee operated, has an internal loss prevention/security staff, whose duties include:
  - Establish security at the corporate headquarters.
  - Establish security standards at the regional offices.
  - Establish security standards for the individual retail company-owned locations.
  - Develop loss prevention standards for all of the individual company-owned retail locations.
  - Investigate incidents of loss and theft, internal employee theft, ensure actual unit sales are the reported sales, develop inventory control standards, etc. for all company-owned locations.
  - Ensure product brand integrity at all franchise locations.
  - Establish programs to ensure weekly/monthly sales are reported accurately from the franchise locations.
  - Incidents of loss and theft and internal employee theft, inventory control standards, etc. are the responsibility of the individual franchisee. Based on the actual retail operation, franchisees can own a single location up to several hundred.
- The regional multiunit retail operation, where a percentage of the locations are company owned and the remaining are franchisee operated, has an internal loss prevention/security staff whose duties include:
  - Establish security at the corporate headquarters.
  - If there are enough units scattered over a large geographical area, there could be a need to have regional offices. If so, establish security standards at the regional offices.
  - Establish security standards for the individual retail company-owned locations.
  - Develop loss prevention standards for all of the individual company-owned retail locations.
  - Investigate incidents of loss and theft and internal employee theft, ensure actual unit sales are the reported sales, develop inventory control standards, etc. for all company-owned locations.
  - Ensure product brand integrity at all franchise locations.
  - Establish programs to ensure weekly/monthly sales are reported accurately from the franchise locations.
  - Incidents of loss and theft and internal employee theft, inventory control standards, etc. are the responsibility of the individual franchisee. Based

on the actual retail operation, franchisees can own a single location or several locations.

- The large, multiunit retail operation, where a very large majority of the locations are franchisee operated, with a few company owned locations, has an internal loss prevention/security staff whose duties include:
  - Establish security at the corporate headquarters.
  - Establish security standards for the individual retail company-owned locations.
  - Develop loss prevention standards for all of the individual company-owned retail locations.
  - Investigate incidents of loss and theft and internal employee theft, ensure actual unit sales are the reported sales, develop inventory control standards, etc. for all company-owned locations.
  - Ensure product brand integrity at all franchise locations.
  - Establish programs to ensure weekly/monthly sales are reported accurately from the franchise locations.
  - Incidents of loss and theft and internal employee theft, inventory control standards, etc. are the responsibility of the individual franchisee. Based on the actual retail operation, franchisees can own a single location or up to several hundred.
- The regional multiunit retail operation and the smaller geographical retail operation have an internal loss prevention/security staff. (Based on the size of the parent franchisor network, the size and scope of the loss prevention/security staff is based on operational budget capacity.) Duties include:
  - Establish security at the corporate headquarters.
  - Ensure product brand integrity at all franchise locations.
  - Establish programs to ensure weekly/monthly sales are reported accurately from the franchise locations.
  - Incidents of loss and theft and internal employee theft, inventory control standards, etc. are the responsibility of the individual franchisee. Based on the actual retail operation, franchisees can own a single location or several locations.
- For the small mom and pop multiunit retail operation to the single unit owner, the presence of a loss prevention/security staff is based on the overall budgeting parameters of the ownership:
  - Security standards are established by the ownership and the development of these policies could be made by an individual who wears many hats in the organization. For the single unit owner, the security standards are developed on the individual need of the store owner.
  - Loss prevention standards and investigations are established by the ownership of the small mom and pop multiunit retail operation and the activity is based on budgetary restrictions.

- Investigation of incidents of loss and theft and internal employee theft, ensuring actual unit sales are the reported sales, developing inventory control standards, etc. could be handled by a small loss prevention/security staff or individual or by an owner who wears more than one hat.

When discussing the two worlds of company-owned retail stores versus franchised locations, the responsibilities of the loss prevention/security staff and that of ownership differ. Someone who owns the retail operation outright has full control. Someone who owns the franchise rights and sells locations to third-party owners has varying aspects of control:

- The franchisor owns the name of the retail operation and can establish standards on raw material purchases, marketing, sales reporting standards, products offered to the consumer, etc.—basically any aspect of the operation that controls the brand integrity of the product being offered to the public.
- The franchisee is responsible for the physical security of the location or locations. If directed by the parent organization, his or her ability to purchase raw material could be restricted to select vendors. The franchisee is also responsible for establishing the individual location loss prevention standards, inventory control, product development, investigating incidents of employee theft, etc. Basically, the franchisee is responsible for location appearance and retail operation as an individual owner of the specific location or locations. What the franchisee does not own is the location name and the product or service that is offered to the public.
- In order to ensure the franchisee is reporting sales correctly the franchisor can use internal loss prevention/security personnel to investigate potential incidents. The franchisor can also use staff to ensure and maintain product integrity standards.

Chapter 6

An Overview of Franchise Operations

Most people go through their daily lives making purchases in a retail store, getting their oil changed from a local garage or a chain that provides the service, checking into a hotel for the evening, visiting a learning center, getting their suit dry cleaned, etc. Within the retail environment, the type of product to be purchased by the consumer is based on what product or service can be offered. Basically stated, can this product or service be marketed to the public and can a profit be made?

As most people go throughout the day, making all types of purchases, they do not know or probably care if the location in question is owned by an individual, company, corporation, or franchisee. Their only concern is product satisfaction, customer service, and a reasonable price.

From the perspective of the large or small retailer where all locations are owned and operated by the organization, concerns are

- Selling marketable products
- Product advertising
- Easy access locations
- Employee and customer safety
- Managing location lease agreements
- Hiring quality associates
- Managing inventory
- Ensuring shrink and theft losses are kept at a minimum
- Ensuring all sales are properly recorded through the register and reported to the main office
- Maintaining the security posture of all retail locations as well as the main and regional offices

From the perspective of the franchisor, where all retail locations are owned and operated by franchisees [1], concerns are

- Developing marketable products that can be sold to the consumer through the franchise locations
- Ensuring that the proper money is collected from franchisee locations to produce an effective product marketing campaign
- Working with the perspective franchisee to select the best retail location, which can be either constructed by the franchisor company and leased or sold back to the franchisee or existing locations leased by the franchisee
- Ensuring all sales are properly recorded through the register and reported to the main office
- Collecting on delinquent franchisee royalty payments [2] and loans

From the perspective of the franchisee, concerns are

- Hiring quality associates
- Raw material and product purchasing to run the internal operation
- Managing inventory
- Ensuring shrink and theft losses are kept to a minimum
- Ensuring all sales are properly recorded through the register and reported to the main office
- Maintaining the physical security posture of their individual retail locations

With traditional retail locations, all of the associates are employed by the corporation. The corporation is responsible for all aspects of the business operation, to include all issues related to fraud and theft. With franchisee/franchisor relationships, the franchisor owns the business or product name while the franchisee owns and operates the individual retail location.

Endnotes

1. Franchisor operations have an income base from selling locations and collecting royalties from weekly/monthly sale of the franchise locations. The royalty monies collected are based on a percentage of the franchisee locations weekly/monthly total sales. Based on the franchise agreement a portion the royalty fees go into the general fund of the franchisor and the remainder are used in the advertising fund. Basically generating advertising revenue to market the product or brand to the consumer.
2. Franchisees pay a percentage of their total sales to the franchisor. These are referred to as royalty payments. Based on the franchise agreement established by the franchisor, franchisees could also be required to pay a percentage of their total sales for the purpose of an advertising fund.

Chapter 7

Franchise Sales Underreporting and Brand Integrity

Introduction

Many loss prevention/security personnel are used to working for retailers where all of the sales locations are owned by the parent company and they have carte blanche access to all operations. This is to include working with individual locations for associate integrity, inventory control and shrinkage, internal location security, and unlimited access to the entire store operation.

In the franchisor/franchisee world, loss prevention/security personnel have no control over many of these aspects for an individual franchise location. Location security, associate integrity, inventory control, and shrinkage and other aspects of the daily operation are under the direct control of the franchise location owner or franchisee.

What the loss prevention/security personnel who work for the parent organization do have control over are the areas of sales underreporting and brand integrity.

What Is Sales Underreporting and Who Are Its Victims?

In a typical retail operation, the goal of the manager/operator is to have the highest number of product sales for a specific location. All of the sales dollars for any traditional retail location become part of the total sales numbers for the entire organization. If the organization has 10 retail locations and the weekly sales for each store are $1,000, the overall sales number for the company is $10,000.

If the same organization were operated from the franchisor perspective, the overall goal would be to have the highest number of product sales for each specific location. Although the main organization or franchisor does not actually own each of the 10 individual locations, the weekly sales of each franchise store are of some concern.

Based on the franchise agreement [1], the individuals operating each individual retail location are required to pay a set percentage of weekly sales to the parent organization. The higher the amount of weekly sales produced, the greater the amount of revenue that flows into the account of the franchisor. A major concern for any franchise-based operation is the accurate reporting of sales by all of their franchisees. If actual weekly/monthly sales are reported as received, the franchisor will receive the royalty fees that are rightly due. If the franchisee reports a lower weekly/monthly sales amount to the parent organization, the franchisor will receive a lower royalty amount than is rightly due.

In order to establish the potential victims of underreported sales, it is necessary to provide an account of what royalty payments can consist of

- Some franchisee-based operations collect a single percentage royalty fee from each location. Based on the franchise agreement and the needs of the parent organization, a single percentage fee is collected on a weekly/monthly basis. Once the single royalty payment is received by the parent organization, the money allocated for the general fund and advertising account is broken down internally.
- Some franchisee-based operations will break the required payments down into two categories. One is the main royalty fee that is collected as part of weekly/monthly sales of each franchise-based location. In addition to receiving a traditional royalty fee, some franchisors also collect what is referred to as an advertising fee. Advertising fees are typically a smaller percentage than the initially collected royalty payment.

Some franchisee-based locations can have an overall 12% weekly/monthly sales royalty fee. If the franchisor has the franchise agreement set up to collect both a royalty payment and an advertising fee, the breakdown could be 10% royalty and 2% advertising fee.

As previously referenced, all royalty fees collected are prearranged based on the agreements made with the signing of the franchise agreement; the actual royalty/advertising breakdowns vary.

Due to how franchisee-based royalty payments are broken down, the victims of franchisee sales underreporting are many:

- The general operating fund of the franchisor. Royalty fees collected are typically deposited into the general fund of the parent organization, with the revenue used to cover the following:
  - Associate hiring, training, and retention
  - New product research and development

  - General operating expenses
  - Expansion (marketing) capabilities
  - Brand integrity inspections by franchisor associates
  - Business development visits by franchisor associates
- The advertising fund. Fees collected as part of royalty-based weekly/monthly sales reported are used to cover the following:
  - Local, regional, and national product advertising campaigns
  - In-store poster type brand advertising material
  - Educating the consumer on new-product releases

Based on the information previously discussed, the victims of franchisee sales underreporting are many. The lower the amount of revenue collected by the parent organization is, the greater the effect on internal business operations. This can lead to fewer location visits by home office associates, which are used to increase franchisee sales and increase the ease of operation and brand identity protection. Franchisees and franchisors work hand in hand to obtain the maximum amount of profitability from each individual franchise retail location.

With the advertising fund revenue, the lower the amount collected is, the greater the impact on all franchisees within the overall operation will be. The marketing department associates with the parent organization might not have the needed funds to effectively market the products being offered. Successful marketing campaigns work by keeping the consumer informed on product locations, product improvements, new products or services, and product superiority.

With a decreased marketing budget based on lower reported overall sales revenue, each and every franchisee in the entire operation becomes a victim of sales underreporting. If the products or services of the franchise operation cannot be successfully marketed, individual franchisees suffer as it pertains to lower weekly/monthly sales numbers.

Sales Underreporting Causing a Negative Chain Reaction

The reasons a franchisee might choose to underreport sales are based on a decision they make. The individual causes of a franchisee choosing to underreport sales are many:

- Individual greed
- Curiosity (Can I beat the system?)
- Need extra cash to pay one or more associates under the table or off the books
- Change in individual home income status (Spouse could have lost a job.)
- Change in local or national economic conditions
- Recent road construction that affects traffic flow into and out of the retail location

- Recent influx of a competitor in the market
- Increase of raw material purchases
- Increase in the franchise fees set by the parent office
- Drastic changes in minimum wage payment requirements for all associates—typically set by the local city or municipality
- Sudden increase in the monthly expenses of the franchisee (e.g., college tuition, DUI conviction, new home purchase, etc.)

No matter the reason that a franchisee chooses to underreport weekly/monthly sales to the franchisor, individual actions could have a negative impact on the entire operation. Two of the main areas where sales underreporting has a major effect on the overall franchisee/franchisor business relationship are

- New product development
- The ability to effectively market the product

Research and new product development are vital in allowing the individual franchise operations to remain competitive in their individual markets. If the franchisor operation begins seeing a decrease in reported sales and royalty fees collected, choices have to be made by the parent company on budget allocations. If the choice is made to maintain the current level of operation, while lowering the amount of assets allocated to new product development, the franchise-based retail operations could suffer in a competitive market.

The other negatively affected area, due to a lower amount of fees collected, is advertising. In order to keep the consumer informed on new products, current discount offers, and other current product-related information, all organizations need to have adequate funds allocated to advertising. This is to include product advertising in print media, television, and online.

If the retail product-consuming public is not informed of the services offered by a specific retailer, its individual market share could be transferred to the competition.

Based on the two previously discussed areas that could have major effects on overall operations, along with other potential issues related to sales underreporting, some or many of the franchisees could see lower customer traffic. With a lower level of customer traffic, weekly/monthly sales could suffer.

Since many franchise-based operations have many franchisees that are one- or two-location owners, these operations conduct business with tight margins. Any change in sales income amounts in the main affected area with the franchisee comes down to profit.

As with the previous discussion on the need for the parent company to maintain a certain level of royalty income to keep operations consistent or growing, the same holds true for the individual franchisee. These individuals all have minimum weekly/monthly income levels that need to be maintained in order to operate their business and cover personal expenses. Any negative change in overall product sales on a weekly/monthly basis causes the business owners to make changes. These changes could be in the form of lowering labor costs, lowering product/raw material costs (discussed in the next section on brand integrity), or lowering the actual amount of weekly/monthly sales reported.

As previously discussed, there are many reasons why a franchisee would choose to underreport sales to the franchisor. If overall sales are down due to cuts in franchisor-based new-product development and advertising, the individual franchise owners will feel the effects. These effects could be one more reason why a franchisee could choose to underreport sales.

As previously discussed, franchisees are small business owners and operate within tight margins. With any change in income due to decreased customer traffic, a franchisee might have to make a choice as to how to keep income levels consistent. Instead of making a change to the current staffing requirements or altering raw material purchases, the choice can be made to keep more money in the franchisee's pocket by reporting a lower than actual weekly/monthly sales amount to the parent organization—basically allowing the intended underreporting activities of fellow franchisees to force the franchisee into making an unethical decision in order to keep his or her current level of household weekly/monthly income. Thus, sales underreporting leads to additional incidents of sales underreporting. No matter what the business or industry is, negative monetary changes have a cause and effect.

Why Is It Necessary to Protect Brand Integrity?

Many consumers have an understanding that a fast-food restaurant is owned and operated just like another one with the same name a few miles down the street. For some fast-food restaurants that are not owned by individual franchisees, this thought process holds true. With franchisee-operated fast-food restaurants called Burger World (fictional name given to support the story), the individual ownership is most likely different. A Burger World on the north side of town might not have the same owner as a Burger World on the south side of town.

As previously referenced, franchise locations are operated as independent businesses. Even though the same business name is on the door, inside resides an independent owner/operator.

The hope of the franchisor is that a consumer will receive the exact same service and product quality when visiting a Burger World on the north or south side of town. The same holds true for a Burger World in Florida and one in California, basically ensuring brand integrity.

In the arena of all franchise-operated businesses, brand integrity is vital for continued success. No matter if the business is a Burger World, one that offers quick oil changes, ink cartridge refills, etc.—the product quality received at one franchise location has to be the same at all others.

For franchise operations in financial trouble, the operator might choose to purchase raw material from an unapproved source in order to save money on raw material purchases and hopefully fool consumers into believing they are receiving a quality (Burger World) product.

When substandard raw material is used to produce a product that is sold to the public, the consumer's expected quality standards suffer. With lower than expected quality standards at some of the locations of a franchise-operated business, the entire operation can be looked upon in a negative light.

In order to protect the brand integrity of a particular franchise operation, it is vital that loss prevention/security personnel work to ensure all franchisees are using only franchisor-approved raw material. Fraudulent raw material could consist of

- Unapproved ice cream
- Low-quality cold cuts
- Low-quality meat for burgers
- Low-quality coffee beans
- Substandard vehicle fluids and parts

No matter the service provided by a franchise operation, it is necessary to protect the overall brand integrity of the entire organization. Lower than expected product quality can lead to decreased foot traffic at the location and, eventually, lower weekly/monthly sales. As previously referenced, sales underreporting by a few can lead to increased underreporting by other franchisees. The same holds true for brand integrity issues. Franchisees cutting corners on product quality can have a negative cause and effect on the entire operation.

Making Sure That All Sales Are Reported (Sales Integrity)

From an investigative perspective it is vital to ensure that sales from franchise locations are recorded in the store register and properly reported to the franchisor. Loss prevention/security personnel, working for the parent organization, can use many investigative tools (discussed through the remainder of this section) to uncover potential issues of sales underreporting.

In order to ensure the success of any franchisor-based sales integrity program, the use of investigative tools has to be common knowledge among the franchisee base. All franchisees in the overall operation should be made aware the parent corporation employs an aggressive sales integrity program. The program needs to be marketed to the franchisee base in a manner of cooperation. The parent organization is cooperating with the entire franchisee base to ensure as much money as possible is collected for continuing operation and growth. With the proper reporting of all sales within the operation, both the franchisor and the franchisees benefit.

Franchisees can then develop an understanding of a cause and effect factor. The actions of a few underreporting franchisees can have a negative effect on the overall operation.

If the sales integrity program is successfully marketed to the franchisee base, it can work to create an added level of cooperation between the two parties—franchisor and franchisee.

What the franchisor wants to avoid in the creation of a sales integrity program is

- Showing favoritism—creating a sales integrity program where some franchisees are immune from random audits, covert brand integrity visits, mystery shopping visits, undercover large purchases, etc.
- Absence of integrity—operating a sales integrity program where potential investigations are overlooked for certain franchisees. Information is developed where a franchisee is possibly underreporting sales. No investigation takes place due to the franchisee being a favorite among select franchisor employees. For the integrity of the sales integrity program, all franchisee operations have to be investigated if suspicion of underreporting develops.
- Only viewed by the franchisee base as negative—investigative personnel in the Security/Loss Prevention Department need to become partners with the franchisees—being available to answer security/loss prevention types of questions, develop and provide various types of retail-based loss prevention sessions, make location visits for the sole purpose of relationship building, etc. A franchisee should not be able to develop an opinion of the Security/Loss Prevention Department that only shows up at the location in a negative posture.
- Only looking to generate underreporting income—the overall goal of the Security/Loss Prevention Department should be to create an environment where 100% of sales reporting takes place and not one that is only concerned with taking down franchisees.

Successful sales integrity programs work best when a team type franchisee/franchisor relationship is created. In addition to the previously discussed relationship-building tactics, security/loss prevention personnel need to work with the franchisees on the understanding of employee theft issues. This is to include discussion and information sessions on

- The types of employee theft within the specific retail operation
- Causes of or reasons why employees steal from their employer
- Proper new-hire screening procedures
- How a franchisee can identify and prevent incidents of employee theft

When it comes to sales integrity within a franchisee-based retail operation, both parties (franchisee and franchisor) have to take a vested interest in the process.

Franchisees need to understand that all incidents of sales underreporting will be aggressively investigated. Additionally, franchisees need to understand the members of the Security/Loss Prevention Department are working to ensure all areas of sales integrity and growth take place. All sales that are properly reported to the franchisor and individual franchisees are in a position to maximize the income potential.

Sales Underreporting Victims Can Be the Parent Organization or an Unknowing Business Partner

As previously discussed, sales underreporting can have a negative effect on income coming into the parent company. This is to include both royalty and advertising fee income. The victims of sales underreporting for this scenario include:

- The franchisor
- The franchisees as far as new product development and remaining competitive
- The franchisees as far as the parent company being able to maintain a successful product marketing campaign

Additional victims of sales underreporting can also include:

- Fellow business partners
- Family members of the underreporting franchisee
- Employees of the underreporting franchisee

Family members and employees of knowingly underreporting franchisees could be affected from a loss of business income or the closure of the actual business. With many franchise operations, willful sales underreporting on the part of the franchisee is a violation of the franchise agreement and cause to terminate the contract. Based on the wording of the franchise agreement, its termination could lead to

- The franchisee having to sell the business
- The franchisee having to pay restitution to the parent organization

If the franchisee is forced to sell the business due to known sales underreporting, the existing employees are out of a job. Franchisee family members are also affected due to a decrease in household income.

Other individuals affected by a franchisee knowingly underreporting weekly/monthly sales could be business partners. Many individuals form corporations as part of a business venture and enter the world of franchise-based operations. With many franchise agreements, it is stated that if any member of the ownership group knowingly underreports sales it is cause for the termination of the overall franchise agreement. Even though one or more of the other corporate partners were unaware of the underreporting activity, they could suffer the loss of the business—basically becoming a victim of sales underreporting, even though they had no knowledge of the activity taking place.

Employee Skimming and Sales Integrity

Employee or associate skimming [2] is nothing new to the retail industry. This holds true for any business that receives cash as part of its daily business operation. Business operations susceptible to skimming can range from restaurants to automotive garages to a medical office receiving cash as part of a copayment, etc. The goal of the dishonest associate is to remove as much cash as possible from the daily operation while avoiding detection.

There are countless retail types of operations conducting business on a daily basis across this country. These operations range from large multi-unit and company-owned retail stores to small and large franchise locations and the single-unit mom and pop family business. The desire of the owners and operators of these various locations is to ensure all cash received into the business, via customer purchases or transactions, makes it into the company bank account. The desire of the dishonest associate is to look for holes in the daily operating system, in an effort to conduct illegal activities.

The theft tactics used by the dishonest associate vary based on the business operation where the cash transactions take place. Within the retail world there are countless types of business operations and their individual operating practices are many. It would be almost impossible to list each and every business operating across the country and its individual susceptibility to employee skimming. In an effort to provide the reader with a broad knowledge of the many skimming-related activities present in the retail community, the focus for skimming education and prevention measures is as follows:

- Sweethearting
- Manipulating the cash drawer
- Taking advantage of customer reward programs

Sweethearting

The word "sweetheart" can be a term of endearment, lead to an upcoming list of "honey do's," or describe a conspiracy to commit theft against a retail organization. It is quite possible associates working for any retail operation remove items from the premises behind the backs of the manager or owner. This is outright stealing and, based on the retail operation, quite risky.

In an effort to conceal the theft of material from the retail location, many associates operating the cash register take to sweethearting.

Sweethearting requires the involvement of at least one other person. This individual, acting as a consumer, will approach his or her fellow accomplice and present one or more items for purchase. Instead of recording all of the items presented for purchase, as with a traditional sale, the individual operating the register might ring a few small dollar items and place them in a store bag. The register operator will also place other higher dollar items into the same bag as the items recorded on the register. The only difference is that the customer is not charged for the high-dollar items.

In the eyes of someone looking over the transaction from a distance, the activity between the customer and employee appears normal.

The same type of activity holds true for a deli type of operation. An accomplice might approach the counter with a tray of entrees and only be charged for a cookie. A friend could have an accomplice who works for an auto maintenance business. The friend has major maintenance done to his or her vehicle and is only charged for an oil change.

With the crime of sweethearting, the manner in which the act is conducted is based on the actual retail operation and the product for sale. The loss from items stolen via a sweethearting operation can have harsher effects on a single franchise location versus a large corporation-owned retail operation. As previously referenced, each and every franchise location is an independent business that operates under tight margins. The higher the overall operating costs of the franchise business are, the lower the profit level is.

In an effort to avoid suffering losses due to associate-based sweethearting, franchise owners should

- Install on-site and off-site monitoring capabilities at each register. During associate loss prevention training programs, ensure that all employees are aware of the register video monitoring system.
- In a retail location where a large number of high-dollar retail items can be purchased, use a third-party receipt verification individual. After the consumer leaves the register but before he or she exits the building, another associate looks over the items in the bag or shopping cart and makes a comparison with the items present and the sales receipt.
- Based on the retail operation and the items available for purchase, some operations can use the lock and key method. In order for customers to obtain smaller high-dollar items, a manager has to use a key to unlock the display counter to retrieve the item. Once the item is selected by the customer, the manager can oversee the register transaction.
- Sometimes associates will bypass the universal product code (UPC) [3] (Figure 7.1) on the particular item and manually attempt to enter a lower item price through the register. This is also a form of sweethearting. In order to

Figure 7.1 Sample UPC.

avoid this type of sweethearting, the retail location should require manager approval for any UPC overrides.

- Managers and owners need to be aware of repeat customers waiting to check out with a particular sales associate.
- Managers and store owners can also look into purchasing various software programs that claim their technology can be used to prevent associate sweethearting. Because this text is not a marketing catalog for specific vendors, retail managers and store owners should research the industry for a program that fits their specific establishments.

Taking Advantage of Customer Reward Programs

The goal of many retail operations is the repeat customer. These are individuals who frequent the establishment on a routine basis. Many repeat customers are attracted to the retail location based on the product offered, the quality of merchandise sold, and the cost. Based on the retail operation, some can count on the repeat customer as part of the daily operation and services offered. Other retail locations attract the repeat customer based on providing the individual with discounted or free product as part of the customer making a set number of purchases over a period of time. This is basically setting up a customer reward program.

Customer reward programs vary depending on the business operation. Many are associated with but not limited to the restaurant industry. Within the retail community, customer reward programs can be associated with the following:

- After 10 sandwich purchases, the next sandwich is free.
- Make 10 smoothie purchases and the next one is free.
- After six oil changes, the next one is free.
- After spending $100 in movie and snack purchases, $10 is credited to the customer's account.
- After making a certain number of copies, the consumer's account is credited with a dollar amount.
- For every $100 in grocery purchases, the customer receives a $0.10 per gallon discount on the next fuel purchase.

As previously referenced, the reward program is based on the product or services offered by the retail establishment. The customer reward is based on making a set amount or number of purchases in order to receive a free item or account credit. With many large retail operations, the entire process is computer based and harder for the associate to manipulate. An example of a popular customer reward program follows.

Across the country there are several large operators of multiplex theater operations. Many of these multiplex theater locations have from 6 to 30 or more screens that each show a different movie. Customers are enticed into signing up for these frequent movie watcher programs by being offered a monetary reward or account credit for making a set amount of ticket and snack purchases over a set period of time. One popular program is that, after the customer makes purchases of over $100, his or her account receives a $10 credit. The credit can be used to purchase additional movie tickets or snack items.

Once enticed to become a frequent movie watcher, consumers can sign up at their local theater or through the company website. Many of these programs require an upfront member fee, as well as an annual renewal fee. (The greater the number of ticket and snack purchases made throughout the year by members, the initial and annual renewal costs can be justified in the minds of the consumers. They might have spent $30 to join and renew each year, but their activity resulted in a large amount of account credits.)

After becoming a member, the consumer is provided with a credit card type card that is swiped after a movie ticket or snack purchase. Once the consumer reaches each spending threshold, the individual's account is automatically credited. During the next visit to the theater, any credits on the consumer's account can be used to lower the cost of the movie ticket or a box of popcorn.

With these types of consumer reward programs, it is hard for a dishonest associate to manipulate the system for his or her own monetary benefit.

Retailers become more vulnerable to employee skimming and theft when the customer is provided with a frequent customer card that is punched or stamped after each purchase. An example of these types of reward programs follows.

Many towns and cities across the country have several different sandwich shops where consumers can purchase their lunch or dinner. In an effort to attract repeat customers, many of these locations offer free product for a set number of previous purchases. Many of these free product offer programs require the customer to make 10 sandwich purchases and then the next one is free—that is, for every 10 sandwiches purchased, the 11th sandwich is free. This offers roughly a 10% discount for an individual making frequent purchases at the specific location.

With a majority of these sandwich locations, customers are provided a business-card-sized repeat customer card. Based on the establishment, the frequency card is marked in some manner for each purchase made:

- Stamped with a location unique identifier
- Hole punched with a location unique identifier
- Initialed by an associate working the cash register

Once the customer reaches the required number of item purchases, the frequency card is presented at the time of payment. Upon presentation, the customer receives the free item.

With any customer reward program, the retailer can attract repeat business and provide patrons with discounted or free product. Reward programs that use a paper-based card that is stamped after each purchase, open the business owner up to potential fraudulent activity. Many of these programs are manipulated by the cashier and customer working in concert to defraud the business and its owners.

As previously discussed with sweethearting, the business associate is manipulating the system to provide a friend with free product or services. After making a sandwich purchase, as previously discussed, instead of marking the customer frequency card with a single purchase, multiple credits are provided to the customer. This allows the friend to complete the number of required purchases without actually making the product purchases.

Additionally, the business associate can provide the friend with several reward cards that have already been properly marked with the required number of purchases to receive free product. This allows the friend to receive countless amounts of free product without making any of the required purchases.

As referenced previously, the larger the retail operation is, the more sophisticated the reward program will be. In many circumstances, this is a true statement and the ability to defraud these programs is limited. What the reader and business owner need to understand, especially in franchisee-owned locations, is that having a large parent operation does not lead to a lower fraud threat level. Many single- or multiple-location franchise operations operate somewhat independently of the franchisor and are allowed to establish their own customer reward program. In an effort to save money, many franchises establish the simple paper-card-based reward programs that are easily manipulated.

Business owners also need to understand that switching the customer reward program to a computer-based operation connected to the point of sale system does not protect the business from potential fraudulent activity. As long as an employee operating the register can go into the computer-based system and add purchase amounts or credits to a customer's reward account, the business owner has allowed an avenue for fraud.

Other computer-based customer reward programs provide the consumer with a key-tag type card that is scanned each time a purchase is made. On the front side of the key-tag card is usually the name of the business and the other side contains a barcode that is unique to the specific customer's reward frequency account. All the customer has to do is present the key card during each purchase in order for the computer system of the specific business to record the transaction.

As long as the card scanned during each purchase belongs to the actual customer making the purchase, the reward system operates as desired. As with any legitimate system, however, associates working within the business can engage in manipulation. A few examples are as follows:

- The business associate creates several bogus customer reward accounts and pockets the key cards. Once the key cards are in the possession of the associate, he or she can scan one of the bogus cards during each transaction for customers not belonging to that business's specific reward program. Once the bogus key cards reach the desired number of purchases or purchase amounts, they can be given to friends or sold to others and redeemed for free product.
- Associates can have their friends, who obtained reward key tags legitimately, give them (the business employee) their individual tags. Throughout each business day, the individual key tags are scanned during customer transactions where the individual is not a member of the customer reward program. Once the reward key tags have reached the number of purchases necessary to receive free product, they are returned to the friends. Typically, once the key tags are returned to the conspiring friends, the associate receives some type of monetary payment.
- The associate can have a single individual involved in the process; the friend creates numerous customer reward accounts using different names. Once several key tag type accounts are created, the tags are given to the associate. All the associate has to do is swipe a key tag for each purchase made throughout the day, as long as the current customer is not a member of the reward program. Once the key tags have registered the required number of purchases, they can be returned to the single coconspirator or sold to other friends or individuals.

From a small business owner's perspective, the more repeat customers the better. The main issue with the scenarios previously outlined is that many of the customers making purchases are single-visit consumers—customers that might visit the retail establishment once or twice a year. If all of these single-purchase customer visits are treated as repeat customer traffic, the reward program is providing free product at a rate that is not consistent with the number of program members who accumulate the required number of visits on a routine basis.

Employees manipulating a well-meaning repeat customer reward program can actually cost the business more in product costs than the intended benefit of the marketing campaign. In an effort to prevent fraudulent activity from taking place in a repeat customer reward program, the location owner or franchisee needs to keep the following information in mind:

- Keep a close eye on the total number of free items provided as a result of the reward program. As time goes by and associates realize they can manipulate the system, a fraud warning could be a drastic increase in the redemption of reward cards. This is especially necessary if the reward program is based on paper or cards.

- If the customer reward program is tied to the swiping of a key tag, use the point of service to create a daily report listing all of the account numbers used each day. The report can also be used to report reward account numbers on a weekly basis. The purpose of the account number report is to look for repetition in account numbers used.
- Look into creating a frequent rewards program that is tied to an app on the cell phone of the individual customer.
- Do not allow associates to manually add reward points to the account of customers through the point of sale system.

Endnotes

1. According to BusinessDictionary.com, a franchise agreement is defined as a legal contract in which a well-established business consents to provide its brand, operational model, and required support to another party for them to set up and run a similar business in exchange for a fee and some share of the income generated. The franchise agreement lays out the details of what duties each party needs to perform and what compensation each can expect. http://www.businessdictionary.com/definition/franchise-agreement.html (accessed July 31, 2015).
2. Skimming in the retail environment involves an employee or employees removing all or part of the cash from a transaction prior to the proceeds from the sale being recorded into the financial records of the organization.
3. A UPC is swiped over a reader on the register counter. Based on the line setup and numbering of the UPC, the actual price of the individual item is revealed.

Chapter 8

Understanding Established Comparable (EC) Sales

Within the retail sales community, success is based around what is referred to as established comparable sales or EC sales. This basically refers to a weekly or monthly sales period that can be compared to the previous year. The goal of the location manager or owner is to ensure the sales for the month of May 2016 are higher than sales for the month of May 2015.

When tracking EC sales, different accounting methods are used for comparison. Sales can be referred to or tracked based on

- The total dollar amount of sales per period tracked. (EC sales for the month of June are up $10,000.)
- Total sales based on percentage. (EC sales for the month of July are up or down 2%.)
- EC sales tracked (percentage or dollar amount) based on certain items within the overall business operation. (Overall store EC sales are up 2% for the month of May, while sales of winter clothing are down 5%.)

EC sales are also tracked or monitored regionally, state by state, nationally, etc. Based on the specific interests of the business operation, managers, executives, and owners will use the tracking method that can best show sales' progress or decline.

The use of EC sales in the franchisor/franchisee community is a key factor when showing overall business growth or decline—basically answering the question, "Is our overall business operation increasing the total sales of product each year?"

When looking at EC sales, those conducting the analysis also need to take into account price changes of product, weather issues, specific marketing programs, etc. Looking to answer the previous question on whether total sales increased, the answer is not based entirely on dollar amounts. A 10% price increase per item sold will likely work to increase the total overall sales amount for the year. However, customers might not like the increase in price and make fewer trips to the stores to make a purchase.

A lowering of the price of a certain item or items can work to the advantage of the store owners and the overall business. A lower price can increase customer traffic and have a positive impact on EC sales.

As previously referenced, harsh weather can have an effect on foot traffic during the winter months and lower sales for that period—another issue that can affect sales in a new marketing campaign. Many franchise-based business operations will work to tie product advertising in with the release of a highly anticipated movie release or game system. If the marketing is successful, managers and owners should see an increase in EC sales.

Business owners and loss prevention personnel need to take a step beyond comparing the local, regional, and national sales numbers with the previous year's activity. It is vital that an analysis of raw material purchased is compared to the sales of the business operation.

Take into account a franchise-based business that has the primary business of selling ice cream. When tracking EC sales, an analysis of total gallons purchased through the distribution centers also has to take place. If EC sales are flat and prices remain relatively unchanged, Store A should have purchased the same amount of overall gallons of ice cream for the two years in the analysis. If EC sales increase, the amount of ice cream purchased should increase. The same holds true for a decrease in EC sales the following year in the analysis period.

When conducting an analysis of ice cream purchased year to year, as compared to EC sales, investigators need to take into account whether sales increase or decrease in line with yield projections per gallon of ice cream. Each gallon of ice cream purchased should provide a set dollar amount of retail sales (yield/usage) [1].

When conducting a yield/usage type of analysis, many questions come to mind that need to be answered:

- Is the number of gallons of ice cream purchased consistent with the sales increase or decrease?
- Did EC sales increase, while the yield/usage analysis projected a higher level of possible overall sales than the amount reported?
- Did EC sales decrease, while the yield/usage analysis projected a higher level of possible overall sales than the amount reported?

The necessity of conducting a yield/usage analysis is vital when store owners, regional managers, investigators, etc. are trying to get a true handle on the actual EC sales:

- Many might choose to look for a sales decrease that most likely took place over an extremely cold and snowy winter.
- Retail sales were lower for a specific geographical region of the country.
- A specific franchise-based operation is reporting decreased sales regionally or nationally.
- A specific franchise-based operation is reporting increased sales regionally or nationally.

In the franchise world, a franchisee can use reported market trends, weather issues, etc. to manipulate the number of sales reported to the franchisor. The title of this chapter is "Understanding Established Comparable (EC) Sales"; with a basic understanding of EC sales, many might accept the sales numbers provided by the franchisee as true based on the weather or reported market trends. In an effort to determine the possibility of sales underreporting, EC sales numbers and yield/usage amounts need to be analyzed in order to get a clear picture of accurate sales.

Take into account the fictitious national franchise operation of Burger World. All of a sudden many consumers have become more health conscious and are changing their eating habits. They might go out for lunch, but instead of visiting Burger World they go to Salad World. Over time, the EC sales for Salad World increase, while the parent company of Burger World reports negative financial news of decreased EC sales. The blame is put on a more health-conscious society.

Many franchisees of Burger World will use local marketing campaigns to increase their sales and look to the parent organization to introduce a healthier product line. Other franchisees will use the negative company-wide sales numbers to increase the amount of money going into their personal bank accounts, while blaming the decrease in EC sales on a health-conscious society. On face value, many in the parent company will accept the lower royalty and advertising funds paid by the franchisee. Their belief is that sales are down across the board. A franchisee who is not entirely honest can use the negative company-wide financial news to underreport the true sales information.

As previously referenced, many franchisees are small business owners and operate one to a few store locations. Changes in overall sales and cash flow will have a negative effect on the overall bottom line. In an effort to maintain the current level of cash flow into his or her personal bank account, a dishonest franchisee will "cook the books"—basically reporting a weekly sales amount that is lower than actual sales during the reported period.

On average, overall sales are down for the franchise operation a few percentage points. Those taking advantage of a decrease in national or regional sales numbers might claim their individual business has suffered a larger drop in product purchases.

Investigators and business owners (franchisors) also need to develop an understanding that an attempt to take advantage of negative business-wide sales numbers is not limited to those franchisees who operate a small number of locations. Based on the integrity level of the individual business owners, an operator of 100 locations could possibly take advantage of company-wide negative sales numbers.

It is also necessary for those who have an involvement in the analysis of reported sales numbers to the parent organization to understand that there are a number of reasons for a decrease in national, geographical, or regional sales numbers:

- A rapidly expanding franchise operation that sells competitive products
- Negative product information that gains national media attention
- On a geographical level, harsh weather conditions
- On a regional level, the opening of a new bypass road
- On a more local level, some type of construction activity taking place

Prior to accepting the decrease in reported sales, investigators need to look at the amount of raw material purchases made by the individual franchisee. During the reported period of decreased sales, the following questions need to be answered:

- Are raw material purchases consistent with the reported sales amounts?
- Why are lower sales reported, while raw material purchase amounts are relatively stable?
- Why is there a large decrease in reported sales, while there is a slight decrease in raw material purchases?

In order to answer the previous questions, a yield/usage analysis can assist in providing the true sales of the reporting periods in question. Also, there is one additional question that needs to be taken into account when looking to understand EC sales:

- Is the decrease in reported sales consistent with the decrease in raw material purchases?

On face value, the lower sales and raw material amounts validate the decreased reported sales. Why would any business owner purchase additional raw material that cannot be sold during the normal course of business? If the sales numbers reported to the parent organization are accurate, logic dictates the decrease in raw material purchases.

If the franchise operation in question intends to use the negative financial information reported by the franchisor to underreport sales, it has an option of using unapproved product or raw material. A large majority of franchise operations require that their store owners purchase product/raw material through authorized distribution centers or through select wholesalers. On most occasions when a franchisee looks to purchase product or raw material through an unapproved supplier, he or she can do so at a price that is lower than that of the distribution centers or select wholesalers. (This is a major issue that could have an effect on the previous discussion on brand integrity.)

All the location owner has to do is report the sales that would be generated from the authorized product/raw material purchased. A quick yield/usage analysis between reported sales and material purchased will show the franchisee is properly reporting the correct sales information. In order to carry out the subterfuge, the franchisee has to track the additional sales generated from the sale of unapproved product and not report this information to the franchisor.

In order to protect against the use of unapproved product/raw material, there are several identification tools available:

- Use known location or geographical industry labor costs [2] for weekly/monthly sales information that can be compared against the reported labor costs. If a location is reporting lower sales information, the loss of customer traffic and decreased purchases should be offset by the need to hire fewer employees. The business owner can choose to keep the current employees on staff, but decrease their hours. Ensuring all franchisees are required to submit monthly profit and loss statements, investigative personnel will have access to what is being reported as labor costs. If the labor costs remain unchanged from months where higher sales were reported, this could be an indicator the location is using unapproved product/raw material. (Investigative personnel need to be aware the franchisee could choose to pay one or more employees off the books or under the table to show a decrease in monthly labor costs.)
- Business consultants, franchisor investigators, company marketing personnel, etc. should also make announced and unannounced visits to the location or locations in question. During these visits it is important to look around the location to determine if only approved product and raw material are present. Individuals making these visits should also look into the dumpsters around the location for the presence of boxes or bags that could have been used to deliver any unapproved product or raw material.
- Many franchisee operations have developed what is referred to as average ticket [3] information. Basically stated, if 10 customers visit a certain location, the overall purchases will be X amount. (The average ticket amount times 10.) Average ticket information is generated over a selected time frame and has been proved to be accurate. Once a person has access to what the average ticket should be for a location in question, a choice can be made to conduct what is referred to as customer counts—basically, having someone sit outside the location in question and count the number of individuals entering the establishment. By counting the number of individuals entering the business during operating hours and having the average ticket amount, a simple math calculation will reveal a ballpark figure of what the sales should be. In order to obtain what is referred to as a quality customer count, the pedestrian

traffic information should be conducted for at least a complete week. Once the average ticket analysis is completed, the projected sales based on the customer count information should be in line with the reported sales from the franchisee. Any large differences where the average ticket analysis reveals a higher than reported sales amount could be clues of a franchisee using unapproved raw material or outright sales underreporting.

- As stated in law enforcement, "Nothing beats a good old stakeout." Sometimes it becomes necessary to sit outside a location in question and take a long look at the activity. If a franchisee is suspected of using unapproved raw material or product, investigative personnel might need to sit outside the establishment to observe the possible presence of unapproved product delivery vehicles. If investigative personnel take to using the surveillance method, backdoor activity during nonbusiness hours becomes necessary. When the location is closed, the store owner or franchisee could choose to unload unapproved raw material into the store using their own vehicle or a rental truck.

When looking at EC sales, the franchisor can only hope for a year-to-year increase. As previously discussed, there are many reasons for changes to EC sales on a national, regional, or local level. With any change to the overall or local EC sales numbers, it is vital the franchisor and investigative personnel work to determine the cause. Is it negative media information against the organization, weather, competition, construction, etc.?

The main issue that the franchisor and investigative personnel need to be aware of is the franchisee using a legitimate cause for a decrease in EC sales to underreport sales.

Endnotes

1. Using a yield/usage type analysis for the ice cream discussion, there should be a benchmark previously established on the raw dollar amount that can be created from the sales of product per gallon purchased.
2. Within any retail establishment it takes X number of employees, working X number of hours (labor costs) to produce X dollar amount of sales. This information (labor costs) can be obtained by analyzing the profit and loss statements of several franchise locations over a set period of time. It is important this analysis be conducted on locations in the same geographical region during a time frame prior to the release of negative company-wide financial information.
3. Average ticket (average sale): the average dollar amount of a merchant's typical sale. The average ticket amount is calculated by dividing the total sales volume by the total number of sales for the specified time period. http://www.infomerchant.net/creditcardprocessing/glossary/ticketsale.html (accessed August 4, 2015).

Chapter 9

Operations Pending Bankruptcy and Lower EC Sales Are a Catalyst for Theft and Sales Underreporting

Introduction

As discussed with the world of franchisee/franchisor relationships, it is a world that is not in line with a typical and consumer-understood retail operation. On one hand, the franchisor owns the overall business name and controls the actual product offered to the public. On the other hand, the franchisee owns the actual individual business location. Even though the franchisee is the legitimate owner and operator of the individual business, the franchisor exercises some control in the actual operation. With this unique business operating setup, both sides have their goals:

- The goal of the franchisor is to have each and every franchisee operate his or her individual business in a manner that leads to increased year-to-year established comparable (EC) sales and quality brand integrity.
- The goal of each and every franchisee is to have the franchisor develop quality and marketable products, sell locations to aboveboard new owners, and establish product-enticing marketing campaigns.

From franchisees' perspective, their worst nightmare is trouble at the main office. For varying reasons, franchisor operations get into financial trouble that has an overall negative effect on the entire operation. This is especially true if the parent organization files for bankruptcy protection.

If the parent organization actually files for bankruptcy protection, its goal is to take the necessary steps to come out of the process better and stronger. An issue for the individual franchisees is the negative public relations aspect associated with an organization having to file for protection. Additionally, parent organizations working through the bankruptcy process cannot effectively operate the overall business operation, including effective marketing campaigns and attracting new franchisees for growth and product development.

With many franchisor organizations going through a negative financial situation, there is also the aspect of having to close locations. Some of the reasons behind the need to close retail locations are as follows:

- The overall franchisor business operation has led to lower EC sales and, for some locations, the drop in income is drastic. Franchisees suffering a drastic decline in sales can choose to sell the operation to a new buyer. With the overall organization in financial trouble, the possibility of attracting new buyers is slim. With the prospect of not being able to sell the location, many franchisees simply cut their losses and close the business.
- With the prospect of lower than desired EC sales in future years, franchisees who have their franchise agreement up for renewal might choose to leave the business.
- In order to stay afloat, some franchisors could choose to raise the franchisee rate of royalty percentages. The hope is that an increase in revenue will help out the parent organization. This might be the case, but for the franchisee, the results will be a decrease of income for the individual business operation. Instead of draining individual savings accounts and using money to keep a failing business above water, the franchisee can choose to close the doors and begin a new business venture.

Instead of choosing to close a franchise-based retail operation, the franchisee could make a business decision to report a lower than actual weekly/monthly sales amount to the franchisor. Franchisees take issue with a decreasing lack of support from the parent office in product development and effective marketing. These same individuals also have to operate one or more retail locations with the parent office making business decisions that lead to negative public perception.

As previously discussed, when a retail organization faces a decrease in EC sales, the individual franchisees have to make hard business decisions in order to remain operating:

- Terminate loyal employees?
- Reduce the working hours of their employees?

- Seek a cheaper outlet for raw materials?
- Initiate a repeat-customer reward program? (Previous discussion has revealed these programs can have their own negative side effects.)
- Report a lower weekly/monthly sales amount to the parent office?

In an ideal world when a storm hits, people hunker down and ride it out. After the clouds clear and a little work is done, operations get back to normal. The hope with a parent organization going through rough financial times or a bankruptcy is that the franchisees will do their best to make ends meet and also adhere to all aspects of the franchise agreement. This is to include correctly reporting sales and only using approved products and raw material. What is unknown to the parent organization is how each individual franchisee will weather the storm.

Terminating Employees or a Reduction in Hours

When hard financial times make their way through any franchisee-based operation, hard decisions have to be made on both sides:

- Franchisors have to make decisions on asset allocation for new product development, franchisee support, and product marketing.
- Franchisees have to make decisions on employee staffing, product purchasing, whether or not to remain in business, and weekly/monthly sales reporting.

One area where business owners have to be concerned, no matter the type of operation, is the issue of terminating associates or reducing the hours of working employees. With the decisions revolving around employee staffing, employers have to be aware of the following:

- The remaining associates will understand the need for a reduction in staff and be thankful they are still employed. Along with this line of thinking, they will also work harder to ensure future employment.
- One or more of the remaining employees who sees a close friend become unemployed may seek revenge on the individual that made it happen. In order to seek revenge for the friend's loss of a job, the remaining employee could make a decision to steal money or product/material from the business.
- Some employees who have had their work hours reduced could be of the mind-set that they still have a job and will work hard and aboveboard to remain employed. However, some employees could have a harder time accepting a reduction in work hours. In an effort to maintain their current living style, they could resort to stealing money from the business to make up for the loss in hourly income.

In order to protect against the loss of business-related material and assets, business owners need to have a loss prevention policy in place. This is especially true for those franchisees looking to identify and prevent employee skimming and theft. The actual loss prevention policy and direction vary per the type of business operation and can be developed based on the fraud/theft discussion topics in this text.

Monkey See, Monkey Do

If a franchisee makes a decision to underreport weekly/monthly sales to the franchisor, the franchisee is aware of the dollar amounts involved. With most franchisees they have an accurate record of the true weekly/monthly sales per location and a record of the reported amounts sent to the parent organization.

From a franchisor perspective, the owners and loss prevention/security personnel have to be aware that one or more franchisees could be underreporting sales, especially for an organization operating through tough financial times or a bankruptcy. Another area of concern for both the parent organization and the underreporting franchisee is the thought process of, "If he or she can do it, so can I."

From the franchisor perspective, the goal is to identify all areas of weekly/monthly sales underreporting through an aggressive royalty assurance program [1]. If the program successfully identifies one or more franchisees underreporting sales, investigative personnel can use one or more of the many tools discussed throughout Section II (Chapters 6–15). These tools can be used to determine an approximate dollar amount of underreported weekly/monthly sales.

One issue that could arise during the sales underreporting investigative process is a franchisee admitting to stealing a lower dollar amount per week/month than discovered. A difference in the identified and claimed weekly/monthly underreported dollar amounts could be based on the following:

- Once it has been determined and proven that a franchisee willfully underreported weekly/monthly sales, an analysis will take place using various individual financial records of the franchisee and varying types of business-related documents. This information is then used to determine an approximate amount of money that was underreported each week/month. This weekly/monthly sales underreported base amount is what will be used to determine the overall amount of restitution due to the franchisor.
- A franchisee makes a decision to report a weekly sales amount to the franchisor that is $2,000 lower than the actual true amount. No matter the actual weekly sales for the business, the franchisee automatically subtracts $2,000 from the total amount. If confronted with evidence that proves the franchisee willfully underreported weekly sales, the investigative personnel could inform the location owner of a different dollar amount. The franchisee could

be informed the investigation revealed the actual weekly sales for the location in question are $3,000.

- Many associates in any business operation watch the owner/manager. In a franchisee-based operation, the employees are aware when the owner or franchisee is present. They are also aware if certain sales are not transacted properly at the hands of the franchisee. If this process takes place in the business, the thinking is, "If he or she can do it, so can I."

Even though the franchisee knowingly underreported $2,000 per week, one or more associates could have stolen $1,000 per week from the operation, leaving the franchisee responsible for all underreported sales during the investigative period in question. (In order to provide more detail as to how the investigative process could determine an approximate weekly underreported dollar amount, refer to the upcoming discussion on yield/usage analysis.)

Reverse Sting

Previous discussion took place on the reality of franchisees making a decision to sell their businesses. This decision could be based on an individual decision to sell the franchise operation for any of the following reasons:

- Seeking a new business opportunity
- A decrease in overall brand-wide sales
- Looking to exit a business where the parent company is seeking bankruptcy protection
- Increased competition in the region from the same or a similar competitive brand
- No new marketing ideas from the parent organization

Based on most franchise agreements, franchisees looking to sell their individual business operations have to give advance notice to the parent organization. From an investigative perspective, knowing which franchise operations are on the market provides an additional investigative avenue for the purpose of identifying underreporting franchisees.

When investigating franchise locations for possibility of underreporting sales, success has been possible using a technique that has been referred to as a reverse sting:

- The parent company's internal investigative staff hires a third-party consulting firm.
- One or more investigators from the consulting firm contact the perspective seller and express an interest in buying the business [2].

- A meeting is arranged between the seller and the perspective buyers.
- At this meeting the selling franchisee will work to convince the buyer the location or locations are profitable. (When advertising the franchise location for sale the franchisee will most likely publish sales information that has previously been provided over the years to the franchisor.)
- The goal of the third-party investigative individuals is to have the selling franchisee provide better than advertised sales information—basically presenting a second set of books.

If the reverse sting investigative process was successful and the selling franchisee provided information of higher than advertised sales numbers, the parent company investigative staff can launch their own investigation into sales underreporting. The goal of the underreporting sales investigation is to prove the selling franchisee knowingly underreported weekly/monthly sales information. If sales underreporting is proven, the franchisor can terminate the franchise agreement, allow the franchisee to continue with the sale, and eventually collect restitution on the underreported sales amounts [3].

Endnotes

1. A royalty assurance program is another name for an aggressive internal loss prevention effort used to identify franchisee-based sales underreporting. Since a large amount of income coming into the parent organization is royalty based, the goal of the program is to assure all franchise sales are properly reported.
2. Individuals looking to purchase existing franchise operations can obtain the information from many different sources. There are many business-related websites where potential buyers can obtain information on franchise operations on the market. Additionally, some franchisor operations will post operating locations for sale on their corporate website.
3. Prior to any franchisor-based internal investigative unit beginning a reverse sting investigation, it is highly advisable to have the operation approved by the internal legal department.

Chapter 10

Using Yield/Usage Programs to Identify Potential Sales Underreporting

Yield/usage programs are successful when investigating franchise operations where raw material is used to develop a retail product. Ideal franchise operations are as follows:

- Bakeries
- Ice cream/yogurt shops
- Sandwich shops
- Quick service restaurants
- Coffee shops
- Restaurants
- Bars
- Quick lube/oil change shops

What makes a yield/usage analysis beneficial in the sales underreporting process is knowing "what goes in and what comes out." In order to shed light on the benefits of a yield/usage analysis, the following breakdown will discuss how the process is used for a bakery type of operation:

- The bakery operation in question sells two main products: donuts and coffee.
- Historical information can provide the investigators how much yield can come from a sack of donut flour, basically stating that a 40-pound sack of donut flour will yield X number of dozens of donuts.
- When looking at coffee, the second major product sold, one or two paths can be taken. The analysis can look at the sizes and numbers of cups purchased or at how many gallons of coffee can be brewed based on how many pounds of beans are purchased.
- With the coffee cup perspective, the theory is why would a franchisee purchase more cups per week than needed? Business operators understand their operation and purchase just enough material for the week in question.
- With the coffee bean perspective, the theory is why would a franchisee purchase more raw coffee than could be sold in a week?
- Another area investigators need to be aware of and analyze with the coffee analysis is the actual weight of the grind used to brew a pot of coffee. All restaurants producing coffee for sale to the public say that theirs is the best and is based on the perfect mix of water and a set ground coffee bean weight. If the coffee-to-water mix established by the franchisor is X ground ounces to X fluid ounces of water, the in-store coffee grinders are set to that ratio. Investigators need to make sure the in-store grinders are producing the required ounces. For locations that sell large amounts of coffee each day, any variation in the grind ounces can have an effect on the yield/usage analysis outcome.
- Based on the program created to conduct the yield/usage analysis, a percentage also has to be set for other product sales. This percentage can be determined by using the menu mix/sales volume of the location in question [1]. If the menu mix/sales volume shows the location in question has weekly sales of 35% in coffee and 35% in donuts, the remaining product sales are 30%.
- Part of the yield/usage analysis also has to consider what percentage of the product produced went to waste. Waste percentages can include throwaways, spilled product, giveaways, etc. Not every cup of coffee produced or donut made is sold through the cash register.

The previous yield/usage analysis provides a basic discussion on how the investigative tool can be used. In order to have a more precise analysis, the computer program created has to be specific to the business operation in question.

In order for a yield/usage analysis to be successful, investigative personnel need to have access to all of the product purchasing documentation for the period under analysis. Thankfully a majority of franchise operations are required by the parent office to purchase their raw material through approved distribution centers, from the actual franchisor, or from selected vendor operations.

One area that investigative personnel need to be aware of is the purchasing of unapproved raw material. As previously discussed, franchisees have been known to use unapproved raw material. Many times this unauthorized raw material is used by the franchisee for a number of reasons:

- Saving money by purchasing a similar but cheaper product (brand integrity)
- Only reporting sales information based on the dollar amounts generated from the legitimate raw material purchases
- Having a business interest in the third-party supplier
- Because of serious personal financial problems, seeking the cheaper purchasing avenues

In order to produce a more precise yield/usage analysis, internal loss prevention/security personnel need to investigate the possibility of a franchisee using unapproved raw material. Investigative personnel also need to understand that a yield/usage analysis is not a smoking gun tool that can be used to terminate the franchise agreement. It is part of a detailed investigative process and a good tool to use to determine a potential restitution amount. The restitution amount can be based on the following:

- The yield/usage analysis period was 15 weeks.
- Investigators collected raw material purchase records for that 15-week period.
- Investigators collected the exact menu board pricing for the items in question from the location in question. Investigators need to make sure the menu prices obtained were in effect during the 15-week analysis period.
- Investigators also collected the 15 weeks of franchisor-reported sales information.
- The yield/usage analysis provided results that there was a difference in reported sales.
- The franchisee reported weekly sales in the 15-week period of $5,000 per week.
- The yield/usage analysis provided results that the raw material produced enough product for $6,000 in weekly sales.
- The total underreported sales for the 15-week period in question was $15,000.
- The parent company usually stipulates in the franchise agreement that all franchisees need to retain business records for a set number of years. The records retention time frame can be used as an estimated window for the period of underreporting.
- If the records retention time frame is three years, a restitution number can be based off a weekly underreporting of $1,000 per week for three years (156 weeks × $1,000 = $156,000).
- Investigators need to take the total underreported sales amount of $156,000 and multiply it by the royalty percentage. If the royalty percentage is 12%, the amount of restitution due the franchisor is $18,720 ($156,000 × 0.12 = $18,720).

Any franchisor operation pursuing an aggressive sales underreporting program has to obtain buy-in from the internal legal department and use the actual wording of the franchise agreement. As each franchise operation offers different products for sale, each franchisor operation has individual and unique franchise agreements.

As previously referenced, the yield/usage analysis is part of the sales underreporting investigation. Additional investigative tools are discussed throughout Section II.

Yield/usage analysis is not limited to franchise-based operations. Company-owned retail locations can also use the process in an effort to determine if skimming is taking place on the part of the employees or location manager. Any retail location that purchases raw material that can be used to create a product for retail sale can benefit from using a yield/usage analysis.

Endnote

1. Sales volume percentage: Managers use sales volume information to compare the number of each menu item sold to the total number of items sold on the entire menu in the same time period. This means that each menu item's sales can be expressed as a percentage of total sales.

Chapter 11

Why the Income Statement/Profit and Loss Statement Is Vital in Detecting Theft/Fraud

As defined by Business Dictionary.com [1], an income statement is "a summary of a management's performance as reflected in the profitability (or lack of it) of an organization over a certain period. It itemizes the revenues and expenses of [the] past that led to the current profit or loss, and indicates what may be done to improve the results."

As defined by Investopedia.com [2], a profit and loss (P&L) statement is

> a financial statement that summarizes the revenues, costs and expenses incurred during a specific period of time—usually a fiscal quarter or year. These records provide information that shows the ability of a company to generate profit by increasing revenue and reducing costs. The P&L statement is also known as a "statement of profit and loss," an "income statement" or an "income and expense statement."

For many, income statements (Figure 11.1) and profit and loss statements (Figure 11.2) are similar in nature and provide the same type of information. It comes down to which terminology the organization and creator choose to use. For the purpose of this discussion, we will use "P&L."

A majority of franchise-based operations require the franchisees to create and submit to the main office a monthly P&L. The rationale behind making this

Donuts Made Simple Bakery Income Statement January 1, 2016 through July 31, 2016		
Income/revenues		
Donut/coffee sales income		$100,000.00
Catering income		$20,000.00
Misc. income		$5,000.00
Total income/revenues		$125,000.00
Expenses		
Raw material purchases		$55,000.00
Labor cost		$10,000.00
Advertising		$2,500.00
Office equipment		$2,000.00
Accounting expenses		$1,000.00
Total expenses		$70,500.00
Net income		$54,500.00

Figure 11.1 Income statement example.

requirement varies per franchisor, as the information in the monthly P&L is used to gain differing types of franchise-based information. From an investigative perspective, some of the information available in a P&L can be used to identify franchise locations for investigation.

When using financial information on the P&L to determine if the numbers reported by the franchisee warrant additional scrutiny, it is important to look at a period longer than one month's worth of data. Based on the varying requirements set by the franchisor as to how many times a year a franchisee needs to supply a P&L, reporting periods can range from monthly to quarterly, biannually, or annually. In order to gain a realist perspective of the sales data reported on the P&L, investigative personnel need to look at a period of at least six months.

Within almost every retail business operation, there are certain percentages assigned to sections listed on the P&L. Some examples are as follows:

- A bakery shop in the Midwest has a cost of goods sold somewhere in the neighborhood of 22% to 25%.
- A coffee shop in the Northeast has a cost of goods sold somewhere in the neighborhood of 30% to 34%.

2016 Donuts Made Simple P&L	
Income	
Sales	$150,000.00
Expenses	
Product purchases	$35,536.28
Rent	$32,588.00
Misc. expenses	$2,617.67
Insurance	$714.00
Utilities	$2,760.00
Phone	$770.63
Maintenance	$60.00
Trash	$420.00
Water	$219.00
License	$89.00
Equipment	$418.00
Alarm company	$403.32
Advertising	$3,290.16
Supplies	$6,122.22
Gifts	$400.00
Merchant fees	$3,052.71
Bank fees	$144.00
Payroll	$13,970.92
Buying trips	$1,967.03
Breakage/theft	$250.00
FICA/medicare taxes	$1,746.47
Other taxes	$519.94
Professional fees	$650.00
Total	$108,709.35
Profit/loss	$41,290.65

Figure 11.2 Profit and loss statement example.

- A sandwich shop in the Southwest has a payroll expense of somewhere in the neighborhood of 26% to 29%.
- A burger shop in the Southeast has a payroll expense somewhere in the neighborhood of 28% to 31%.

Even though the percentages previously listed are fictitious, each type of franchise-based organization has a neighborhood figure for costs of goods sold, payroll, etc. When conducting an analysis of franchisee P&L statements, for the purpose of identifying locations for possible sales underreporting, the main information provided is labor costs, followed by cost of goods sold.

Looking at the reported labor cost and cost of goods sold numbers is important for the following reasons and could raise questions:

- Are the labor cost percentages listed on the P&L in line with the known market averages? Labor costs that are higher or lower than market averages could be possible indicators of underreporting activity.

- Are the labor costs well below the known market averages? Lower than normal labor costs could be an indicator the franchisee is not reporting true payroll expenses. The franchisee does have labor costs above what is listed on the P&L, but these associates are paid off the books or under the table. The money used to pay select employees in cash could possibly come from unreported sales income.
- By looking at the low labor cost numbers on the P&L, is it possible for the franchisee to be open for business during the hours of operation? This question is a continuation of the previous discussion and the answer could shed light on possible sales underreporting.

Investigative personnel need to be aware that the franchisee could be operating the business or multiple locations with the assistance of several family members. The lower than normal labor numbers could be correct because the family members are not receiving a weekly paycheck.

When looking at the labor cost numbers, do they answer the following questions?

- How many employees are needed per shift to successfully operate the specific business?
- What is the hourly wage being paid to the varying levels of employees? A cook will most likely be paid a higher hourly wage than a person bussing tables.
- What are the total number of operating hours for the analysis period in question?
- Do the reported payroll costs support the staffing levels needed to operate the business during the reporting period in question?
- Are the labor costs well above the known market averages? It is possible the franchisee is reporting accurate labor cost amounts on the P&L. What he or she may be failing to report are the actual sales amounts. As with the previously asked question, does it make sense to operate a business with such high labor costs that do not support the amount of related sales? As previously referenced, many franchise operations are small businesses and operate within tight margins. If a franchise is paying a certain number of individuals to operate the business, they are not doing it out of charity. The sales are present to support the working associates. What is not present are the true reported sales amounts.
- Are the cost of goods sold percentages listed on the P&L in line with known market averages? Costs of goods sold that are higher or lower than market averages could be possible indicators of underreporting activity.
- Are the costs of goods sold well below the known market averages? Lower than normal cost of goods sold could be an indicator of sales underreporting. The franchise is reporting material expenses as received from the approved suppliers. What the franchisee is not listing on the P&L is the additional cost of goods

sold expenses from the unapproved suppliers. When looking at a very low cost of goods sold percentage on the P&L, the following question has to be asked: Can the franchisee produce enough product from the raw material amounts purchased and achieve the weekly sales numbers reported? If not, then the franchisee is purchasing additional raw material from an unapproved supplier.

- Are the costs of goods sold well above the known market averages? Higher than normal cost of goods sold could be an indicator of sales underreporting. By knowing that X amount of raw material purchased yields X dollar amount of potential weekly sales, it becomes probable the franchisee is only reporting a certain percentage of total weekly sales.

As previously discussed with developing a yield/usage analysis program, it is also important to develop an additional program for raw material expenses and potential sales. This type of program takes time to develop and is based on using data developed through conducting an ongoing process of yield/usage investigations.

In an effort to ensure all franchisees in the organization are aware of an aggressive royalty assurance program, it becomes necessary to conduct random yield/usage analysis investigations. This process is to include requesting product purchasing information for aboveboard franchisees and inserting this information into the yield/usage analysis program. With many of these random investigations, the results will show the amount of raw material purchased is consistent with the weekly sales reported.

The purpose of conducting the random yield/usage analysis investigations is twofold: as referenced, to keep all franchisees aware of the ongoing royalty assurance program and to collect data to build the program comparing material expenses and potential sales. The goal is to locate a range number of material expenses that can be used to ballpark a potential weekly sales amount. An X amount of raw material purchased yields X dollar amount of potential weekly sales.

In addition to concentrating on the labor and cost of goods sold information listed on the P&L, additional categories require analysis:

- The bottom line (net income) of any P&L requires attention. This is especially true if the P&L shows a low net income over a period of time. The main question that needs to be pondered is: "Why is this individual continuing to operate a franchise that is barely profitable?" Investigative personnel also need to look at the big picture and determine other sources of income for a specific franchisee. Franchisees might be partial owners of other business operations, have a spouse with a high-paying job, have other sources of income, etc. Two good sources that can be used to determine other sources of income for a specific franchisee is the franchisor business consultant [3] that works directly with the franchisee or information obtained from a detailed background investigation. (The benefits of an individual and business background investigation are discussed later in Section II.)

- The cost factors associated with operating the business are higher than normal for the amount of sales and income reported. At times some individuals will report the true cost of doing business, while working to conceal the actual income received through the business. All of the information listed on the P&L is accurate, except the total sales and net income. P&L statements of this nature could be a good starting point for a successful underreporting investigation.
- It is important to look over all of the line items listed on a P&L. At times individuals will list all of the cost associated with operating the business and not think through their actions. It is possible a franchisee will list all of the supplier cost of raw material. One line could be for the expenses associated with the approved supplier and another line for the cost of an unapproved vendor. Even though the franchisee is providing all raw material cost information, he or she is not truly reporting the associated sales.

With the discovery of more than one source of material expenses, the issue of brand integrity comes into question.

When conducting a P&L analysis it is important to understand how the various reported costs are related to the sales information provided. Investigative personnel need to look at the P&L from the perspective of a business owner and ask the question, "Are the numbers reported on the P&L consistent with a successful business operation?" Any inconsistencies could be an indicator of sales underreporting.

Endnotes

1. BusinessDictionary.com. http://www.businessdictionary.com/definition/income-statement.html (accessed August 5, 2015).
2. Investopedia.com. http://www.investopedia.com/terms/p/plstatement.asp (accessed August 5, 2015).
3. Business consultant is one of many names assigned to individuals who work directly for the franchisor; their duties include working with the franchisee on business development, marketing, store operation, expansion, etc. Many of these consultants have developed a close relationship with the franchisees in their network.

Chapter 12

Using Franchisee Tax Documents for Identifying Sales Underreporting

As previously referenced, franchise operations are set up as small businesses. The owners can choose what business entity works best for them. Their choices are as follows:

- DBA or "doing business as." This is basically an individually owned operation where the business name is separate from the name of the actual owner: John Doe operating as Johnny's Donuts. With this type of business setup, the individual owner is completely responsible for the entire operation, including any debt. Additionally, the owner is not protected by any type of corporate umbrella in case of a lawsuit. If this type of business setup has more than one owner, it is classified as a general partnership. All business-related income and losses are filed as part of the owner's individual tax return.
- Limited liability corporation (LLC). An LLC is the simplest form of incorporating a business and has the benefit of being a corporation, while operating as a partnership. The owners are protected under the corporate umbrella, while business-related profits and losses are filed as part of the owners' individual tax returns.
- S-corporation or S-corp. An S-corp has the benefits and prestige of an actual corporation, but it is limited to no more than 100 shareholders. The owners,

who can be a single owner, are provided an umbrella of protection as it relates to being a corporate entity. Tax-related issues are filed under the corporate name.

- C-corporation or C-corp. A C-corp is the truest of corporations with which many are familiar. The corporation can have unlimited shareholders, has an established board of directors, can buy and sell property, etc. The corporate entity is the business and not the individual. From a lawsuit perspective, the owners are protected by the corporate umbrella. All tax-related issues are filed under the corporate name.

The best source of information that can be used as part of the underreporting process are the individual and business related tax records of the franchisee. As previously referenced and based on how the business is structured, the company's financial information can be filed via a corporate structure or as part of the franchisee's individual tax return.

When conducting a financial analysis of a franchisee's business operation, the main purpose is to determine if the individuals in question can support themselves. Based on the types of tax forms filed, they all contain financial information and assets available to the individual franchisee. The question is whether this franchisee can support the current way of life based on their financial situation.

In order to answer this question, a detailed financial analysis has to take place via personal and business tax records for at least a period of three consecutive years. Ideally, assume the financial analysis is taking place for Johnny's Donuts in June 2016. Those conducting the financial analysis would look at the tax records from the years of 2013, 2014, and 2015.

To provide the reader of this text with each and every point to look for when conducting a financial tax form analysis would require the entire book being written based on a single topic. The purpose of this text is to inform the reader on the benefits of conducting a tax-form-based financial analysis. When conducting this type of financial analysis, it is important to know what documents to obtain and the income avenues to look for.

Based on how the business is structured, investigative personnel need to ensure the following tax forms are obtained:

- Individual 1040 form
- Schedule A (form 1040) itemized deductions
- Schedule B (form 1040/1040A) interest and ordinary dividends
- Schedule C (form 1040) profit and loss from business
- Schedule D (form 1040) capital gains and losses
- Schedule E (1040) supplemental income and loss
- Schedule H (form 1040) household employment tax
- Schedule R (form 1040/1040A) credit for the elderly or the disabled
- Schedule SE (form 1040) self-employment tax

- Schedule EIC (form 1040/1040A) earned income credit
- Form 1041 US income tax return for estates and trusts
- Schedule A (form 1041) charitable deductions
- Schedule B (form 1041) income distribution deduction
- Schedule K-1 (form 1041) beneficiary's share of income, deductions, credits, etc.
- Form 1065 US return of partnership income
- Form 4562 depreciation and amortization
- Form 8949 sales and other dispositions of capital assets
- Form 8917 tuition and fees deduction
- Form 8829 expenses for business use of your home
- Form 1120 (US corporation income tax return)
- Form 1120S (US S-corporation income tax return)
- Schedule D (form 1120) capital gains and losses
- Schedule G (form 1120) capital gains and losses (schedules D and G cover different variations of capital gains and losses)
- Schedules M-1 and M-2 (form 1120-F) reconciliation of income (loss) and analysis of unappropriated retained earnings per books

An in-depth tax form-based financial analysis will be conducted based on the various forms as they apply to the business in question. As previously referenced, each franchise operation is an individual small or large business and has several options for filing structure. Smaller individual location owners and up to the multi-location owners will most likely be structured as a DBA or an LLC. With these two types of structures, the tax forms and schedules that apply to them are the 1040/1040A/1041.

Within the world of franchise-based operations, there are franchisees that own several hundred locations and are structured as a C-corp or S-corp. These business operations file tax forms and schedules related to form 1120.

When conducting a tax form analysis on franchisee operations, a very large majority will pertain to businesses structured as a DBA or an LLC. With the very large multiunits, C-corp and S-corp operations are businesses within themselves. They operate with a chief executive officer (CEO), a chief financial officer (CFO), other executive level positions, a Legal Department, a Human Resources Department, and a Loss Prevention/Security Department.

From an underreporting perspective, these types of operations govern themselves. From a franchisor loss prevention/security perspective, any sales integrity issues will be conducted on the part of the locations' associates or managers. It is possible the largest of a franchisee-based operation could willfully underreport sales, but the likelihood is very low. What is more likely to take place is the skimming of sales on the part of individual location managers and employees.

When conducting a tax-form-based financial analysis, the key items to look for are sources of income, to include business income, investment income, capital gains, tax credits, etc. It is also important to look for business expenses and losses.

The key number to look for is income minus expenses/losses and it is necessary to answer the question, "Can the franchisee support his or her current lifestyle?"

Investigative personnel need to be aware of loan-based information contained within the various tax forms. The franchisee can show a write-off expense for a business loan repayment. The bottom-line number could also show that the franchisee has been living off $20,000 a year for the past three years. It is quite possible the business loan taken out by the franchisee is being used to support his or her current lifestyle (living off credit).

Ideally, being able to obtain the credit report of the franchisee in question can help to answer many questions. Unfortunately, franchise agreements do not allow for this type of invasion of privacy. It is possible that the franchisee could provide a recent credit report. Prior to asking a franchisee for a personal credit report, investigative personnel need to obtain approval from their internal legal department.

In order to conduct a detailed tax form financial analysis, investigative personnel need to look to their internal accounting department, legal department, or auditors. There could also be investigators within the loss prevention/security staff with detailed financial knowledge. There is also an option of hiring an outside accountant or a certified public accountant (CPA) to conduct the analysis. Additionally, some third-party investigative firms have the knowledge base on staff to conduct a detailed tax-form-based financial analysis.

If the franchise agreement allows for the collection and analysis of tax documents, investigative personnel should also collect all state tax forms. The main purpose of reviewing the individual state tax forms is to ensure the reported income and loss numbers are consistent. It is quite possible a franchisee might report certain financial information to one entity and not to another—that is, honesty with the state and lying to the federal government.

Chapter 13

Understanding the Franchise Agreement

Based on the franchisor, its legal department, corporate officers, etc., each franchise agreement is different as it pertains to the brand name owning organization. The wording of the actual franchise agreements for Burger World is consistent, the only difference being in the individual owners' names and specific store information.

The one thing all franchise agreements have in common is wording on the specific business operation, products to sell, what records to file with the corporate office, record retention time frames, basic operating procedures, etc. Basically, what can the individual franchisee do as far as using the brand name on the sign, maintaining brand integrity, complying with all laws and regulations, etc.?

From the perspective of the franchisor, the franchise agreement also defines its ability to monitor the business operation: issues such as franchisor access to the business, ability to audit the business, ability to work between the franchisee and business consultant, etc.

From a loss prevention/security perspective it is important that each member of these departments gain a detailed understanding of the actual agreement. Other pertinent information that could be contained in a franchise agreement is as follows:

- The franchisee may or may not enter into a business with another franchisor. If allowed, most agreements restrict operating a competitive franchise business operation.
- The franchise agreement could also restrict a franchisee from opening a similar business operation that is not part of another franchise business. On more than one occasion franchisees have used money collected from underreporting sales to open up a similar business operation.

- Resale rights of the location: can the franchisee sell the business prior to the ending date of the agreement and, if so, does the franchisor have a right of first refusal?
- Limitations and restrictions on signage and in-store advertising material: many franchisors require franchisees to post only parent company product advertising signage in the location.
- Franchisee rights to sell branded material to third-party outlets: can franchisee A produce donuts for production and sell them in its Donut World location and also sell additional product to John Doe's Service Station? John Doe's Service Station then sells the donuts to its customer base. Many agreements allow the selling of product to third outlets, but limit the use of the brand name. John Doe's Service Station can sell the donuts but cannot advertise that the donuts are from Donut World. Other franchise agreements allow the selling of product to a third-party outlet and the use of the Donut World name. Based on the franchise agreement, the franchisee is required to pay the franchisor royalty payments for third-party outlet product sales. These percentages could differ based on the use of the producing company's name in selling the product.
- Information on the required royalty and advertising fee percentages based on the amount of total sales for the period in question.
- Many franchisors have business-related schools that are used to train new franchisees and their staff on store management, product production, advertising, etc. These agreements require the franchisee or its representative to have received the required training. If the franchisee elects to have a manager receive the required product training and the manager leaves the operation, someone else from the company has to become certified.
- The use of trademark information: the franchise agreement stipulates when and how franchisees can use trademark information for advertising and business promotion purposes.

Based on the franchisor and the franchise business operation, the wording and stipulations of the franchise agreements vary. The information previously discussed about the wording of franchise agreements is pertinent for loss prevention/security personnel to understand. Through speaking with business consultants, surveillance activities, and conducting background checks, the information discussed provides investigative personnel avenues to uncover franchisee misconduct and potential sales underreporting.

Chapter 14

What Can Be Found in an Asset Search/ Background Check

Introduction

There are many aspects of conducting an underreporting investigation of a franchisee and his or her network. With the continuing increase in technology, investigative companies are able to uncover more and more information about individuals and businesses. The wealth of information that can be located is very beneficial as part of an underreporting investigation.

The purpose of an underreporting investigation is to determine if the franchisee is properly disclosing all sales information to the franchisor. When taking a look at the profit and loss (P&L) information, the bottom-line number is net income. How much money is the franchisee making per franchise location? Once it has been determined how much income the franchisee is generating from operating the franchise retail locations, investigative personnel have to conduct an asset search/ background investigation. The purpose of these types of franchisee-related investigations is to see how their money is spent. The questions to be answered are

- Is the franchisee living beyond his or her means?
- Can he or she support the current lifestyle?

In order to completely answer the previous questions, investigative personnel need to develop a complete understanding of the franchisee's assets and family-related expenses. From the family-related expenses side of the discussion, investigators need to answer the following questions:

- Does the franchisee have younger children in private school?
- Does the franchisee have older children in college?
- Does the franchisee have more than one residence?
- Does the franchisee have a vacation home?
- What vehicles are owned by the franchisee and his or her family members?
- Does the franchisee own a boat, motorcycle, jet skis, small plane, etc.?
- Has the franchisee or a family member gone through a DUI/DWI recently?
- Is the franchisee caring for an elderly or sick relative requiring constant medical care?

The answer to many of the previously listed questions can be provided through two sources. The first source of information is the franchisor-related business or operations consultant. As previously referenced, these individuals work closely with the franchisee on all aspects of the business. Many business consultants develop a close relationship with franchisees and have detailed knowledge about the franchisees' households. The business consultant might have information on the franchisee having kids in private school or in college, other owned real estate or personal property, personal family issues, etc.

The other source of franchisee expense-related information can be uncovered through a detailed asset search. In addition to locating information on franchisee-related household expenses, investigators also need to develop an understanding of income sources by gaining answers to the following questions:

- What are the other sources of income into the franchisee's household?
- Does the spouse have a job outside the franchise business?
- Does the franchisee own rental properties?
- Is the franchisee involved in other business ventures?

As previously discussed, the business consultant can provide detailed personal franchisee-related information. In addition to obtaining information from the business consultant, investigative personnel need to conduct a detailed asset search and background investigation.

Asset searches can be conducted on an individual in question, as well as on corporations. The type of financial information that can be obtained follows.

Individual Asset Search

- Property information (rental homes, vacation homes, beach house, etc.)
- Real estate and deeds

- Mortgage information
- Bank account information (Laws pertaining to the research and discovery of bank accounts are constantly changing. However, depending on the investigative firm hired, the amount of financially related information that can be uncovered is almost unlimited. When researching bank account information, caution needs to be used on the legality of the information uncovered. Another item of note is that asset search information uncovered is not going to be part of a law enforcement type of investigation requiring previously issued search warrants. If the underreporting case eventually goes to trial, any financial information that will be used can be located through the discovery process.)
- Brokerage and investment accounts
- Foreign asset searches (can be conducted on individuals and businesses)
- Off-shore bank accounts
- Personal property (vehicles, boats, yachts, other watercraft, fine art, etc.)
- Motor vehicle/watercraft/aircraft registration and liens
- Business ownership and associations
- Accounts receivable
- Uniform commercial code (UCC) filings and liens

Corporate Asset Search

- Corporate-related real estate holdings and deeds
- Corporate-related mortgage information
- Dun and Bradstreet records
- UCC filings and liens
- Corporate-related vehicle registration information

In addition to conducting an asset search, investigators will also want to have a background search on the individual and his or her related business operations. Information that can be uncovered through a detailed background search is as follows:

- Employment information (the franchisee, spouse, and family members)
- Contact information (addresses, phone numbers, etc.)
- Additional addresses related to the franchisee (rental properties, vacation homes, etc.)
- Tax-related liens (state and federal; individual and corporate)
- Criminal records
- Bankruptcies and judgments (individual and corporate)
- Information on corporate officers and other staff members

The main purpose behind conducting an asset/background search is to answer the question: "Where did the individual get the money?"

This question becomes important if the related search information uncovers a lifestyle that cannot be supported by the income associated with the franchise-owned businesses. By conducting a detailed background investigation and speaking with the business consultant, a determination can be made on additional sources of income into the household. Once all sources of income are determined, the following questions require answers:

- Are the franchisee and his or her family living beyond their means (vehicles, homes, recreational equipment, etc.)?
- Are family expenses (personal, financial, medical, educational, etc.) greater than the known sources of income?
- Have recent family-related incidents (DUI/DWI, arrested for other offenses, etc.) caused a drain on the family resources?

Once it has been determined that the franchisee in question has expenses greater than income sources, it is quite possible sales underreporting is taking place.

As previously discussed, there are numerous reasons why franchisees choose to underreport sales. Once the decision is made to underreport sales, based on the amount concealed, the franchisee has the following income benefits:

- Based on the weekly/monthly sales concealed from the franchisor, the franchisee is saving the royalty percentage amount. If the franchisee underreports $2,000 a week in sales and the royalty percentage is 12%, this is $240 he or she does not have to send to the franchisor.
- Staying with the $2,000 weekly underreported amount, the franchisee also saves on paying state and federal taxes—basically putting $2,000 of unreported income into his or her pocket.

This is why it is important to compare reported sales to the franchisor with the income amounts on the tax returns. If the franchisee is concealing sales to the franchisor, he or she is most likely keeping this information from the state and federal governments, although I have conducted underreporting investigations where the franchisee reported accurate sales information on federal tax forms and fraudulent data to the franchisor. If federal and state tax records are eventually collected as part of a sales underreporting investigation, the first comparison has to be between the franchisee-reported sales numbers and the sales income listed on the tax forms.

Based on the size of the franchisor operation and the individual franchise locations, sales underreporting incidents can and have been related to large dollar amounts. Looking at the $2,000 underreporting figure previously discussed, the franchisee is failing to provide payment to the franchisor in the amount of $12,480 a year ($2,000 × 12% = $240 × 52 weeks = $12,480).

To place the need to conduct a complete underreporting investigation into perspective, the following case information is provided:

- A franchise business located in the Southeast operated three bakery type locations.
- There were three individuals listed as partners on the franchise agreement.
- Over the period of a number of years, at one of their three retail locations the franchisees did not report half of their total sales. Their accurate weekly sales were around $32,000 and they only reported around $16,000 in sales per week.
- At the two other retail locations the underreported weekly sales were about $4,000 per store.
- On the federal tax forms for the business, the franchise-related income was in line with the sales amounts reported to the franchisor.
- The money that was not reported to the franchisor or to the government was used to finance a bakery business in the Northeast.
- The three underreporting franchisees removed enough money from their three franchise locations in the Southeast and opened two bakery locations in the Northeast.
- These Northeast bakeries were in operation for a few years.
- Using a three-year investigation period analysis, the franchisor was not paid royalty fees in the neighborhood of $449,280 ($24,000 per week in underreported sales—all three locations—and using a 12% royalty fee for 52 weeks per year for three years).
- A total of $24,000 ($16,000 + $4,000 + $4,000 = $24,000) × 12% = $2,880 × (52 × 3) = $449,280.

The case information previously discussed did in fact take place and it is part of underreporting incidents that take place across the country. In an effort to identify all aspects of underreporting franchise locations, a detailed asset/background search is necessary.

Chapter 15

Hiring a Third-Party Sales Integrity Company/ Mystery Shoppers

Introduction

As previously discussed, third-party firms can be hired to conduct asset/background searches on franchisees and their businesses. It is also possible to hire third-party firms for the purpose of managing the sales integrity/royalty assurance program of a franchisor. Many of these firms are staffed with professionals with years of experience in the underreporting/brand integrity arena.

Franchisors can choose to have one of these firms manage their entire sales integrity/royalty assurance program or do so on a smaller scale. A franchisor might choose to look at select franchisees or implement a royalty assurance program regionally.

In addition to hiring a third-party firm for the purpose of conducting detailed underreporting investigations, the option also exists to have mystery shopping performed. Like the name states, a mystery shop is a visit to a retail location by a third-party. Based on the nature of the business in question, a person or people enter the establishment and conduct one or more transactions that are industry specific. The purposes of conducting mystery shops at a retail location are many:

- To ensure all associates offer a high level of customer courtesy
- To ensure customers are provided with a detailed sales receipt
- To check cleanliness of the property, location appearance, etc.

- To check on the professionalism of the staff and management
- For restaurants, to check on cleanliness standards, food safety, whether three sinks are used to wash glasses, etc.
- To verify product standards and brand integrity
- To determine if unapproved product is being sold
- To determine whether all sales are properly processed through the register

Mystery shopping service organizations can provide franchisors (at times franchisees checking out their own locations) valuable information on how the businesses are being operated.

Many mystery shopping organizations will collect a check sheet from the company requesting their services or create one to provide to the client once all the covert purchases or location visits have been completed. Check sheet information can include:

- Employee courtesy
- Professional appearance of employees
- Location appearance
- Transaction activity details
- Receipt provided and sales properly recorded

A good starting point for any underreporting investigation is with one or more mystery shops. These shops can be target specific or randomly selected. For the purpose of conducting underreporting investigations, an ideal area to target with the mystery shop is product purchases—ideally, large dollar amount product purchases. An employee or owner is more likely to fail to ring in a $100 large donut order purchase versus a single cup of coffee.

Video Surveillance/Large Purchases

Based on the nature of the retail organization, there are two good services that can be provided by third-party sales integrity companies. One is the use of video surveillance and the other is conducting large product purchases. As previously discussed, making large retail product purchases is a good starting point for a sales underreporting investigation.

If a franchisor organization is going to hire an outside vendor to conduct large product purchases, it is also a good idea to capture the transaction on video. With the technology available to conduct undercover videos, investigative personnel are also able to conceal their activities. Years ago, the size of the smallest video recording camera was the size of a kid's lunch box. Today, the technology has been reduced to a recording device the size of a shirt button.

The purpose behind conducting video surveillance is to have tangible proof. A franchisee can be told he or she was observed selling product without ringing the transaction through the register. With this situation, it is one person's word against the other's. If the transaction is captured on video, the franchisee will have a hard time explaining why the person on the video is not him or her.

In addition to using undercover video for large product purchases, it can be used for the following retail activities:

- Conducting surveillance of bartenders' activities. Are they ringing sales, sweethearting customers, pocketing tips, using an accounting system for the purpose of stealing money [1], etc.?
- Conducting surveillance of a vehicle oil change shop. The person conducting the surveillance will most likely have an opportunity to look around the shop while waiting for the service to be completed. While in the specific location, the undercover investigator can look for signs of selling nonapproved items, off-branded merchandise, the proper ringing of sales, etc.
- Conducting surveillance of quick service restaurants (QSRs). Many of these locations sell donuts, burgers, tea and coffee products, etc. Many sales are cash transactions that provide an opportunity for the sale not to be registered.

These types of operations also allow for customers to sit at a table in the restaurant while they consume their purchase. While sitting in the restaurant, the investigator can have the covert camera recording the customer transactions and register activity.

No matter the type of franchise-based retail operation, the use of video surveillance opens up windows of investigative opportunity. The need to use covert video surveillance is based on the imagination of the vendor and the franchisor loss prevention/security section.

I would caution against recording the audio portion of any covertly recorded retail transactions. The laws differ between states on one or two-party consent. Prior to making a decision to record the audio portion, it is advisable to check with the internal legal department or outside counsel.

Building Blocks

The overall purpose of any detailed sales underreporting investigation is putting the case together. The more evidence that can be developed and presented, the stronger the case will be. As previously referenced, the purpose of any sales underreporting investigation is to prove the franchisee or his or her associates willingly failed to report sales. With a majority of the information discussed in this section, the investigators are assembling the building blocks necessary to build an airtight case. The more investigative tools used, the stronger the case will be.

Endnote

1. Employees looking to steal money in the retail and restaurant industry will develop their own counting system to keep track of cash not processed through the register. With a register cash drawer, the fifth coin slot will be used to place random coins as part of a counting process. A penny represents a dollar, a nickel represents five dollars, etc. Bartenders might use a glass of straws and an empty glass. Each straw taken from the full glass and placed in the empty glass has an assigned dollar amount. No matter the method used, at the end of the shift the employee knows how much cash to pocket.

III
UNDERSTANDING FRAUD/THEFT IN THE RETAIL INDUSTRY

Chapter 16

Understanding Differences between Franchise and Company-Owned Operations

Introduction

From an external perspective, many thieves/shoplifters do not know the difference between a company-owned and a franchised retail location. All they know is that a majority of retail locations offer a goldmine of opportunity for theft. For many individuals looking to commit retail theft, their only concern is being able to remove as much merchandise as possible while avoiding detection. They have little or no concern as to the foundation of the retail location or what individual or entity will suffer the loss.

As discussed in Section II, there is a difference in the ownership, loss responsibility, purchasing, hiring, training, etc. between traditional company-owned stores and franchise locations. In the traditional retail company-owned locations are individual retail stores that are owned and operated by the organizational or corporate entity. The owners of these retail organizations are responsible for the entire operation, to include:

- Inventory purchasing
- Location development and construction
- Employee hiring and training

- Advertising and marketing
- Business expansion
- Hiring and training of security/loss prevention personnel
- Individual store access control and security
- Loss prevention training and the development of procedures
- Any losses related to shoplifting and employee theft

For the franchise-operated retail locations, there is a separation between the actual location owners and the parent organization. With franchised business operations, the franchisor owns the business name, but not the individual retail locations. With some franchise operations, a portion of the individual retail locations is actually owned and operated by the parent organization. These are referred to as company-owned locations. The retail locations in these types of operations that are not owned and operated by the parent organization are owned by franchisees.

With franchise operations, the individual location operators own everything but the business name. This is owned by the franchisor, which allows the franchisor the ability to dictate some of the operating requirements to the franchisees. Outside of the company name and franchisor-dictated operating requirements, the franchisee is responsible for the business operation. This responsibility includes:

- Inventory and purchasing raw material
- Development of raw material into retail products
- Employee hiring and training
- Scheduling and payroll
- Day-to-day business operations
- Location security for employees and customers
- Loss prevention

With franchise operations the franchisor maintains the following responsibilities:

- Building name design and display
- Products to be sold, with pricing windows
- Maintaining brand integrity
- Dictating the royalty and advertising percentages to be paid by the franchisee

Although there is a separation of responsibilities between company-owned and franchised retail operations, they both offer products for sale to the public. Both types of operations have to open their doors, advertise, offer quality merchandise for sale, set competitive pricing, hire and train associates, etc. As previously referenced, on face value a large majority of the shopping public just sees a retail operation.

When looking at the two types of retail operations from a security/loss prevention aspect, there is a distinct difference. To address the two operations from a theft/fraud perspective, the following questions need to be answered:

- Is there a difference in product/services offered between company-owned and franchised locations?
- Would a company-owned or a franchised retail operation be more susceptible to shoplifting/theft?
- Is a company-owned or a franchised operation more susceptible to internal theft?

Is There a Difference in Product/Services Offered by Company-Owned and Franchised Operations?

A majority of company-owned retail operations are just that: retail operations that sell clothes, electronics, grocery items, household goods, etc. If a random, off-the-street consumer were asked to provide retailer store names, many of the responses would be

- Target
- Sears
- Bloomingdales
- Macy's
- Walgreens
- Safeway
- Bed, Bath & Beyond

The provided list of names could go on, but the answers will be along the same lines. These types of retail operations are all company owned with many stores in shopping malls, strip malls, or large store stand-alone locations.

If the same off-the-street consumer were asked to provide the names and products offered by franchised operations:

- Many would refer to fast food and restaurant operations.
- Many would be hard pressed to name a franchised retail operation that offers products and services as the previously discussed and known company-owned Target-like stores.

For those answering the franchised question, they would be correct. When looking at franchise-based retail operations, the types of products and services offered are

- Quick-service restaurants
- Restaurants and sports bars

- Automotive repair and oil change operations
- Hardware stores
- Vitamin and health-related stores
- Package shipping operations
- Hotels and motels
- Education and child-learning operations
- Hairstyling and haircut operations
- Businesses offering financial and tax services
- Pet product supplies

To answer the previously asked question, there is a difference between the two types of operations as far as products and services offered.

Would a Company-Owned or a Franchised Retail Operation Be More Susceptible to Shoplifting/Theft?

When looking at both types of operations and the products and services offered to the general public, the answer is company-owned operations. The rationale is the actual size of the various retail operations, the products offered for sale, and customer traffic. Major retail giants like Target and Best Buy, throughout their thousands of retail locations, offer items that are more attractive to shoplifters.

As discussed in detail in Section IV, organized retail crime is a major threat to the retail industry. Organized retail crime operations consist mainly of well organized groups that exist for the purpose of stealing merchandise from retailers. Based on their past history, organized retail crime operations have favorite types of items they target for theft. These targeted items are sold through numerous retail operations and are selected by these groups because they are easy to resell. Some of the popular retail items that are typically stolen by organized retail theft operations are

- Various types of clothing items, like handbags, jeans, designer-brand clothing, etc.
- Grocery types of items like diapers, cigarettes, protein and energy drinks, wine and liquor items, and infant formula
- Household items, such as vacuum cleaners, mixers, coffee makers, etc.
- Electronic items, such as cell phones, digital cameras, laptops and tablets, televisions, etc.
- Over-the-counter medications, such as allergy medicine, various types of pain relievers, diabetic test strips, weight loss pills, etc.
- Other items, such as makeup, pregnancy testing kits, hand lotions, electronic toothbrushes and razors, etc.

Although popular for theft by organized retail theft operations, these types of retail items are also stolen by the lone shoplifter. These lone shoplifters also steal smaller types of items from retail and grocery stores for personal use.

When looking at the types of retail merchandise items that are targeted for theft and the services offered by many franchise operations, it is easy to see that company-owned retail locations are more susceptible to shoplifting.

From franchisees' perspective, as discussed in detail in Section II, their major theft/fraud losses take place as a result of dishonest employees working alone or in collusion with outside sources.

Is a Company-Owned or a Franchised Operation More Susceptible to Internal Theft?

No matter the type of retail operation, company owned or franchised, both are ideal targets for internal theft. As long as the retail business has a need to hire employees to conduct day-to-day operations, there is a susceptibility to internal theft. As discussed with the main components of retail-related shrinkage, employee theft makes up the largest percentage of overall losses. These employee theft-related losses can and do occur in all types of retail operations.

From the perspective of company-owned retail operations, the shrinkage percentages apply across the board. Employee theft accounts for 43% and shoplifting makes up 40% of the shrinkage loss [1]. With franchise-based retail operations, the breakdown of the shrinkage-related percentages is unknown. Based on the retail item makeup of franchise operations, they have a lower threat percentage for shoplifting-related losses. This is not to say that shoplifting does not take place at franchise-based retail operations, but the related shrinkage percentages are most likely not in the 40% range.

What is more of an accurate percentage number pertaining to the overall shrinkage loss amounts for franchise operations are internal losses. Franchisee employees are more likely to steal from their employer through register skimming, sales underreporting, product theft, and sweethearting.

As stated, all retail operators have to face the issue of shrinkage-related losses. The company-owned retail operator has to address shrinkage-related losses due to shoplifting and employee theft. The franchisee has a lower threat level for customer shoplifting and a greater threat level for employee theft issues.

Endnote

1. "US Retail Workers Are No. 1…in Employee Theft." http://fortune.com/2015/01/26/us-retail-worker-theft/ (accessed September 14, 2015).

Chapter 17

Understanding Large Retail Operations Fraud/Theft Prevention Structures

Introduction

As discussed in Section II, franchise location owners are responsible for security and loss prevention operations. This setup differs from a traditional retail operation where all fraud/theft directives come from the main office. Even though the manager of a single company-owned retail location is responsible for that individual store, operating procedures are mandated from the corporate office. This is to include location security, inventory control, employee training, loss prevention, etc.

For many of the large, well known retail operations, their operational structure is as follows:

- The main office houses many of the higher end company executives, including the security/loss prevention managers. Out of this location, individual retail store operating directives are created and forwarded to the various location managers.
- Based on the overall size of the company-owned retail operation, many have what is referred to as regional offices. Within these offices, the regional directors of security/loss prevention reside and have geographic responsibilities for a select number of retail stores.

- Based on the overall size of the company-owned retail operation, many have what are referred to as district offices. Within these offices they could have a district manager of security/loss prevention, who has the responsibility over a group of stores in a smaller geographical location.

In addition to the office setup structures, a majority of large retail operations employ security/loss prevention personnel who have the responsibility over a set number of retail locations. These associates usually operate out of a home office and report up through either the district or regional office. Their responsibilities include overseeing the day-to-day security and loss prevention operations for their assigned retail locations. Many of their responsibilities include:

- Ensuring the security/loss prevention policies are followed in each retail location
- Monitoring the shrink numbers for their assigned retail locations
- Establishing and monitoring antishoplifting programs in individual retail locations
- Delivering employee training programs at the store level for the areas of security and loss prevention

Based on the actual retail operation, the individuals performing these functions operate under differing titles. Some of the titles are

- Loss prevention specialist
- Loss prevention analyst
- Loss prevention auditor
- Security/loss prevention manager
- Loss prevention associate
- District loss prevention manager
- District security/loss prevention manager
- Regional loss prevention manager
- Regional security specialist

No matter the title assigned, the functions of these positions have the same end goal: protecting the organizations associates and assets of the organization.

Additional Security/Loss Prevention Benefits of Large Retail Operations

In addition to having a large and well structured security/loss prevention operation and team, many multistore retail organizations reap the benefits of having sufficient operating budgets. From a budgeting standpoint, security/loss prevention managers can ensure they have

- Adequate staffing of security/loss prevention personnel
- The ability to create theft and loss prevention operating guidelines
- The ability to create theft and loss prevention training programs
- The ability to use the latest product tracking technology
- The ability to use the latest antishoplifting prevention technology
- The ability to install and operate video surveillance technology at their retail locations

Having all of the aforementioned benefits of a large, multiunit retail operation does not make a business immune from loss. It does, however, create a barrier of protection that makes it harder for losses to take place.

Who Can Better Protect Property and Prevent Losses—Company-Owned or Franchised Operations?

The benefit of a company-owned operation is having the ability to dictate policy from the corporate office down to each and every retail store. Store managers are made aware of the organization's security/loss prevention policies and are mandated to follow the established procedures. These store managers also receive the benefit of the supporting security/loss prevention personnel, who also work for the large organization.

When looking at large franchise operations that have a comparable number of retail units, they also have security/loss prevention associates in their employ. Unlike those hired by the company-owned operations, security/loss prevention associates of franchisor organizations have a much different function. Part of their duties, like those working for company-owned retail operations, is to protect the personnel and assets of the parent organization.

When it comes to the individual franchise retail locations, these security/loss prevention associates have no operational authority. They are hired by and work for the franchisor and can work in an advisory capacity for the individual franchise locations. As far as setting policy for individual store security/loss prevention, this is left up to the franchisee.

Based on the size of the operation (one to a hundred locations), the security/loss prevention operation is based on the budgeting allocations of the individual franchisee. The efforts placed toward operating an effective security/loss prevention program reside on the shoulders of the franchisee.

To answer the posed question of who can better prevent losses, company-owned and -operated retail locations have the upper hand if they are part of a large, multiunit organization. As the company-owned retail operation goes down in size, budget constraints can have a negative effect on a security/loss prevention program.

It is also important to look at the threat level of theft/fraud as it relates to the retail product offered to the general public:

- A large (company-owned) multiunit retailer that sells general merchandise has a threat from customers stealing property. There is also an internal threat from employees stealing merchandise and working in a sweethearting operation with one or more accomplices.
- For a large (company-owned), multiunit retailer that has a product line in the fast food industry, the threat of customers taking items from a shelf for the purpose of shoplifting is minimal. However, the threat of employees stealing raw material, underringing sales, recording "no sale" transactions, and working in a sweethearting operation is great.
- An individual franchise operation that specializes in selling bakery type products has a low threat level of customers stealing items. The greatest threat comes from employees underringing sales and working in a sweethearting operation.
- An individual franchise operation that specializes in automotive maintenance has a low threat level from customer theft. Its loss potential resides in employees stealing inventory items, product switching [1], not ringing up all sales, and working in a sweethearting operation.

Large, company-owned retail operations definitely have the upper hand from a security/loss prevention perspective. They have the tools and internal personnel that can be used to create a strong loss prevention program. The same holds true for large, multiunit, company-owned operations that operate in the food industry. They have the ability to create well organized loss prevention programs. As the overall size of the company-owned retail operations goes down, the loss threat level rises. This is due to smaller operating budgets for using technology and for hiring security/loss prevention personnel.

No matter the size of the franchisor operation, the individual franchisees have a greater loss threat coming from the inside. The types of products offered to the public provide an avenue for internal losses to take place.

It is also necessary to look at the motivation behind protecting the bottom line for each type of business:

- Company-owned retail operations have to look at the bottom line of the organization. All of the assets used in the prevention of theft/fraud come off the company books. The same holds true for the loss of property when it comes to theft/fraud. It affects the company-owned organization's bottom line.
- Franchised operations have two bottom lines to consider. Franchisors need to ensure all of their franchisees are accurately reporting all sales and are

making the correct royalty payments. The individual franchisee has to worry about the individual bottom line, while making sure that employees are properly ringing all sales and are not stealing raw material and merchandise.

As far as determining where the greater theft/fraud threat lies between company-owned and franchised operations, the answer can be found in the motivations of the company owners and the individual franchise operators. Whoever uses the information and assets necessary to ensure all retail items are sold at the recorded price, while protecting the integrity of the inventory, can better protect the operation from theft/fraud.

Endnote

1. Product switching is selling an accomplice a lower priced product, while providing him or her with a similar item with a higher price tag. Using the automotive maintenance example, one could use the selling of tires. The customer can purchase a cheap brand of tires at a low price and the friend working in the shop places an upper end brand of tires on the vehicle.

Chapter 18

Understanding Shrinkage

Introduction

In order to control the profit margins in any retail operation, it is vital that the issue of shrinkage be understood and controlled. As previously defined, shrinkage is "the loss of inventory that can be attributed to factors including employee theft, shoplifting, administrative error, vendor fraud, damage in transit or in store and cashier errors that benefit the customer" [1].

A large percentage of the overall shrinkage numbers resides in shoplifting and employee theft, basically accounting for about 80% of the problem. The other 20% of shrinkage comes from administrative errors, vendor fraud, items damaged in transit, and cashier errors. In an effort to address the roughly 20% of the shrinkage causes, company due diligence is necessary. Organizations need to ensure the following:

- Administrative errors are not simply overlooked errors in the recording of merchandise into the business and product sold, basically ensuring the accounting accuracy in the organization's inventory. The merchandise in the retail operation can be the typical items for sale on the counter items like socks, shoes, clothes, food items, etc. The merchandise can also come in as raw material that needs to be converted into retail sale items. This is mainly the issue for food-based operations. The question, "Do the 20 buns and hotdogs processed through the system eventually become 20 actual sales of hotdogs to customers?" needs to be answered.
- Vendor fraud as part of the shrinkage number comes from inaccuracies in the material receiving process. Vendors looking to game the system will provide invoicing documents detailing larger amounts of product being delivered than what is actually received.

- Inventory items damaged in transit can occur prior to the material arriving at the retail location or while it sits in the inventory system after the delivery is accepted.
- Cashier errors that benefit the customer could be part of innocent employee errors or ones that involve intent on the part of the associate.

As previously referenced, proper due diligence is a vital tool in lowering the percentages for the other causes of shrinkage.

Administrative Errors as Part of Shrinkage

Once the individual retail location enters the newly received material into the inventory system, the integrity of the items has to be maintained. Beginning with the receiving of material at the retail location's door, there has to be some type of dual control, with the delivery accuracy numbers of material or product being received. If possible, more than one person needs to be charged with providing an accurate count of delivered items, while having a separate person enter the received numbers into the inventory system.

In an effort to avoid administrative types of classified errors of inventory material, store managers and owners need to establish a dual control accountability system. Have at least two trusted store employees conduct separate counts of the delivered material/product. Once their independent counts have been completed, they need to be compared and match. If there is a discrepancy between the independent material/product counts, the process needs to begin again. Once an agreed upon, dual controlled verification is completed, the delivered material/product can be signed for.

At no time should a store manager, independent owner, or franchise operator allow the delivery driver to provide an invoice for the material/product being delivered and take it at face value.

Once the material/product is entered into the inventory system of the retail establishment, there needs to be some type of continued accountability. This accountability process needs to begin with the physical aspects of the business operation. Based on the location and size of the retail establishment, there needs to be some type of fencing/access control around the part of the operation where deliveries are made. In addition to establishing access control procedures, it is also necessary to establish some type of video monitoring system. This is to include continuous monitoring of vehicle traffic into and from the loading dock area, the actual material/product delivery area of the operation, and the actual in-store inventory area.

It is also a good idea to establish control procedures where employee parking lots are not located near the loading dock area. Employees working in the loading dock area should also be required to enter through the front doors of the retail establishment and walk back through to the loading dock area. Once the loading dock employees' shifts are over, they need to be required to exit the retail location through the front doors.

Retail store managers and owners need to ensure that the trash disposal area is not located in the same proximity as the delivery/loading dock area. If possible, the trash receptacles should be maintained in their own controlled area away from the material/product delivery area. Store managers and owners also need to establish trash control policies for the retail location:

- Establish a flat box policy. All cardboard boxes need to be flattened prior to being taken to the dumpsters.
- Establish a dual control policy as far as bulk amounts of trash being taken to the dumpsters.
- Never allow the same one or two employees to take out the trash.
- Ensure clear plastic trash bags are used in trash receptacles throughout the retail operation.

Retail operations also need to establish the following inventory control procedures:

- Develop an internal tracking system of moving items from the retail location's inventory and into the sales area. At no time should the same person who transfers material from the inventory area and into the sales system be the same person who updates the inventory control system.
- For restaurant retail operations, tight control needs to take place on raw material in the inventory system. If possible, there needs to be some type of access control system initiated for access to where the inventory items are maintained. No matter the type of access control system, managers and owners should be able to see employees and the times they entered the room where the inventory items are stored.

Over a period of time restaurant owners and managers can get a tight handle on sales patterns and the approximate amount of raw material items to purchase each week. This information needs to be used and compared to the weekly/monthly material order forms. In an extra effort to prevent the overordering of raw materials, there needs to be a dual control system in operation before all orders are placed. Additionally, restaurant managers and owners need to stay on top of the items maintained within the store inventory by using scheduled and unannounced audits.

Vendor Fraud as Part of Shrinkage

As previously discussed with "Administrative Errors as Part of Shrinkage," vendor fraud can be controlled by ensuring accuracy in the delivery process. Receiving retail operations need to establish a dual control item delivery accountability system. At least two employees perform a separate count of material/product being delivered and cross-verify the information.

Retail managers and owners also need to ensure the material/product employee counts match with the invoicing documents. It is possible that verifying associates can agree on the exact amounts of material/product entering the retail location. These amounts also need to be compared to the amounts listed on the invoices. Once all of the numbers match, the shipment can be signed for.

Retail establishments not cross-verifying the actual material/product counts against the invoicing documents run the risk of being billed for material that was never received.

Inventory Items Damaged in Transit as Part of Shrinkage

Part of conducting the material/product counts when shipments are received at the retail location is to verify the integrity of the items. Retail establishments receiving a television with a cracked screen or a bakery location taking possession of a bag of flour with a large tear in the side are basically spending money on items that will not provide the desired profit level. Although more time consuming, detailed inspections of all delivered material/products need to take place.

Damaged in transit also accounts for items that currently reside with the inventory system of the retail location. Almost all retail type business operations will suffer some type of material/product loss from some type of breakage.

From an accounting standpoint it is important that broken and damaged items are quickly identified and noted. Accounting principles allow for the monetary write-off of damaged items from the financial statements and an eventual deduction on the organization's income tax return.

From a safety and property protection standpoint, it is necessary that a video surveillance system be installed in the inventory area. This is necessary to ensure that employee horse-playing is not causing the property damage, as well as the unsafe handling of merchandise. A good example is one employee trying to carry an item that requires a two-person lift and carry.

Installing a video surveillance system also works as a deterrent to employee theft.

Cashier Errors That Benefit the Customer as Part of Shrinkage

Pricing errors happen within the retail industry. The register system shows a different item price from the one listed on the item in question. With most retail operations, the customer is allowed to make the purchase at the lower price displayed or advertised.

Cashiers errors also consist of

- Incorrect handling of the money transaction: returning more cash to the customer than was due
- Not paying attention to the scanning process to ensure that the items scanned are correctly referenced on the display screen (See discussion on barcode fraud later in Section III.)
- Failure to properly correct scanning errors that benefit the customer (The customer is attempting to purchase two like items, but the cashier scans three items. While correcting the overscan, the cashier removes two of the items from the system and the customer eventually gets charged for one of the items instead of the intended two.)
- Misusing the register scales for weighted items, thus benefiting the customer

Cashier errors that benefit the customer can be attributed to honest mistakes where additional employee training could serve to prevent future incidents. Cashier errors that benefit the customer can also be part of what is referred to as sweethearting. This is where a store associate is working with a customer/accomplice/friend to provide merchandise at a lower than advertised price. Some examples of sweethearting in the retail industry are as follows:

- A customer brings numerous small-dollar items to the register. During the scanning process the cashier moves items over the scanner. In order for the scanned items to be read by the register system, it is necessary the cashier moves the UPC [2] (Figure 18.1) directly over the scanner. Once read, the item type and price are shown on the register display. With this type of sweethearting, the cashier only places the UPC in the correct position to record a limited number of items. The remaining items are moved over the scanner, but not in position to be properly read. At the end of the transaction, the customer pays only for the items that were properly scanned.
- In many supermarket operations certain items have to be weighed. Based on the weight of the item, there is a corresponding price. Additionally many

Figure 18.1 Sample UPC.

supermarket items that require weighing are placed in small plastic bags, before being taken to the register. Once at the register, the cashier moves the plastic bag to the scale and enters a specific product code. With the product code and the item weight, the transaction price is recorded through the register and displayed. With sweethearting, the cashier partially lifts the plastic bag off of the scale while entering the product code. The practice records a lower item weight, resulting in the customer paying a lower overall item price.
- Items sold within the supermarket industry require an item count to be put into the register. An example would be the purchase of bananas. The customer brings ten bananas to the register. The cashier enters the code for bananas, but only enters an item count of two. The register display shows the customer made a banana purchase, but at a lower quantity than what went into the paper or plastic bag.
- In the restaurant/bar industry sweethearting is a common practice. A customer spending an evening sitting at a bar drinking decides to pay the check. During the evening the customer consumes a total of eight beverages, but when the check comes he or she is only charged for one. With this type of sweethearting operation the customer pays for the single beverage, but leaves a very large tip. At the end of the transaction the customer winds up paying a lower price than if he or she had paid for all eight beverages. The employee receives a large tip (usually in cash) and the restaurant/bar receives payment for a single beverage.

Sweethearting has been and will be an issue for the retail industry for years to come. The problem is that it is an easy practice to complete and one that is difficult to detect. Some possible sweethearting prevention deterrents are as follows:

- All employee theft/fraud prevention begins with the new-hire and associate orientation process. (See Chapters 2 and 3 in Section I.)
- Install video surveillance systems over the store's register systems. Associates need to be made aware of the monitoring process and the owner's/manager's ability to remotely monitor all customer transactions.
- Establish a receipt and purchase verification system at the store's exit. More and more retail operations have employees located at the exit doors. Once a customer reaches that point he or she is asked for the sales receipt. The items on the sales receipt are compared with the items in the shopping cart. This practice works to prevent employee sweethearting as well as shoplifting.

Employee Theft and Shoplifting, the Other Main Causes of Shrinkage

As previously discussed, employee theft accounts for 43% of the losses attributed to shrinkage. Additionally, shoplifting accounts for 40% of the losses attributed to shrinkage. When looking at the previously discussed shrinkage topics of administrative errors, vendor fraud, item damage, and cashier errors, the remaining two issues of employee theft and shoplifting need to be the main areas of concern for all retail operators. Many of the issues related to identifying and preventing employee theft and shoplifting follow in Section III discussions.

Endnotes

1. Shrinkage definition. https://www.google.com/search?q=retail+shrinkage+definition&ie=utf-8&oe=utf-8 (accessed September 14, 2015).
2. A UPC is swiped over a reader on the register counter. Based on the line setup and numbering of the UPC, the actual price of the individual item is revealed.

Chapter 19

Employee Theft

Introduction

No matter the industry or type of business operation, organizations that need employees to conduct day-to-day activities run the risk of those associates using their position for personal gain. These can be employees working in the following industries:

- Retail industry. Retail employees have many avenues to use to steal money and assets from their employer. These avenues include stealing property/merchandise from the business, taking food items from a restaurant employer, taking cash from a sales register, and using customer credit card information for personal gain.
- Restaurant industry. Restaurant employees have many avenues to stealing money and assets from their employer. These avenues include stealing cash from the sales register, taking food items from the restaurant, conducting sweethearting operations with a fellow conspirator, and using customer credit card information for personal gain.
- Financial industry. Financial institution employees have many avenues to use to steal money and assets from their employer. These avenues include embezzlement, abstraction [1], misapplication of funds [2], or basically stealing the assets of the financial institution through various means.
- General business operation. These operations function as many nonfinancial or retail businesses. Many of these businesses have some type of cash flow through the business, use suppliers/vendors, and have inventory items that have value. The employee theft issues for these types of operations are embezzlement, vendor collusion, kickback schemes, theft of property, etc.

No matter the types of industries previously discussed, all need employees to complete their day-to-day operations. As discussed throughout this text, employees use many tactics in an effort to steal from their employers. The retail industry is not immune from the threat of employee theft and, as previously discussed, the prevention barriers need to be erected at the front door of the business.

Proper Hiring Procedures for Retailers

Two major issues faced by retail managers and owners are the cost of hiring and training new associates and the turnover rate within the industry:

- On average it takes around $3,000 to hire and train a replacement associate making $10/hour in the retail industry.
- The retail industry employee turnover rate is around 67% for part-time employees [3] and around 60% for all associate positions.

Retail managers and owners are faced not only with the issues of high employee turnover rates, but also with the associated cost factor. Additionally, management decisions have to go into addressing and preventing retail location shoplifting and employee theft.

From a management perspective, is it better to

- Maintain the same dollar amount levels of retail employee hiring and training?
- Live with the high retail employee turnover rates that lead to continuous interviewing, hiring, and training and hope that there is some longevity?
- Accept the high retail percentages of shoplifting and employee theft?

Or should retail managers and owners work to develop an understanding of why there is a high employee turnover rate? By developing an understanding, perhaps the following questions could be answered:

- Would a retail crew of team-oriented associates work to ensure lower levels of shoplifting and employee theft?
- Would a retail crew of team-oriented associates maintain a longer level of longevity and commitment?

When looking at some of the reasons as to why there is a high employee turnover rate in the retail industry, the following points need to be understood and addressed:

- Employees in the retail industry are continuously faced with the antiquated staffing policies of yesteryear. Management dictates that each and every employee will work the same types of hours each week: some days, some evenings, all employees have to work weekends, etc. Instead of mandating a strict policy of "we all have to work the same shifts" schedule, managers and owners need to understand that each associate is a different person with varying commitments. By getting to know the retail associates, managers and owners can work to make them and their commitment part of the retail team. A retail associate attending the local community college will most likely maintain a commitment to a manager willing to schedule shifts around his or her class and study schedule. Retail managers and owners need to develop an understanding of the new millennial workforce and how to make their thought processes a better fit within the overall operation.

- Store goals need to be everyone's goals. Directives can come down from above on sales goals, store goals, increased customer counts, etc. These directives can also come from within for smaller unit or single unit locations. The direction of the retail location and committed goals need to be part of the overall team's success. If a manager is issued a goal-oriented directive, it has to become the team's directive. Employees need to be included as being part of the overall team environment and not just a cog in the wheel. If success is achieved by one, it has to be celebrated by all.
- Newly hired retail associates need to be educated on the focus of the location and the associated job duties. When a new associate is hired, managers and owners need to spend time with this individual discussing what sets this retail location apart from the rest, such as the focus of the retail location, a desire to develop a positive interaction with a customer base, and plans for growth. Newly hired associates need to be trained properly by one or more seasoned employees, with a focus on developing a team aspect. Simply hiring an individual on Monday morning, showing him or her a few videos, and placing the employee in the stockroom in the afternoon does not show a commitment to their future success. Do not just point out that this is the way it is done, but explain why it is necessary. Managers and training associates also need to ask the question, "Do you have any ideas?"
- Newly hired retail associates need to be immediately made to feel part of the team. The newly hired and quickly trained stockroom associate might briefly interact with a few associates during the day, but there was no leadership encouragement to meet and interact. Retail managers and owners need to spend the time getting to know the newly hired associate and then spend the time going around to the other location employees and making personal introductions. Make the new associate feel a part of a team and one that is dedicated to success.
- Retail managers and owners need to understand that the worker of today will not be satisfied with the same old boring daily routine. An associate spending four shifts a week working in the stockroom, with no light at the end of the tunnel, will quickly become bored with the job. Retail managers and owners need to implement some type of job rotation policy for their

associates. Develop a mix-it-up type of working environment. (As discussed in Section I, job rotation policies work to lower the potential for employee theft.) Retail associates also need to be provided opportunities to think. Have them develop an understanding early on that their opinion matters and work-related improvement suggestions are encouraged.

- Retail managers and owners also need to make sure that they are hiring the right people. An introverted individual might not be the best person to place on the store floor in a customer-interactive sales environment.
- Retail managers and owners need to develop programs in which associates can see growth in their future. They are part of a special team—not just a name on the time card [3].

In addition to the previously discussed reasons as to why there is a high turnover rate in the retail industry, managers and owners also need to understand the individual employee. These are employees of a younger or millennial generation that has a focus on social media and constant interaction. Younger associates are constantly interacting on various social media venues throughout each and every day, discussing their daily activities, work-related issues, successes, failures, etc.

Making associates part of the retail team environment can carry over into the social media discussion. Happy and committed millennial associates are more likely to boost the brand (retail store) through social media discussions—basically boosting the company's social media presence by discussing their happiness with the organization, the products being offered for sale, and the company's culture and mission.

Retail operations that create a positive team environment are also working to create brand loyalty. A recent study revealed that 62% of Millennials are more likely to become loyal to a company (retail store) if they can engage with the brand on social media [4].

As previously discussed, retail theft/fraud prevention programs begin at the front door of the business by conducting background checks of all new applicants and, as discussed in Section I, walking the newly hired individuals through the company's code of conduct and conflict of interest policies. But as previously referenced, a focus has to be placed onto creating a working environment that focuses on retention. Without coupling the two operating procedures—background screening and creating a retention environment—retail managers are faced with the high dollar amount cost of a high retail employee turnover percentage.

Rationalization of the Potential Stealing Employee

According to Cambridge Dictionaries Online, the word "rationalize" is defined as "to create a reason, explanation, or excuse for something" [5]. When looking at the definition of this word and the main causes of high employee turnover rates in the retail industry, these two provide a catalyst for theft/fraud. Employees quickly hired, poorly trained, and thrown into the workforce with a perceived belief of not being cared about or having a path to success provides an immediate pathway toward rationalization.

In a retail environment that is imbued with the causes for a 67% employee turnover rate, many thoughts and beliefs can be rationalized. Some of these thoughts include:

- If they do not care about me, why should I care about them?
- I am just a full-time equivalent (FTE) [6] and not an active team member.
- I am just a part-time equivalent being used to fill a coverage void in the stockroom.
- If I am not cared about at work, why should I care about people stealing?
- If they are not going to pay me what I am worth, I will find ways to make up the difference.
- I am sure I am not the only uncared about employee taking what is rightfully his.

In order to combat the threat of employee rationalization and to build the barriers necessary to prevent internal theft/fraud in the retail environment, the following employee/operating policies have to be understood and implemented:

- Ensure each and every new employee is thoroughly vetted and properly trained.
- Create a team-based working environment for all associates.
- Develop an understanding of the theft-/fraud-related threats in the retail environment.
- Use security/loss prevention tools to combat theft/fraud in your retail environment.

Retail managers and owners need to make a business decision early on if they are going to accept the status quo and continue their operations with a high employee turnover rate. If not, the retail theft/fraud prevention process has to begin with the new-associate hiring process. Prior to making an offer of employment, each applicant has to be sufficiently vetted.

Once hired, the employee has to be thoroughly trained in the position or positions within the retail operation and be made part of a working-team concept.

Getting Hired to Steal

Within the retail and restaurant industries, individuals will apply for open positions for the sole purpose of stealing. The stealing can be related to employee theft issues such as skimming cash from the register or sweethearting merchandise/product to friends and family members.

Although popular among the retail industry and entry level positions, no single business entity is immune. People have been known to get hired for the purposes of theft/fraud in the financial, manufacturing, entertainment, etc. industries. All they are looking for is to get a foot in the front door.

By having this knowledge in mind, it is important for all parties involved in the hiring process to ensure detailed background investigations are conducted. The need for such investigations should not be reserved for mid- to high-level company positions. Detail needs to be included for all new-hire verification programs.

With many entry level retail positions, hiring managers and owners rely on the applicant's resume and job application for previous employment information and whom to contact for verification. For example, for an individual looking to get hired at a local sandwich shop, the following factors have been known to take place:

- A prospective employee completes the job application.
- The prospective employee provides information on previous positions held.
- Along with the prior employment information, the applicant provides the names and phone numbers of former managers.
- As part of the new-hire verification process, the sandwich shop manager/owner calls the phone numbers provided.
- Once the phone has been answered, the sandwich shop manager/owner asks to speak with the applicant's former manager whose name has been provided by the applicant.
- Once on the phone, the former manager provides a glowing recommendation for the applicant.
- After a few successful verification calls, the applicant is hired.
- After a few weeks on the job, it is determined the newly hired individual has been stealing product, skimming money from the register, and sweethearting product to friends.
- The recently hired individual is terminated.

After terminating the stealing employee, the sandwich shop manager might reflect back on the hiring process. This individual might find it hard to believe the applicant received such glowing recommendations from former employers. What the sandwich shop manager fails to recognize is the tactic used by the job applicant: providing the names and phone numbers of individuals with whom he or she had supposedly previously worked.

On the part of the sandwich shop manager, the failure resided in accepting the names and phone numbers provided by the applicant. Waiting on the other end of the phone line were accomplices of the applicant. These individuals were waiting for the call by the sandwich shop manager. Once contacted, their job was to provide a positive recommendation.

In order to prevent this type of scenario from taking place, those involved in the verification process should not call the phone numbers provided by the applicant. In an effort to obtain the correct phone numbers, a simple call to directory assistance or a visit to the previous employer's website would have provided the correct phone numbers. Once the correct phone numbers were obtained, a few simple questions would have revealed the applicant never worked for the location(s) in question.

Although the scenario provided is simple in nature, it is based in reality. Anyone making preemployment verifications has to conduct proper due diligence and take it upon himself or herself to

- Verify any phone numbers provided. Do these numbers belong to the business name provided?
- Verify the previous manager names provided. Do these individuals actually work for the businesses in question?
- Verify the business name provided. Is it an actual operating business?

People looking to commit acts of theft/fraud by getting hired to steal have the time necessary to create a verifiable background. Proper due diligence on the part of those conducting prior employment verifications can work to save their employer from monetary loss and embarrassment.

Endnotes

1. Wrongfully taking or withdrawing money, funds, and credits with the intent to injure or defraud the bank. https://medvinlaw.com/federal-charges-for-theft-embezzlement-misapplication-by-bank-officer-or-employee-in-alexandria-virginia/ (accessed September 13, 2015).
2. Misapplication of funds is the willful and unlawful use of funds or credit of the bank, made with the intent to injure or defraud the bank. https://medvinlaw.com/federal-charges-for-theft-embezzlement-misapplication-by-bank-officer-or-employee-in-alexandria-virginia/ (accessed September 13, 2015).
3. "Eight Reasons Why Retail Employee Turnover Is So High." http://www.retailwire.com/discussion/17354/eight-reasons-why-retail-employee-turnover-is-so-high (accessed September 13, 2015).
4. "Six Ways to Attract and Retain Millennial Workers." http://www.cio.com/article/2925344/hiring/6-ways-to-attract-and-retain-millennial-workers.html#slide7 (accessed October 14, 2015).
5. Rationalize. http://dictionary.cambridge.org/us/dictionary/english/rationalize (accessed October 14, 2015).
6. According to BusinessDictionary.com an FTE is defined as "the ratio of the total number of paid hours during a period (part time, full time, contracted) by the number of working hours in that period Mondays through Fridays. The ratio units are FTE units or equivalent employees working full time." In other words, one FTE is equivalent to one employee working full time. http://www.businessdictionary.com/definition/full-time-equivalent-FTE.html (accessed October 14, 2015).

Chapter 20

Retail Theft/Fraud Identification and Prevention Measurers

Introduction

Within the retail location, along with the services provided by outside sources, managers and owners have many tools at their disposal to identify and prevent theft/fraud issues.

As previously referenced, the building blocks to an effective theft/fraud prevention program begin at the front door of the retail operation:

- The first block is laid by initiating a detailed new-hire background verification policy.
- Additional blocks are then built on the foundation as they relate to informing all associates up-front of what is expected of them through the organization's code of conduct and conflicts of interest policies.
- More and more blocks are then added to the strength of the building as new associates are immediately made to feel they are part of a team.
- Along with initiating a team environment in the retail operation, associates also need to feel they are needed and have growth potential.

As part of the requirements of working for any organization, employees need to know what is expected of them in their day-to-day duties. In addition to their basic job duties, they also need to be informed of what is considered proper conduct and potential conflicts of interest.

As discussed in Section I with the need to have newly hired employees acknowledge and sign code of conduct and conflict of interest documents, the same requirement has to reside in the retail community. The wording of these documents will be different from those of a general business operation and can be written to reflect proper employee actions in a retail environment.

To continue the theft/fraud prevention building program, managers and owners need to look at operations within their walls and also outside the front door for additional assistance.

Benefits of Using Mystery Shoppers

Within the retail and services communities, some refer to media-based marketing firms for information on their specific business operation. These operations are also referred to as business review sites. No matter the name, anyone can go online and post details of an experience he or she had at all types of retail operations.

When it comes to the accuracy of the information posted on these websites, there are individuals on both sides of the fence. One of the main issues against 100% believing the information posted is the ability of the person posting to be anonymous. However, many individuals post comments to these websites with the best of intentions and try to be accurate in their analysis.

On the other hand, there are many reasons why individuals will post negative information about specific retail locations. Some of these reasons include:

- Someone is mad at a former friend that works at a specific retail location.
- Stock boy Joe just ended a relationship with Betty Complainer's best friend.
- Someone is just having a bad day.
- Betty Complainer's father is the manager at a competing restaurant.

No matter the reason why people choose to post untrue information about a retail experience, managers and owners need to exercise caution when reading negative reviews. This is especially true if the information posted pertains to employee integrity issues, employee theft, brand-integrity [1] issues, etc.

In an effort to get a true handle on issues within a retail operation, managers and owners need to look to using one of the numerous mystery shopping organizations [2] around the country. The many services provided by mystery shopping organizations include:

- Enter a specific retail location and make a product purchase.
- Enter a specific retail location and make it a point to interact with a targeted store associate.
- Enter a specific retail restaurant location to test the quality of service.

- Enter a specific retail restaurant location and test the quality of the product served.
- Enter a specific retail restaurant/bar and act like a patron for an extended period of time.

The benefits of using a mystery shopping company from a theft/fraud perspective are many. Based on the target of the retail location visit experience, it can be determined whether:

- Employees are conducting register activities in a manner consistent with company policies.
- Employees are correctly recording all sales, especially the transaction conducted by the mystery shopper.
- Employees are sweethearting items at the sales register.
- Bar employees are correctly recording all beverage transactions.
- Customers are provided with a valid and current register receipt.

Business managers and owners have also had success in the past by having friends and relatives shopping their locations. Although these people are not industry-educated mystery shoppers and are not trained on completing investigation reports, they can still observe questionable activity.

If it is determined there is questionable employee activity within the retail establishment, security/loss prevention personnel can take the next step in the investigative process. This step pertains to using other types of business verification services or a private investigative company.

Benefits of Using an Investigative Company

Within the industry, there are numerous investigative firms that can conduct covert duties on suspicious employee activities. The purpose behind using investigative companies is to obtain documentation [3]. Mystery shopping employees can observe and provide written reports on the activity witnessed. Trained investigators can also complete observation reports, as well as documenting the observed employee activity on video.

A growth in technology has taken the video camera from a shoulder-held Hollywood production type of device to something that can be concealed within a pair of eye glasses. This technology allows investigators the ability to conceal their intent, while blending into the background or foreground as a normal customer.

While acting as a normal customer, investigators can use a hidden video camera to document the following questionable retail activities:

- A fast food or quick service restaurant establishment manager/employee is failing to properly process large item transactions. With many fast food restaurant operations, customers always place large orders in advance of actually needing the product. In addition to placing the large order, the customer designates a time for the order to be purchased and picked up. With a normal large order transaction the customer enters the location, pays for the large purchase, and exits with the food items. When the customer makes the payment, the restaurant employee conducts the transaction like all of the others, processing the transaction through the store register. On numerous occasions the customer enters the location, pays for the large item transaction in cash, and exits the establishment with the purchase. With many of these types of cash transactions, the store manager or employee takes the money and provides the customer with the purchase. Instead of processing the cash transaction through the register, the customer is provided with some type of handwritten receipt and the store associate pockets the cash. When using video surveillance, these types of dishonest employee activities are recorded as part of the investigative process.

- A fast food or quick service restaurant employee or manager is suspected of not ringing all customer transactions. These transactions are suspected to take place during busy restaurant times, when there is a lot of customer activity around the sales counter. Many repeat or daily customers enter the establishment and make the same food or beverage purchase each morning. One or more store employees recognize the repeat customers and know what they typically purchase and that the customers typically make cash payments. When processing these types of small-dollar cash payments, the suspect employee can ring the transaction as a zero or no sale. All the employee needs is for the register drawer to open, so he or she can make change for the customer. Throughout the busy period the suspect employee can keep ringing numerous zero or no sale transactions. He or she can also choose to leave the cash drawer open as long as many in the line of customers are paying with cash. Based on the fast food restaurant setup, a trained investigator can sit at a table posing as a regular customer. While the investigator is at the table consuming the items purchased, he or she has the ability to record numerous customer transactions. The goal is to capture on video the cash transaction, the open register drawer, and the register display screen.
- Bar investigations provide an ideal climate for using video recording. An investigator sitting on a bar stool can capture the activity of the associates working in the bar area. This is important if one or more bar employees are suspected of not ringing customer sales or of sweethearting.
- Video surveillance can also be used for restaurant operations where it is suspected one or more employees are delivering product to undisclosed locations. A good example would be a bakery operation where the location manager is delivering dozens of donuts to several local hotels each morning. The manager is accepting payment for the product, but the daily transactions are not processed through the register. Trained investigators can observe the

product being loaded for delivery. Once the product is loaded, the investigators can follow the delivery vehicle and eventually watch the merchandise being unloaded while capturing the activity on video.

- In addition to using video surveillance for capturing various types of suspicious restaurant activity, it can also be used in the traditional retail environment. A good example would be conducting video surveillance of loading dock activity—especially if one or more store employees are suspected of removing delivery items from the store prior to their being placed into the inventory system. One or more employees could be removing store items and placing them in personal vehicles parked around the back door of the business. These employees could also be placing store merchandise into the dumpsters at the back of the location. After the shift has been completed, the employee retrieves the merchandise from the dumpster and loads it into his or her vehicle. The dishonest employee could also contact an accomplice to retrieve the stolen merchandise.

The opportunities to use video surveillance to detect retail incidents of theft/fraud are unlimited. Based on the suspicion of the crime being committed, retail security/loss prevention personnel and the private investigator can find a way to conduct the covert video activity.

One area of caution is in the use of capturing audio activity during the covert investigation. The laws differ between the various states as to the number of parties who must consent to have their conversations recorded. Some require one-party consent, while others require two-party consent.

It is highly advisable that store investigative personnel consult with their in-house or contract legal counsel prior to conducting any type of covert audio recording.

Tracking Established Comparable Sales

Established comparable or same-store sales is a tracking method for retail locations that have been open for at least a year. It is basically taking a time frame of operations and comparing it to the same period in the previous year. Comparable sales periods can be for twelve months, six months, a quarter, or a seasonal time frame.

Retail store managers and owners traditionally look at established comparable periods to determine the trends within the location by answering the following questions:

- Are sales up for the period or year?
- Are sales flat for the period or year?
- Are sales down for the period or year?

In order to answer these questions, it is also important to blend into the analysis other market-related trends:

- Have there been new store openings within the past year within a close proximity of the location being analyzed?
- Have competitive retail locations been opened within the past year within close proximity of the location being analyzed?
- Has there been any lengthy road construction in and around the location of the store being analyzed?
- During the winter months, were there long periods of extreme weather?

Additional sales-related information also has to be included into the established comparable analysis:

- Did the chain or location being analyzed conduct a large and well-advertised sales promotion?
- Was there a big change in a popular product/food lines for the chain or location being analyzed?
- Were there pricing changes (increased or decreased) within the chain or the location being analyzed?

From the perspective of retail store managers and owners, the goal is to have established sales increases year after year or period after period. Unsatisfactory comparable sales trends can be analyzed from a retail management perspective, with the hope of reversing the numbers in a positive direction. (Refer to Chapter 8 for detailed discussion on the topic.)

Understanding Internal Retail Store Trends

It is important for security/loss prevention personnel to take an interest in the tracking of established comparable or same-store sales numbers. What might be perceived by management as negative information resulting from internal decisions could actually be the result of an increase in shoplifting and/or employee theft.

One specific period that security/loss prevention personnel need to keep a close eye on is the Christmas or holiday period. Within the retail industry, this is the six-week period from mid-November through the end of December. Traditionally during this holiday period both shoplifting and employee theft are on the rise. There can be many reasons for the holiday period increase, but it is a good prevention idea not to accept it as a cost of doing business.

The same thought (loss prevention) process has to be maintained throughout the year. As previously discussed with the possible attributing factors to a change in established comparable numbers, security/loss prevention personnel also have to look at trends within the location being analyzed:

- Has there been an unexpected increase in employee turnover?
- Have staffing issues led to a decrease in employee training?
- Have staffing issues led to less strict new-hire verification procedures?
- Has there been a large change in the store management?
- Has there been an increase in the hiring of high school-aged associates, coupled with an increased level of high-school-aged customers?

As previously discussed, employee turnover has been an issue for the retail community. Based on the location's historical data, security/loss prevention personnel can develop an understanding of the turnover percentage numbers for specific retail locations. Based on a basic number, changes in turnover trends can be easily obtained.

Higher than normal employee turnover numbers can lead to changes within the workforce that can work to change a previously established team environment. Employees not believing they are part of a team might not have the attitude necessary to protect the integrity of the location's assets.

Significant retail location turnover numbers can also lead to a suspension of or dialing down in the amount of new-employee training. As previously discussed, newly hired employees who feel they have been thrown to the wolves might not form an alliance with their place of employment.

In addition to a downturn in new-hire training, it could also be possible there has been a change in the amount of scrutiny given to new applicants. In an effort to quickly fill open positions, retail managers might choose to conduct a cursory new-hire verification process. This mind-set can quickly lead to having members of the retail team who were not properly vetted.

In addition to having drastic changes within the retail staff, increased changes in the store and department management positions can also work to increase the levels of insecurity among associates. Constant changes in management philosophy can work to have a negative effect on employee morale and their commitment to protecting the organization's assets.

A major issue for security/loss prevention personnel, when it comes to asset protection, is a commitment from retail store management. Ideally, retail store managers find a balance between reaching set sales numbers and ensuring the integrity of the location's assets. In an effort to ensure this type of management commitment, security/loss prevention personnel need to develop relationships with store and department managers. Part of these relationships is making management personnel a part of the security/loss prevention team. Working in concert to prevent both internal and external theft, store managers and security/loss prevention professionals can achieve lower percentages of in-store shrinkage.

Retail store managers, owners, and security/loss prevention personnel need to be aware of hiring high school aged employees. Many of these younger individuals prove to be quality associates and conduct themselves in the most professional manner while at work. On the other hand, there is a percentage of teenaged associates who work in the retail industry as a benefit to themselves and their friends. Sweethearting among younger associates, especially high school aged employees, is a major issue for retailers. This includes the traditional retail locations and especially fast food operations.

Retail location managers, owners, and security/loss prevention personnel need to stay on top of locations with an overabundance of teenage associates. Location managers and owners also need to be aware of customer activity between teenage associates and teenage patrons. The following situations provide areas of concern:

- An increase in younger shoppers, during the same time frames when teenage associates are working.
- Younger associates interacting with customers of the same age in an overtly friendly manner.
- Younger customers purposely waiting (e.g., in longer lines) for store cashiers of the same age.

Although the previously mentioned youth-related situations could be innocent in nature, teenaged employee sweethearting always has to be an area of concern.

Employees Using Local Situations for Their Personal Benefit

As previously discussed, established comparable sales could be down at certain retail locations due to road construction. The same holds true if a retail location (traditional or fast food) remains open for business during a remodel. During these inconvenient periods, retail managers and owners understand there will be a negative impact on sales. An additional area for concern for all parties involved is savvy employees using this information for their own personal gain.

Certain retail employees also understand that sales will decrease during various types of construction activity. With this knowledge, they could increase the incidents of product theft and sweethearting. The thought processes are the following:

- Management is going to concentrate on creating special sales promotions to increase store customer traffic.
- Management is going to understand that the decrease in store register sales is related to the construction activity.

- Management might be more concerned about keeping the store open during the construction period than keeping an eye on suspicious employee activity.

No matter the season, specific location-related incidents, or the time of year, it is necessary that the loss prevention posture remains forever vigilant.

Endnotes

1. Brand integrity is important for the retail community. Many retail organizations rely on customers having a good experience at any of their locations. A customer having a bad experience at a Burger King in Florida might not stop at a Burger King in Ohio the following week. The customer has developed a negative perception of the entire brand.
2. Full disclosure: I have no vested interest in any mystery shopping operation. I have in the past hired more than one mystery shopping company in an effort to get a reading on employee integrity issues.
3. Full disclosure: I have no vested interest in any private investigative company. I have in the past hired and used investigative companies to document questionable employees on video.

Chapter 21

Retail Shrinkage Prevention Measures

Introduction

As previously discussed, the goal of any retail store is to develop a team-based environment. Part of this team-based environment is to make all associates part of the theft/loss prevention program. This begins at the front door through a detailed new-hire verification program and continues with letting employees know what is expected of them, as well as ensuring that they understand and sign store code-of-conduct and conflict-of-interest documents. Once inside the operation, employees need to have a belief that their opinions matter and there is a progression path for individual growth.

In addition to creating an employee-friendly working environment, it is necessary to create operating policies that focus on lowering internal theft and shoplifting.

Involve All Associates in Customer Awareness

It is a common practice for many to go into a retail establishment and feel like a ghost. Store associates are only concerned with their task at hand and are not paying attention to the activity around them:

- The employee stocking shelves with merchandise has eyes fixed between the loaded cart and the shelves where the product is being placed.
- Two floor employees are having a conversation about an upcoming sale and are ignoring the customer traffic.
- The store has four registers open and manned by individual associates. The issue of concern is that there is limited customer traffic looking to check out.

No matter what is going on in the retail location, store associates need to be aware of customer activity in the store. Customers need to be greeted by store associates as they make their way through the store. It is also a good idea for sales associates to approach customers to ask them if they require assistance.

The purpose of having a customer-aware sales staff serves two purposes:

- It goes to show the retail establishment is involved in customer service.
- It also lets customers know they are noticed. For the honest customer, the service and attention aspect is appreciated. For those looking to steal, it lets them know they are being observed.

In addition to the basic aspects of customer awareness, it is also a good idea to train retail associates on the potential traits or mannerisms of a shoplifter. Within the retail community there are many suggestions as to actions or traits exhibited by potential shoplifters. Some of these traits or mannerisms include:

- A customer wearing bulky clothing, especially if it is not suited to the weather (a customer wearing a raincoat on a clear day).
- A customer who is jumpy when approached by a retail store employee.
- A customer who appears nervous and is sweating for no apparent reason.
- A customer who is constantly looking around rather than at the merchandise.
- A customer who enters the store early in the morning or right before closing.
- A customer who watches the store employees more than looking at the merchandise.
- A customer who works to avoid being approached by store employees.
- A female shopper carrying a very large purse.
- Groups of individuals who enter the store together.

In addition to the traits discussed, shoplifters have also been known to

- Enter as a group and separate once in the store. One or more members of the group work to create some type of disturbance. While the store associates are addressing the disturbance, other group members are concealing merchandise.
- Purchase an item and exit the retail location. The item or items in question are removed from the shopping bag and placed in their vehicle. The customer then conceals the shopping bag and receipt and reenters the retail establishment. Once back inside the retail store, the shoplifter selects the same item or items and places them in the shopping bag. The customer then exits the store with the same recently purchased items in the store shopping bag. If questioned by store staff, he or she has a recent and valid receipt.
- Enter the retail location with a store shopping bag concealed on him or her. The shopping bag is quickly filled with merchandise and the shoplifter exits

the establishment. The hope is that a store employee, seeing the store shopping bag, assumes the customer just made a purchase and is heading to a vehicle.
- Enter the retail location with a store shopping bag concealed on him or her. The shopping bag brought into the store is lined with aluminum foil and is quickly filled with store merchandise. Once the shopping bag is filled with merchandise, the shoplifter quickly exits the store. The purpose behind lining the shopping bag with foil is in order to bypass the sensors placed at the store's exit doors. The purpose of these sensors is to detect an active electronic article surveillance tag. If detection is made, an alarm sounds. When the shopping bags are lined with foil, the sensors cannot detect an active surveillance tag located in the bag.

Once all retail associates have been educated in the necessity of maintaining an alert posture while at work, the store can benefit from a better customer experience and more eyes watching out for shoplifters and their known activities.

Understanding Popular Theft Items

In Section IV, discussion takes place on organized retail crime or organized retail theft. Organized retail crime groups specialize in shoplifting on a mass scale. They take the items stolen from retailers and sell the merchandise through various markets. In an effort to ensure success in the selling of stolen merchandise, these well-organized retail crime groups have a list of favorite items to steal. Many of the items on the popular list of retail items to shoplift are

- Popular grocery store items are cigarettes, energy drinks, expensive liquor and wine, baby formula, diapers, laundry detergent, razor blades, and electronic razors.
- Over-the-counter items include pain-relieving pills, weight loss pills, diabetic test strips, various allergy medications, and pregnancy test kits.
- Health and beauty items stolen are teeth whitening strips, electronic toothbrushes, and high-end makeup items.
- Clothing items include various types of designer clothing, high-end denim items, designer handbags, and furs.
- Items for the home include vacuum cleaners, high-end electronic mixers, and other types of kitchen counter appliances.
- Electronic items include electronic toys and games, GPS devices, digital cameras, cell phones, laptops, tablets, electronic reading devices, LCD monitors, and batteries.

In addition to the provided list, individual retail stores should develop lists of items lost due to store shrinkage. Many of these items could be unique to the actual store.

In an effort to prevent the shoplifting of known popular retail items, store managers and loss prevention personnel need to ensure these items are located in easily observed areas within the store. It is also advisable to keep the popular shoplifting items behind counters or on locked shelves that can be accessed by store associates. Additionally, store video surveillance systems need to be concentrated on the store locations where the popular shoplifting items are located.

Using Technology to Prevent Shrinkage

Video Monitoring

One of the main technology-based items retailers can use as a deterrent to employee theft and shoplifting is video monitoring. To begin, each and every customer entering the location needs to view himself or herself entering the retail establishment. Monitors should be mounted from the ceiling and these screens need to show a clear picture of customers entering through the front doors. The monitors should be placed in a position inside the entryway doors where they catch the customer's eye. Entryway monitors work to show all individuals entering the retail location that they and their activity are being recorded.

In addition to entryway surveillance monitors, video cameras need to be placed throughout the store. When the cameras are placed in the retail location, the installers need to ensure the following areas are covered:

- All exit doors.
- The loading dock or rear store areas where product is delivered. (All activity in these areas needs to be covered, including delivery vehicles, drivers exiting these vehicles, product being brought into the establishment, employees working in the delivery area, etc.)
- The entire product storage/inventory room.
- Doors used by store associates when the trash is taken out.
- The trash/dumpster areas in the back of the store.
- The retail floor, paying attention to potential blind spots and high-value item areas.
- Over the cash registers.
- In the customer service area of the store.
- In the product return area of the store.

During the new-hire employee orientation process, associates should be shown the video monitoring area in the store. The security/loss prevention personnel need to walk the new associates through the monitoring process and how the video systems work. Educational detail needs to be concentrated on the ability of the actual cameras: their pan/tilt functions and the ability of screening personnel to zoom in on specific customer activity and the cash registers. This process works to show all associates that the activity of the entire retail establishment is constantly being monitored. Showing coverage of the entire retail operation to all associates lets the employees know there is no place to hide potential suspicious activity.

Hopefully the video surveillance area is manned by one or more security/loss prevention personnel during the hours of operation. Having an unmanned video surveillance room provides investigative personnel someone to look for only after the crime has taken place. Having the ability to monitor customer activity from the back room of the retail store allows security/loss prevention personnel to follow suspicious individuals—hopefully catching them in the act, rather than after the fact.

Electronic Article Surveillance (EAS) Tags

EAS tags (see Figure 21.1 [1] for examples) are items that are affixed to material items and can be placed in other types of retail items. The purpose behind retailers using EAS tags is that they act as deterrents to shoplifting. Once an EAS tag is placed into use:

- It works as an active electronic device within the walls of the retail operation.
- After the retail item is brought to the register for purchase, the tag is removed by the cashier (using a special tool) or scanned and deactivated.
- If a customer attempts to exit the retail establishment with an active EAS tag, an audible alarm sounds when the item passes through one of the various types of antenna devices located at the exit doors.

Figure 21.1 Examples of EAS tags.

Security Locking Hooks

More and more retailers are using wall display protection items, such as security types of locking hooks (see Figure 21.2 [2]). These hooks can be affixed to display walls or pegboards. Once the hooks are properly placed on the display walls, retailers can load product. These retail items are usually smaller/high-theft items, such as ink cartridges, thumb drives, video games, razors, batteries, etc.

By using the security locking hooks, customers are allowed easy access to view the products. In order to remove one or more items for purchase, customers need the assistance of a store employee. Store employees possess the tools necessary to unlock the locking device and provide the requested product to the customer.

For retail operations that are sectioned off into specialty areas, it should be company policy that items secured by locking devices be purchased in the specific department. This prevents the high-value item from being pocketed by the customer on the way to the front of the store. Many retailers might choose to not use EAS tags for items that are secured on a security locking hook.

Product Tie-Down Devices

In order to protect high-dollar items like cell phones and digital cameras, retailers are using various types of product tie-down devices. The devices operate with a retractable cord, allowing customers the ability to pick up and view items. For security purposes, one end of the cord is affixed to the display table and the other end is secured to the retail item.

If a customer wishes to purchase one or more of the items secured with a product tie-down device, he or she needs the assistance of store personnel. Retail store employees can easily unlock the security device, handing the product to the customer for purchase.

As discussed with the use of security locking hooks, customers should be required to pay for the merchandise in that specific retail department area of the store.

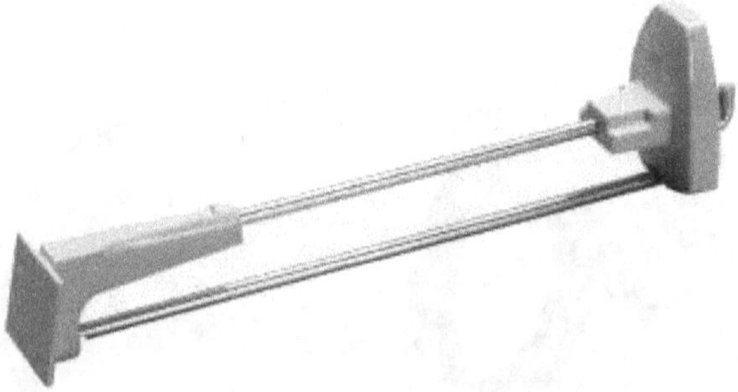

Figure 21.2 Example of a security locking hook.

Using Package Inspection at the Register or Exit Door

A popular shoplifting technique is for a person to enter a retail establishment and locate an item that is displayed in a large box. The shoplifter removes the item from the box, while being careful not to alter the outside appearance of the container. Once the large product box has been emptied, the shoplifter makes their way around the store and places small items into the box. Once the shoplifter is satisfied with the amount of merchandise placed inside the box, it is resealed in a professional manner. The shoplifter then takes the box full of merchandise to the cashier for checkout. The hope of the shoplifter is that the cashier uses the hand barcode reader and scans the box while it stays in the shopping cart.

This is also a popular method for shoplifting in a grocery store environment. Individuals will select big box items for sale in a grocery store and remove the item inside. As they make their way around the grocery store, the shoplifter places specialty items into the box. Popular grocery items to conceal are

- Premium cuts of meat
- Seafood items
- Deli meat

As with the retail method, the box or container is resealed and taken to the register with the same hope that the boxed item is hand scanned and not removed from the shopping cart by the cashier.

In order to prevent this type of theft, retailers need to establish a policy where all items are placed on the checkout counter. The retail or grocery store can also establish a product inspection policy at the register or by the employee checking sales receipts at the exit door. Even though the boxed item gives the appearance it has not been tampered with, the actual weight of the product could be a giveaway.

Controlling Product Returns

Retailers suffer losses from various types of item return scams, committed by both customers and employees. In order to control and prevent losses from taking place through product return fraud, retailers and security/loss prevention personnel need to develop an understanding of the methods used on both sides of the register:

- An unsupervised employee can initiate a product return at his or her register. All the employee needs is the product code or actual item to scan as part of the item return. After scanning, the employee completes the return according to policy and simply pockets the cash amount of the returned product. In order to prevent this type of employee-related theft from taking place, a second set of eyes needs to be part of the return process. The internal register system should not allow a single employee to initiate and fully complete an item return. Based on the internal register system, there needs to be a requirement for a manager to personally enter a return authorization code or use a management key.

- If possible, retail establishments need to designate a separate section of the store for product returns. This needs to be an area of the store that can be accessed immediately upon a customer entering the building. It should also be an area of the store that is constantly monitored by video surveillance cameras showing the activity of customers approaching and waiting at the return counter. Video cameras also need to constantly show the activity of employees working the return counter. If possible, retailers should place a monitor on the back wall of the return counter. The activity displayed on the monitor should show the actual customers making the return and the items being presented.
- A popular method of shoplifters is to make a product purchase, obtain their receipt, and exit the establishment with the item in a store shopping bag. Upon arriving at their vehicle, the customer places the purchased item in the car and reenters the store. Once back inside the store, the customer takes the same type of item to the return counter and presents the retail item and a sales receipt that was issued by the retail store. The hope from the customer standpoint is that the employee will process the item return as a normal course of business. What the employee needs to be concerned with is completely inspecting the sales receipt and immediately questioning the reasoning for the item being returned within a short time of being purchased.
- An effective method retailers are using to combat return fraud is allowing customers to return merchandise purchased with a credit/debit card without a sales receipt. All the customer needs to present is the item being returned and the credit/debit card that was used at the time of purchase. The internal computer system links the two pieces of information together, which shows the item in question was actually purchased with the credit/debit card being presented. Information can also be displayed on the time and date of purchase, the sales register where the transaction took place, and the sales associate. In an effort to add integrity to the process, customers should be required to show proper identification linking them to the name on the credit/debit card.
- All retailers need to have established product return policies. This information can be placed on the receipt header and be clearly posted in the area of the store that accepts returns. Included in the return policy should be information on the customer needing to present a valid register receipt, the time window from purchase to return, if the store is providing a gift card for the amount of purchase if no receipt is presented, etc. Retailers need to use caution if they are establishing a return policy where store gift cards are provided if no receipt is presented. Policies like this encourage thieves to steal merchandise and then return it at a later date. Once these individuals obtain the store gift cards, they are later sold through various online websites for cash.

Never Assume Shrinkage Is from Shoplifting

Although it might seem confusing in nature, it is possible management and security/loss prevention staff could be misidentifying shrinkage. Losses in items off the retail floor are usually quickly attributed to customer theft. With this type of internal thinking, more loss prevention assets are diverted to combating shoplifting. Concentrating video and covert surveillance into identifying and stopping shoplifters is always a good plan, but an overconcentration in one store area could open the door in other areas, such as:

- Employee theft from inventory items not yet placed on the retail floor.
- Employee sweethearting of retail items to friends and family members.

With the percentages of employee theft and shoplifting so close in the overall shrinkage numbers, equal amounts of loss prevention concentration need to be applied across the board.

Endnotes

1. EAS tags images. https://www.google.com/search?q=eas+tags&tbm=isch&imgil=h-71KPGGndQflM%253A%253B3acwa9834dXSLM%253Bhttp%25253A%25252F%25252Fwww.hansab.com%25252Fproducts%25252Feas-labels-and-tags&source=iu&pf=m&fir=h-71KPGGndQflM%253A%252C3acwa9834dXSLM%252C_&biw=1366&bih=657&usg=__G9U_BAO2AzhkjDwP1LTf62pk4o8%3D&ved=0CEoQyjdqFQoTCMD8w-a80cgCFUrxYwodlosB_Q&ei=e2wmVoDTJMrijwOWl4boDw#imgrc=h-71KPGGndQflM%3A&usg=__G9U_BAO2AzhkjDwP1LTf62pk4o8%3D (accessed October 19, 2015).
2. Security locking hook. https://www.google.com/search?q=pegs+locking+hooks&sa=X&biw=1366&bih=657&tbm=isch&imgil=WBgI2hiU-a2w-M%253A%253BwOIfKOAuh5S5cM%253Bhttp%25253A%25252F%25252Fwww.americantheftprevention.com%25252FInVue-S3-Locking-Security-Hook-p227.html&source=iu&pf=m&fir=WBgI2hiU-a2w-M%253A%252CwOIfKOAuh5S5cM%252C_&usg=__KlKNyVTqTrE9PRA7SJXImU7nw0w%3D&ved=0CD4QyjdqFQoTCJWakonC0cgCFVfaYwodETsBjw&ei=AnImVpWRFte0jwOR9oT4CA#imgrc=WBgI2hiU-a2w-M%3A&usg=__KlKNyVTqTrE9PRA7SJXImU7nw0w%3D (accessed October 19, 2015).

Chapter 22

Identifying Loss in the Retail Restaurant Industry

Introduction

When most consumers are asked about what constitutes the retail industry, many will refer to stores where clothing, electronics, and other like items are sold. One area that is usually overlooked is the restaurant industry. As previously discussed, there is a difference in certain restaurant chains as some fall under the company ownership umbrella and others are franchised. With some restaurant chains, companies have both owned and franchise locations.

No matter the type of ownership setup, all brands of restaurants suffer losses due to

- Employee theft
- Customer theft
- Vendor fraud

Within the restaurant industry there is a breakdown as to the various types of operations:

- Traditional restaurants with the sole purpose of selling food products.
- Traditional restaurants with the purpose of selling food products, coupled with a full bar area.
- Full-bar establishments, with a small portion of the menu aimed at selling food products.
- Quick service restaurants (QSRs) or fast food establishments.

No matter the type of restaurant setup, all types need customers entering the facilities to make product purchases and employees to serve the needs of the patrons and to turn raw material into a marketable product. As discussed with retail operations thus far, questionable employees and dishonest customers are major parts of the formula leading to retail shrinkage. Within the retail restaurant community, the same parts of the shrinkage formula exist.

Tracking Established Comparable Sales

As discussed, within the retail industry, it is important for all parties involved to keep an eye on established comparable sales. This is especially true for restaurant operations.

With traditional retail operations, many brands operate in large locations with thousands of square feet of sales space. Retailers work to ensure that as much of the floor space as possible is used to display merchandise. Sales counters, shelving, and large stockroom areas allow a constant turnover of merchandise.

In traditional restaurant and QSR locations, the customer service space is much smaller compared to many traditional retail operations. Restaurants, restaurant/bars, and QSRs are sales restrictive due to the following factors:

- Restaurants have a set number of tables at which to seat customers.
- Restaurants normally have a server-to-customer table ratio. Servers can only provide quality service to a set number of tables and, due to staffing issues, some tables can go unused during slow periods.
- Restaurant/bars and bars also have a limited number of seats for customers.
- Only one meal can be served per filled seat in a restaurant. The retail multi-unit display factor does not come into play.
- All restaurant and bar operations are restricted by customer turnover time frames. It takes time to serve full meals to full tables of customers. Some customers also choose to remain at their table once their meal has been completed. The same is true for bar operations: Some patrons might stay in a seat for a single beverage while others choose to sit for hours.
- QSR operations can only serve product to a limited number of customers due to the number of registers and amount of counter space available.
- QSR service is also based on the speed in which kitchen staff can put orders together.
- With QSR bakery operations, product sales are based on the number of cashiers operating registers. These operations also have to work with situations where certain products are sold out for the day.
- All restaurant/bar operations also operate according to customer peak periods. Most have busy lunch and dinner time frames, with limited customer traffic in between.

- No matter the type of restaurant operation, all are constricted by seating, customer turnover time frames, product availability, menu pricing, peak and off periods, etc.

Developing an understanding of the constrictions that limit the amount of restaurant sales per day adds to the importance of keeping track of established comparable sales. In addition to keeping an eye on comparable sales numbers, all types of restaurant operations need to track their cost-of-goods-sold numbers.

Tracking Cost of Goods Sold/ Sales Ratio and Food Costs

Cost of goods sold in the restaurant industry is a simple formula:

Beginning inventory + purchases – ending inventory = cost of goods sold

$6,000 + $3,000 – $4,000 = $5,000

It is very important for restaurant personnel to track the weekly/monthly cost of goods sold (COGS) numbers. This number has to be compared to the weekly/ monthly restaurant sales numbers. This comparison provides a sales ratio percentage:

COGS/sales = ratio percentage

$5,000/$9,000 = 56% sales ratio

Another important percentage number in the restaurant industry is the food cost percentage:

Cost of goods sold/food sales = food cost

$5,000/$15,900 = 31%

Within a traditional restaurant operation, the food cost percentage is around 30%.

Restaurant managers, owners, and security/loss prevention personnel need to understand and track the previously discussed sales numbers and percentages. Unlike franchise operations where the franchisees report internal sales information, company-owned restaurant sales numbers can be tracked through the internal company systems.

Security/loss prevention personnel need to take the previously discussed sales and cost percentages and develop benchmarks. The benchmark information is based on historical and geographical operating information for restaurants open for at least one year. Once the benchmark numbers and percentages have been established, concerned parties can compare specific locations to the overall company averages.

Additionally, there are several resources where investigative personnel can obtain industry-specific benchmark standards. The information provided pertains to a majority of aspects in the restaurant industry, including:

- Types of operations: full service, table service, QSR, etc.
- Payroll percentages based on type of operation.
- Beverage costs, food costs, alcohol costs, etc.
- Acceptable levels of operating profit.
- Sales projection information.

The goal for anyone looking at COGS, sales ratios, and food costs is to look for

- Consistency in operations, leading to increasing sales numbers
- Outlier locations that have numbers that are not consistent with other similar operations
- Higher than average cost numbers
- Sales numbers that are not in line with product costs

Retail restaurant units that have cost and ratio numbers that are not in line with the other locations in the overall operation could be indicators of

- Poor management practices
- Employee theft of raw material
- Employee theft of developed product
- Extensive product waste
- Employees sweethearting product and/or alcohol to friends
- Sales underreporting by management
- Employees skimming cash from the register

It is important for investigative personnel to conduct an investigation into restaurant locations that have cost and ratio numbers out of line with the established benchmark data.

Creating Yield/Usage Programs

The benefit of having restaurant operations for company-owned operations is the known factor of product received. The product received could be in the form of prepackaged menu items or raw material, such as flour for donuts in a bakery operation.

Over the years investigative personnel have been successful in creating yield/usage programs in an effort to determine a projected sales number. The yield/usage programs are specific to the type of restaurant and have to be created with that fact in mind. The overall goal of the program is to determine restaurant-specific information, such as:

- Counting waste, how many pints of beer does a keg yield?
- Counting waste, how many donuts can be baked from a 50-pound bag of flour?
- Counting waste, how many sandwiches can be made from a standard bread order?
- Counting waste, how many spaghetti meals can be created from a large box of uncooked pasta?

With yield/usage programs, the information going in is based on the specific restaurant operation. The information should include:

- Tracking the raw material of main product items (flour into donuts, pounds of coffee beans into cups of brewed product, etc.).
- Tracking shipped whole main product items (pieces of chicken, fish, beef, etc.).
- Menu item costs.
- Waste factors.
- Number of weekly reporting periods.

Although not an easy process, yield/usage programs can be used to determine underreported sales amounts. The fact that X amount of product and raw material should produce X dollars of sales should be compared to the actual sales numbers reported. If the yield/usage sales projections are greater than the sales numbers reported, it is possible the location manager is not reporting accurate sales numbers. This could be an indicator of someone skimming money from the register or an outright process of deception.

Tracking Voids and "No Sale" Numbers

Two popular methods used by employees to steal money from a retail operation are voiding transactions or using the "no sale" function to open the register drawer. Typically scenarios are as follows:

- A customer makes a purchase in a QSR for six dollars and pays in cash. The cashier completes the transaction as usual (without providing a register receipt). Once the customer leaves the restaurant, the cashier voids the transaction and pockets the cash.

- During busy QSR periods customers enter the establishment for their morning cup of coffee. Many of these consistent customers know the exact cost of their favorite purchase and have the money ready. A savvy cashier could also know the busy times and the consistency of cash-paying/single-item purchase customers. All the cashier needs to do is hit the "no sale" function to have the cash drawer open. With the open drawer, the cashier uses it for making quick change. Instead of numerous sales being processed through the register, the money is pocketed by the employee.

Throughout a typical day in a restaurant, there comes a need to void a transaction or open the register to make change. What investigators need to develop is a benchmark window of acceptability:

- Are five voids per shift acceptable?
- Are five "no sale" actions per shift acceptable?
- Are six voids per shift unacceptable?
- Are six "no sale" actions per shift unacceptable?

Ideally, the restaurant operation should have a policy in place where a management override is necessary to void transactions or to use the "no sale" function.

Tracking Sales Based on Specific Employee Shifts

As long as individual restaurant operations are within the windows of acceptable costs, ratios, and sales numbers, many could assume all within the operation are acting aboveboard. Because of gaps in acceptable numbers and percentages, a restaurant operation could be operating within the number range. Even though the particular operation is within the range, the numbers could be just above the bottom line.

With company-owned operations, investigative personnel have information at their fingertips as far as specific register data. Hopefully, in each individual restaurant operation, employees are required to have their own identifier code to operate a register. By assigning each employee a specific code, individual register activity can be observed.

As referenced, the entire restaurant operation could be operating within acceptable ranges. What also could be taking place is that a single employee is using the register as a personal ATM.

Investigative personnel need to develop programs that track specific employee sales numbers per shift worked. The following could be discovered:

- Throughout the QSR there are typically three associates working the front serving line, taking orders, and processing them through the sales registers. At the end of the busy shift, the three register sales numbers are consistent with the established sales benchmarks. What is overlooked is that two of the three operating registers had consistent sales numbers—sales numbers that were much greater than those of the person operating the third register. If this type of situation takes place here and there, it could be an outlier. If the variances are continuous, the employee operating the third register could be skimming sales and sweethearting.

- Bar operations are also prime areas where employee register login data should be tracked. During busy bar times each employee working should have pretty consistent login and processed sales numbers. Large variations between employees working during the same shifts in a bar setting could be a prime indicator of sweethearting.

If customer traffic is consistent throughout a sales period, the register numbers should be somewhat consistent. If not, investigators have located an indicator.

Dangers of Being a Hands-Off Manager

Managers in company-owned restaurant operations (traditional, carry-out, QSR) need to create an understanding among their staff that no one working for the restaurant knows exactly when the manager is going to show up. Many retail restaurant managers have a set weekly work schedule, so all employees know when the manager is going to be present. With this setting, windows of opportunity are created for employees to operate outside normal procedures, especially when it comes to sweethearting product for friends and family.

A manager who follows a set schedule is being hands off because he or she does not have a handle on the entire business operation. The manager knows employee operations and customer activity while he or she is in the restaurant, but is clueless as to what takes place before arriving and after leaving.

- Every city in the country has at least one high school. During the fall season, Friday nights are dedicated to football games. After the home games, students flock to various types of QSRs that have a primary product of ice cream, sandwiches, other handheld foods, etc. If these QSR operations are only staffed with two or three employees who attend the same local high school, there is a possibility that product is being sweethearted.
- Some restaurant/bar operations have sporadic customer traffic after the lunch rush and before dinner. During many of these periods, management is most likely not working. What is most likely to take place is one or more bartenders sweethearting drinks to friends.

The examples provided have been known to take place in the absence of management. The following needs to take place to avoid product loss:

- Corporate security/loss prevention personnel need to understand what can take place with hands-off management. After developing this understanding, they need to have conversations with retail managers working locations they have a responsibility to oversee.
- Restaurant managers need to maintain a rotating work schedule and create an atmosphere in which the employee base does not know when the boss is going to be around.
- Restaurant managers and security/loss prevention personnel need to have surveillance cameras installed that can directly observe the operations and all register transactions. Managers and security/loss prevention personnel need to have the ability to remotely access the monitoring devices. This remote monitoring ability has to become common knowledge among all employees.
- Employ the services of mystery shopping companies to get feedback on employee/customer activity when management is not present.

Chapter 23

Convenience Store Theft and Fraud

Introduction

Previous discussion has taken place on identifying and preventing theft/fraud as it relates to traditional retail operations and restaurant businesses of all sizes. One area in the retail industry that operates a combination of the two is the convenience store. Convenience stores are also referred to as C stores.

Convenience stores of today offer services to the retail public in the areas of

- Traditional retail merchandise (clothing, games, toys, etc.)
- Grocery store merchandise
- Fuel and vehicle maintenance items
- Propane
- Cooked food and bakery items

Convenience stores operate in a world that incorporates almost every aspect of the retail community. In addition to offering a wide variety of services, convenience stores are also faced with the following issues that are conducive to theft/fraud:

- Many operate on a 24/7 schedule.
- Many are open on all holidays.
- Store size and budgets do not allow shifts to have a large number of employees working.
- Employees perform many functions that are individual positions in traditional retail operations.

- Due to customer activities and potential deliveries, employees can be easily distracted.
- Many times there is only one employee working.
- Employees are trained in numerous functions to keep the business operating.
- Unlike many traditional retail and restaurant operations, robbery is an issue.

Based on the parent company of the convenience store, there are three levels of individual operation:

- All locations are company owned.
- All locations are franchised.
- Some locations are company owned and the remainder are franchised.

No matter the type of convenience store setup—company owned or franchised—each individual location operates as an understaffed, self-sufficient full retail establishment.

From a theft/fraud perspective, convenience stores differ from traditional retail operations with regard to causes of the overall shrinkage number. As previously discussed, the two big factors of traditional retail shrinkage are split: about 40% employee theft to 40% shoplifting. With convenience stores, the employee theft number averages around 70%. Some estimates have the employee theft percentage in the 60% range, while others are in the high 70% to the low 80% range. No matter the actual employee theft percentage number, convenience store owners or franchisees have an antitheft/-fraud mountain to overcome.

In addition to employee theft being part of the convenience store shrinkage percentage, vendor theft/fraud and customer shoplifting are the other major factors. According to the National Association of Convenience Stores, vendor fraud issues account for 15% to 20% of shrinkage [1]. Estimates of shoplifting percentages that make up the overall convenience store shrinkage number range from 15% up through 30%. No matter the exact convenience store shoplifting percentage, owners and franchisees face a major loss potential through their own employees.

Addressing Convenience Store Employee Theft

A majority of industry experts place the percentage of convenience store employee theft at over 50%. Even if only half of the shrinkage-related convenience store losses is due to employee theft, this is the main area that needs to be addressed.

When addressing the convenience store employee theft percentage, it is important to develop an understanding of where ownership operation can place the greatest line of defense. As previously discussed, franchisees operate as individual owners and are responsible for a large majority of the overall business operation, including:

- Employee hiring
- Employee training
- Implementing loss prevention procedures
- Establishing delivery acceptance procedures
- Establishing inventory control and audit procedures
- Purchasing video surveillance systems
- Monitoring and reviewing video surveillance
- Monitoring register activities

At the opposite end of the spectrum, company-owned convenience stores have a management system in place. This system includes a main office, as well as regional and district offices, all staffed with security/loss prevention personnel. With company-owned convenience stores, management and loss prevention personnel can

- Track sales and register activity
- Develop and deliver security/loss prevention training
- Develop security/loss prevention policies and procedures
- Monitor in-store video surveillance activity

Whether company owned or franchised, convenience store operations all come down to employee staffing levels. As referenced with many convenience store operations, there are times when there is a single employee working. In order to ensure the convenience store owner or franchisee the best defense against employee theft and sweethearting, the hiring process should include detailed applicant screening and a thorough background investigation. (Refer to Chapter 2 for detailed discussion on background investigation programs.)

From an Internet search on preventing employee theft or from speaking with industry experts, several tools and tips can be found. No matter which article is read or to whom one speaks, the number one tool to prevent employee theft is to hire the right people.

Once individuals are hired in a convenience store operation, it is necessary for all parties involved to look at the situation. With traditional retail and restaurant operations, employees work in an environment with almost constant co-worker interaction. In the convenience store world, many employees find themselves working alone. This is especially true for employees working the midnight to dawn shift.

As discussed with traditional retail and restaurant operations, the goal is to create a team working environment. With most convenience store setups, creating this type of environment is almost impossible. In lieu of being able to create the desired team setting, convenience store owners and managers need to become more involved in getting to know their employees. This includes:

- Getting to know the individual through continuous conversations
- Understanding any hardships the individual might be going through
- Paying the employee a visit during those long overnight shifts
- Developing the store work schedule around individual employee commitments

Developing relationships with employees places a thought in the backs of their minds that it is harder to steal from a friend.

Once they are hired, it is also a good idea to pay convenience store workers at a higher rate than they could receive at other local business operations. The increased wages show the employees that their time and experience are appreciated. It could also work to add an increased level of store loyalty.

Convenience store owners, along with security/loss prevention personnel, need to ensure that individual locations are completely monitored by video surveillance, including the parking lot, all entry and exit doors, and any fuel dispensing areas. Additionally, the entire store area needs to be covered, including the register and stockroom areas. Surveillance cameras need to be positioned over each register so that all activity can be recorded and remotely monitored.

In order to ensure the integrity of all convenience store employees, they should be made aware of the camera positions and the owner's ability to remotely monitor store activities.

Preventing Convenience Store Shoplifting

Convenience store employees need to be trained to offer a word of welcome to all customers entering the location. Greeting each and every customer places him or her on notice that his or her presence has been noted. Along with requiring all employees to personally greet every customer, a video monitor screen should be hung from the ceiling just inside the front door. The activity displayed on the monitor should show in real time each person entering the store. By walking through the front door, the customer will see himself or herself walking into the establishment. This lets each customer know that activity is being monitored.

In order for store employees to be able to monitor all customer activities in the location, mirrors need to be mounted from the ceiling in a position that allows store employees to see customer activities at other ends of the store from where the employees are positioned.

Convenience store employees also need to be trained on what to look for as it relates to potential shoplifters:

- A popular method, especially for smaller convenience stores, is to use a group of people. Once inside, members of the group split up and go to separate sections of the store. This activity takes place knowing that one or two employees cannot successfully monitor the activities of a large group of people in the store. A popular prevention tool used by some stores that are in the close proximity of local high schools is to limit the number of students allowed in the establishment at one time. Convenience store owners and managers have erected door signs that read: "No more than three school-aged kids are allowed in the store at the same time."

- Watch for customers entering the store pushing a stroller or carrying large bags or a backpack.
- Be aware of customers who enter the location that appear nervous or jumpy, are constantly looking around, check out the activity in the mirrors, keep an eye on employees, etc.
- Be aware of what appear to be two friends entering the store, especially if they split up and one goes to the back of the store, while the other approaches the counter. The goal of the customer approaching the counter is to engage the employee in a conversation, taking the employee's eyes off the other activity in the store. If the employee is visually occupied, the other friend is placing merchandise into his or her pockets or backpack.
- Convenience store managers, owners, and security/loss prevention personnel should have employees train them. These individuals need to take the time to speak with employees about where they see vulnerabilities. This goes back to the "thinking like a thief" theory and asking employees, who spend hours in the store, how they would go about stealing from this particular location. Many times, information will be revealed that can be used to train other employees on shrinkage prevention. Speaking with associates in this manner also lets them know they are part of a team and their opinion is valued.

From a management and loss prevention standpoint, convenience stores need to ensure the product setup protects items of a high retail value. If possible, all high-dollar/high-value items need to be placed behind the counter in a place where only employees have access. By having the employee retrieve the high-dollar item and hand it to the customer at the counter, payment can be easily made and a potential theft is avoided.

Understanding and Preventing Convenience Store Vendor Fraud

The most popular method of vendor fraud for convenience stores is delivery shortages. These shortages could be the result of

- The vendor purposely sending the wrong amounts of merchandise to individual convenience stores
- The delivery driver removing merchandise between the warehouse and the convenience store

- The accidental loading of merchandise that is not in line with the invoicing documents and the items placed in the delivery vehicle
- Individuals at the convenience store not conducting a proper count of the merchandise being delivered
- Store employees accepting the correct amount of merchandise being delivered, removing product once accepted, and altering the documentation
- One or more store employees working in concert with the delivery driver to short merchandise upon delivery

Whether accidental, purposely on the part of the supplier/driver, or in conjunction with store personnel, this is an issue convenience store managers, owners, and security/loss prevention personnel need to be aware of and stay on top of.

For merchandise shortages that begin at the warehouse, it is not important who initiated the intent, including the vendor and/or the delivery driver. What is important to the convenience store owner, manager, or franchisee is the integrity of the amount of delivered and accepted merchandise. Convenience store representatives need to ensure they maintain the integrity of the shipment once it leaves the back of the delivery vehicle and as it comes through the back door.

From the perspective of the convenience store leadership, they have to establish strict delivery procedures overseen by the most trusted of employees. These procedures need to include:

- Not accepting the merchandise counts printed on the delivery documents at face value
- An internal dual control system for delivered item counts that match all related documentation
- Determining who is allowed to accept and sign for delivered merchandise
- Strict agreements with vendors on delivery times (Convenience stores should not accept deliveries when only a single employee is working.)

In addition to developing delivery procedures, convenience store operators also need to

- Designate the door at which deliveries will be accepted
- Ensure a video surveillance system is installed that captures all activity outside the delivery door and into the store
- Ensure designated convenience store personnel can remotely monitor the camera activity

For preventing employee collusion with delivery personnel or their direct involvement with delivered merchandise theft, refer to the previous discussion on addressing convenience store employee theft.

Maintaining an Audit Presence in the Convenience Store Operation

Once the product has made its way through the back door and into the store inventory, there is still a need to maintain the integrity of store inventory. Inventory audits should be conducted on a routine basis, but not on an exact schedule. Store employees should not know when store audits have been scheduled, but should be aware when they are taking place. Those designated to conduct inventory audits should be limited to owners, franchisees, or highly trusted management personnel.

Additional integrity can be added to the audit process by using an outside independent third party on a periodic basis—maybe once a year or every six months, a fresh pair of eyes in the store for the inventory audit. This process can be especially helpful for convenience store operations that are company owned or for franchise operations where the franchisees are not directly involved with their stores. Some large franchise operations operate with a detailed internal management system, with no daily or weekly interaction with the actual locations or store managers.

With many convenience store operations, the sales, ordering, and inventory process is somewhat consistent. As part of the inventory process, what is being looked for is a change in that consistency:

- Are item orders increasing while weekly sales remain consistent?
- Are item orders increasing in line with a rise in weekly sales?
- Are item orders consistent and the weekly sales numbers declining?

Management is looking for the ideal situation of increasing orders that are in line with a rise in weekly sales. Any other trends can reveal the following:

- Possible vendor shortages of delivered merchandise
- Possible employee theft of merchandise while it is in the inventory system of the store
- An increase in shoplifting
- An increase in shoplifting and/or employee theft as a result of a large, sudden change in store personnel (hasty hiring coupled with the inability to properly train new associates)

Within the convenience store industry, the only acceptable trend for owners and franchisees is to increase merchandise orders and sales. Any other variations identify issues for concern. To avoid these concerns, managers, owners, franchisees, and security/loss prevention personnel need to ensure each and every convenience store adheres to the following:

- Proper new-employee vetting and training
- Creating a team environment

- Employing effective anti-employee-theft technology
- Employing effective antishoplifting technology
- Preventing vendor fraud
- Creating an effective audit process

Protecting Customers from Credit/Debit Card Skimming

Individuals' placing skimming devices on ATM machines is becoming a serious issue for financial institutions. These skimming devices are made to look like they are part of the ATM and are placed in a manner that the customer does not notice anything suspicious during the banking transaction.

For ATM skimming to be successful, thieves place the devices into the card reader area of the ATM. Once installed, the device reads the ATM card information after it is inserted into the machine. Additionally, a pinhole camera is installed outside the ATM for the purpose of capturing the account holder's PIN.

After the thief has the user's credit/debit card account information and PIN, he or she can then create fraudulent cards or go shopping online.

Because of the success of using skimming devices on ATMs, they are now being used at the gas pump. With a large majority of convenience stores offering fuel services to their customers, it is vital that all employees be educated with an understanding of the threat.

Although the actual convenience store is not liable for the theft of the customer's credit/debit card information, it is important that employees not allow the fuel pumps to be the catalyst for fraud.

In an effort to detect and prevent this type of fraudulent activity, convenience store employees need to

- Inspect the individual fuel pumps for tampering around the credit/debit insertion area
- Look for foreign devices that can be used as a skimming device
- Look for foreign devices that can be used as a pinhole camera
- Monitor the cameras trained on the fuel service area and look for individuals that might be installing skimming devices
- Monitor the cameras trained on the fuel service area and look for individuals that are retrieving the skimming devices and pinhole cameras

Endnote

1. National Association of Convenience Stores. http://www.nacsonline.com/Pages/default.aspx (accessed October 22, 2015).

Chapter 24

Creating and Delivering Effective Loss Prevention Training

Within the retail industry a percentage of regional, district, and store managers have not received any type of formal loss prevention training. Additional store employees who have never received any type of loss prevention training are general employees or cashiers. The lack of training issue is also a problem for those working in franchisee types of operations. Since a majority of franchise operations consist of franchisees owning from one to several retail stores, they have no formal internal operation to create a training program.

The rationale behind a lack of formal loss prevention training in the franchise industry is obvious. Within the world of company-owned retail operations, there are many excuses given:

- Time constraints—some feel an employee's time can be better utilized in developing customer relations and sales.
- With a high employee turnover ratio, it is a waste of time to keep training associates who are going to eventually leave.
- The store has cameras installed, along with shoplifting prevention technology. What good would lecturing loss prevention information to employees serve?
- Some think, "From a regional level position, I have learned over the years how to prevent theft in a retail store."

- Others think, "A bunch of 'wanna-be' cops cannot teach a 30-year retail professional any new information."
- There may be a management mind-set of not looking at the cost/benefit factor of associates and management receiving loss prevention training. Will the time spent receiving loss prevention training pay off through the money and merchandise saved from having a workforce dedicated to protecting the organization's assets?
- It is an issue that has not been addressed by the security/loss prevention department. Department members feel they are the experts and the only ones who can effectively prevent losses and that training retail store managers and staff can only work as a detriment to the current loss prevention program.
- The thinking may be that management will never approve the development of and the time required to deliver the program to the retail staff.
- Some personnel may think, "We have always operated this way, so why confuse everyone with new policies and procedures?"

No matter the excuse given, the reasons why each and every retail operation does not engage in loss prevention training work to create a recipe for continued losses. In order to overcome any excuse given, it is up to loss prevention professionals to convince the corporate office and upper management that training is needed. Within the retail industry there are plenty of statistics from industry professionals on the losses associated with retail theft/fraud. Additionally, there are several loss prevention and fraud awareness organizations that have worked years developing retail-industry-specific statistics on the loss prevention threat facing the industry.

For company-owned operations it is up to security/loss prevention personnel to collect the following:

- Internal data on company-wide shrinkage numbers that can be presented as a whole and also drilled down to regional and district specifics
- National shrinkage numbers specific to the retail industry, to include total dollar loss projections, as well as data on the areas of total shrinkage percentages, like employee theft and shoplifting
- How a team approach can be beneficial in lowering retail shrinkage numbers
- Known traits of a shoplifter
- Known tactics of and preferred theft items of organized retail crime groups
- Organized retail crime threats to industry-specific retail operations (Does the specific retail operation stock items preferred by professional shoplifting groups?)
- Projected savings that can be achieved by creating a team-based approach to retail shrinkage and, based on the overall retail operation sales and inventory numbers, what additional savings can be achieved

Once the necessary information is collected, it is up to security/loss prevention managers to sell the need for loss prevention training. A simple tool to present to management is a cost/benefit analysis showing the potential long-term savings that can be achieved by having a retail staff educated about loss prevention.

Security/loss prevention professionals and retail management can also reap the benefits of the carryover effect from having all retail associates attend loss prevention training classes. A retail associate educated on the organization's posture to prevent overall shrinkage will most likely think twice before committing acts of employee theft or sweethearting. As previously discussed, show the retail associates what can be observed by the video surveillance system. Simply telling a person the retail store is under constant video surveillance might not provide a clear picture of what exactly can be observed. Showing a cashier that security/loss prevention personnel have the ability to pan down to see exactly what is being processed on a specific register does provide a very clear picture.

Other motivational carryover effects of a retail staff educated on loss prevention is in the actual numbers related to how an effective loss prevention program can ensure

- Larger profit dollars that can be used for employee benefits
- Larger profit dollars that can ensure continued operation of the overall retail business
- More dollars devoted to product development and marketing
- Job security

All retail store employees need to see the relationship between shrinkage prevention and individual benefit. All retail operation managers, directors, and executives need to be educated on the shrinkage prevention and individual benefit factor. With an effective loss prevention program, a team environment can be created. The team environment factor has to be a major selling point for security/loss prevention personnel looking to get an employee training program approved.

Chapter 25

Creating the Ideal Loss Prevention Team

When it comes to preventing shrinkage-related losses in the retail industry, questions arise as to which type of department should be established. Is it better for the organization to hire in-house security/loss prevention professionals or contract out the entire operation? What about a combination of the two—part proprietary and part contract?

When looking at establishing an in-house security/loss prevention team versus using contract services, there are many questions to be answered:

- The first question is cost. Is it cheaper to hire a contract agency, since employee benefits are paid for by the parent organization? Typically it is cheaper to hire contract organizations due to the hiring organization not having to pay for benefits. The contract company is hired at a set price, based on the agreed upon contract. The contract company also has to pay the related hiring and training expenses of the investigators. If the decision is made to go with a contract company, further questions arise.
- The second question is loyalty. Where would the contract investigators' loyalty reside? Will the hiring company come first?
- The third question is legality. Can the contract investigators operate under the same liability protection umbrella as an in-house employee? Is the hiring organization liable for the actions of the contracted investigators?
- The fourth question is the integrity and reputation of the contract organization. Does the contract organization pay its personnel the bare minimum? Are they properly trained? What are their backgrounds? How about their

education? Do they belong to professional industry-related associations? Are they professional?

- The fifth question comes down to due diligence. What is the cost factor pertaining to conducting a full investigation of the contract organization? Can the hiring organization set a minimum education and experience requirement, based upon the agreed upon contract price? Can the hiring organization set a minimum standard on how detailed the background investigation should be for all contract investigators?
- The sixth question comes to the contract itself. What are the chances of getting out of the contract if the performance is unsatisfactory? Is the organization locked in for the time frame agreed upon?
- The seventh question comes down to supervisorial authority. Will the hiring organization have any directional authority over the contract investigators?

When using the services of a contract organization, many questions arise in the beginning and throughout the length of the contract. What the hiring company has to look at is the overall cost factors associated with hiring in-house or using an outside agency. What might seem like the cheaper option of using a contract organization could become more costly and burdensome in the long run.

On the other hand, there are many professional security/loss prevention companies that work with retailers worldwide in a very professional and cost-effective manner. When making the decision, the hiring organization has to

- Conduct a cost/benefit analysis
- Exercise great due diligence
- Consult with its legal and human resources departments
- Get references
- Have more than one face-to-face meeting
- Understand all aspects of the agreed upon contract

It is also possible to find satisfaction in using a combination of the two by having an in-house security/loss prevention department that hires contract investigators on an as-needed basis. Using this method, the retail organization can choose to hire outside companies for specific operations. Using contract companies for specific missions also requires the hiring organization to ensure that

- It is contracting with a professional and experienced organization.
- All aspects of the specific mission are understood and the investigators have the experience necessary to complete the job.
- The investigative staff have all of the state-required certificates and licenses.
- The hiring organization can withhold payment for unsatisfactory performance.

As previously discussed, investigative agencies can provide services to retail operations. Some of these services include:

- Mystery shopping
- Surveillance operations
- Covert video surveillance
- Customer counts
- Sales integrity investigations
- Sales reporting investigations
- Reverse sting operations

Using the services of investigative companies on an as-needed basis can prove to be beneficial to retailers. This is especially true for specialty types of investigations where the expertise resides outside the retail operation.

Chapter 26

Brandjacking

Brandjacking is an activity whereby someone acquires or otherwise assumes the online identity of another entity for the purposes of acquiring that person's or business's brand equity [1].

From a retail perspective, brandjacking is a serious issue and one that is expected to grow for years to come. Brandjacking takes place when unauthorized individuals sell bogus or counterfeit brand name merchandise, without permission. It also includes the development of unauthorized retail company websites that are created to have shoppers believe they are visiting the site of the legitimate organization.

As the world of online shopping continues to grow, so will the illegal activity of brandjacking. Some interesting statistics as they refer to ecommerce are as follows:

- In 2014 about $1.2 million was spent online every 30 seconds.
- In 2013 brands and retailers lost around $350 billion to online counterfeiting of products and merchandise.
- In 2018 the Internet will have an influence on around 60% of all retail purchases [2].

What makes brandjacking such a serious issue for retailers and manufacturers is the broad-based aspect. The actual crime cannot be filed down to a specific targeted retail entity or product line. The many areas associated with brandjacking are as follows:

- Individuals will create bogus or counterfeit websites in the name of legitimate retail operations. The intent is to have online shoppers believe they are making purchases from a known and trusted source. What they are actually doing is providing their name and account information to a nonreputable source.

- Brand name products and merchandise are popular items consumers purchase over the Internet. The goal of the consumer is to make a purchase of an item that has a specific and recognizable brand name. Some popular brand name product items are purses, luggage, clothing accessories, etc. For some consumers there is a certain level of prestige that goes along with wearing or using certain brand name merchandise. With brandjacking, the online shopper is led to believe he or she is making a specific brand name item purchase. What the shopper is actually purchasing is a similar item, made of a lower quality material that bears the specific sought-after brand name.
- Auto supply parts are becoming popular items consumers shop for over the Internet. Consumers shop online for the convenience, sometimes lower costs, and not having to leave their homes. Going with this rationale, why not shop for needed auto parts online? As with the brand name merchandise discussion, consumers shop for a particular auto part based on the reputation of the manufacturer. If the desired purchase is made through a brandjacked website, the consumer is most likely purchasing items made of substandard material. From a vehicle safety standpoint, the purchasing of these products can lead to the car not operating properly or crashing. Vehicle brake pads are a popular item that is easily counterfeited and sold to unsuspecting consumers. These counterfeit items are made with compressed wood and sawdust, instead of the required composite material. Installing these bogus brake pads on an automobile can lead to a braking failure and an eventual crash.
- Consumers make purchases of electronic items on a regular basis. Most people do not notice the Underwriters Laboratory (UL) label on electronic products, but it is there. What the UL label works to ensure is that the quality of the item meets the industry standards for safety and manufacturing. With brandjacking, individuals are selling low-quality electronic items, like toasters, safety strips, cell phone chargers, etc., online. The items being sold are made to appear to the consumer as brand name items that bear the appropriate UL labeling. What is actually taking place is the use of fake UL labels affixed to the substandard electronic items.
- Actual companies are also being targeted for brandjacking. One example is companies that offer mystery shopping services for other business operations. A particular business wishes to have a third-party company shop its operation for various reasons—for example, to check on customer service quality, the ringing of sales transactions, product quality, etc. A popular brandjacking trick is to advertise for open mystery shopping positions in certain geographical areas. The individuals conducting this type of fraud will use the name of legitimate and industry-known mystery shopping organizations. They will contact and hire individuals to work as mystery shoppers, in the name of the legitimate company. The newly hired mystery shoppers are asked to check the customer service quality of a local money transfer company. The mystery shopper is sent a cashier's check and told to deposit

the item into his or her personal account. The individual is then asked to immediately withdraw a large portion of the check amount and conduct a wire transfer. After completing the wire transfer, the mystery shopper is told to keep the remaining amount of the deposited check as payment. Within a few days of conducting the wire transfer, the check is returned as being counterfeit and the mystery shopper is out the amount of money transferred. These duped mystery shoppers then contact the legitimate mystery shopping organization seeking restitution. They are not provided restitution, because both the individual and the mystery shopping company have become victims of brandjacking.

With the crime of brandjacking, there are more instances than those previously discussed. The actual crimes are up to the imagination of those committing the brandjacking schemes. With these varying types of schemes, the end results are many:

- Companies that specialize in the manufacturing and selling of quality brand name merchandise now have customers who believe they were sold substandard items. The reputation of the legitimate organization has been tarnished and the customers are in the possession of a lower quality product.
- Retailers are having fraudulent websites created in their good name, with low-quality merchandise sold. At the end of the day, their quality reputation is tarnished.
- Consumers are in danger of purchasing automotive and electronic items that are substandard. The purchasing of these items can lead to safety hazards in the home and create a potential for vehicle accidents.
- Companies can have unsuspecting individuals hired in their good name to perform various types of services. Typically, the individuals fraudulently hired are duped into conducting activities that are not in line with the actual services provided by the legitimate organizations.
- If an individual or group of people take the time to create a bogus website in the name of a legitimate retail organization, they will most likely use the customer's name and financial data to commit additional crimes. Unsuspecting customers can have their names used for the purpose of identity theft and their credit/debit card information used to make unauthorized purchases.

What makes the crime of brandjacking an issue for today and the future resides in the Internet shopping habits of consumers. A majority of consumers begin their Internet product search by looking for a particular item and not a specific retailer's name [2]. Once a particular item is located, the unsuspecting consumer is taken to a counterfeit or brandjacked website. Believing they have been directed to the website of a legitimate retailer, customers make their purchases.

In an effort to prevent the crime of brandjacking, retailers and other organizations need to constantly search the Internet. The searches need to include:

- Unauthorized websites using the name of a legitimate retailer—for example, if the retail company is known as ABC Clothing, conduct detailed searches using the name of ABC clothing.
- For brand name products, Internet searches need to be made for specific items. Those conducting the search need to ensure consumers cannot be directed to counterfeit websites claiming to sell the specific brand name items.
- Any business that hires employees needs to search the Internet for job advertisements in its good name. All advertisements need to be legitimate and initiated by the actual business.

It is important that all business owners, franchisees, security/loss prevention professionals, etc. understand how the Internet can be used for fraudulent purposes—especially for the crime of brandjacking. It is up to all of these individuals to work to protect the integrity of their specific operation.

Endnotes

1. "Brandjacking." https://www.google.com/search?q=brandjacking+definition&ie=utf-8&oe=utf-8 (accessed October 28, 2015).
2. "Protect Your Brand from Online Threats." http://www.retailfraud.com/protecting-your-brand-from-online-threats/ (accessed October 28, 2015).

EXTERNAL FRAUD/ THEFT

IV

Chapter 27

Organized Retail Crime/Theft

Organized retail crime/theft has been a problem for the retail industry nationwide for years. Based on the many national security-/fraud-related associations or law enforcement agencies discussing the problem, the threat terminology refers to the issues as organized retail crime or organized retail theft. Whether using the terms "crime" or "theft," both refer to the same type of problem. For the purpose of the discussion in this text, we will refer to the issue as organized retail crime (ORC).

It is hard to nail down a beginning date when ORC received its official title, but shoplifting and stealing in the retail industry have been taking place since the inception of individuals placing merchandise on a shelf for sale to consumers. When looking for an inception date for ORC, one can reflect on the early days of mob violence across the country. An argument can easily be made that the Al Capone types of gangs in Chicago and the various mob families in the New York City area were all involved in varying types of organized retail crime. Their specialty revolved around stealing large amounts of merchandise during the delivery process to the individual retail location. These early incidents can also be referred to as cargo theft, which is discussed in Chapter 28.

In addition to hijacking merchandise delivery vehicles on the way to the retail store, others developed ways to steal large amounts of selected items once they were made available for sale to the general public. This activity is now referred to as organized retail crime.

For the official beginning time frame when ORC was recognized as a major issue facing retailers, the best guess can be around 20 years ago. In May of 2014, an article released by the National Retail Federation (NRF) discussed that organized retail crime has been an issue for the better part of 15 years [1]. Also in 2014 the

NRF released its 10th annual survey results on ORC [2]. Information in this report (discussed later in this section) provides shocking data on the crime and its effects on law enforcement and the retail industry.

When discussing ORC, some get confused with what separates this crime trend from simple shoplifting. US Legal.com [3] defines shoplifting in the following way:

> Shoplifting is a crime of theft governed by state laws, which vary by state. Businesses lose billions of dollars annually as a result of shoplifting. Shoplifting laws generally define shoplifting as taking or intentionally paying less for an item than the sale price. Shoplifting can include carrying, hiding, concealing, or otherwise manipulating merchandise with the intent of taking it or paying less for it. Shoplifting laws also may be defined to include changing price tags, committing refund fraud, removing a shopping cart or any other commercial property from a store location, or intentionally using an illegitimate form of payment. An intent to shoplift may be sufficient for a shoplifting charge to be brought, even if the shoplifting was not fully carried out.

A more basic definition of shoplifting by The Free Dictionary.com [4] is "theft of merchandise from a store or business establishment."

Organized retail crime has been defined as "groups of people engaged in illegally obtaining merchandise in substantial quantities through both theft and fraud for the purpose of reselling. These crime rings generally consist of 'boosters,' who methodically steal merchandise from retail stores, and fence operators, who convert the product to cash or drugs" [5].

Looking at ORC from a federal perspective, the definition from Congress is

- Violating a state ban against shoplifting or retail merchandise theft—if the quantities of items stolen are of the amount that would not normally be purchased for personal use or consumption—and stealing for the purposes of reselling the items or reentering them into commerce;
- Receiving, possessing, concealing, bartering, selling, transporting, or disposing of any property that is known to have been taken in the violation outlined above;
- Or coordinating, organizing, or recruiting persons to undertake either of the two violations outlined above [6].

Based on the previously discussed definitions of shoplifting and organized retail crime, one is a simple crime that can be committed by a single individual. Most shoplifters steal one to a few items, normally for personal use. Organized retail crime is committed by groups of well-organized individuals looking to steal large numbers of items for the purpose of repackaging and reselling the items for drugs or money.

The continued growth of ORC groups and their success has also gained greater attention from law enforcement and the retail community. Retailers and law enforcement still look to combat the incidents of shoplifting. Retailers still employ internal loss prevention/security personnel to prevent shoplifting and other related crimes. Twenty or thirty years ago, these investigative personnel had the time to concentrate on identifying the individual shoplifter. Retail employees were trained on issues related to the threat of shoplifting and the steps that could be taken in the store to prevent these acts.

Now, retail industry focus is on identifying ORC rings and figuring out their tactics and the popular items they like to steal. Additionally, law enforcement and retail associations are making ORC a top priority. As previously referenced, the NRF began conducting an annual survey of retailers for the purpose of discussing ORC. In 2015 the organization published its 11th annual survey.

The purpose of the organized retail crime survey by the NRF is to gather information from loss prevention professionals working in the retail industry. Participants are sent a list of questions by the NRF. Those retailers wishing to participate in the survey provide detailed answers and send their information back to the NRF. Once the completed surveys have been returned, the information is analyzed and compiled into the annual results. Information contained within the survey results is as follows:

- A summary of key findings
- The impact of ORC on retailers and the community
- A discussion on the resources needed by retailers to combat ORC
- A discussion on various laws associated with ORC
- How legislation affects the retail community
- A discussion on ORC trends in cities across the country
- A discussion on the popular retail items targeted and stolen by ORC groups [7]

In addition to the efforts put forth by the NRF in fighting organized retail crime, several national and regional associations have developed. These associations have been formed on national and regional bases and within numerous states. For additional information on the many ORC associations, please refer to Appendix A.

Along with the various associations identified in Appendix A, many of these groups develop and hold seminars developed with the purpose of discussing organized retail crime, prevention measures, crime trends, new legislation, etc. Readers of this text can obtain additional information on seminars or conferences related to ORC by visiting the websites of the associations listed in Appendix A.

Organized retail crime usually consists of individuals known as boosters and fences. Boosters are individuals who enter the retail locations for the purpose of stealing merchandise. They have been known to work alone or in groups. Once the boosters steal merchandise from the retail operations, the items are later sold to individuals referred to as fences, who pay a price that is generally lower than the actual retail price. Fences will typically pay boosters between 10% and 30% of the actual retail price of the items stolen.

Most organized retail fraud rings are looking to steal specific items. Many boosters enter retail establishments with what is referred to as a "fence sheet"—a list of items provided by the fence to the booster. By having a fence sheet, the booster knows he or she is not wasting time stealing items that cannot be sold.

As organized retail crime has grown over the years, law enforcement and loss prevention and security personnel have developed an understanding of the popular items boosters are looking to steal—items that have been successfully repackaged and sold through various venues. Some of the most popular theft items for ORC groups include:

- Grocery items, including energy drinks, cigarettes, infant formula, higher priced liquor, teeth whitening strips, electronic razors, razor blades
- Clothing items, including designer handbags, higher end denim clothing, furs
- Electronic items, including laptops, tablets, cell phones, digital cameras, LCD monitors, GPS devices, video systems, and games
- Home goods, including high-end vacuums, quality mixers, kitchen counter appliances, laundry detergent, electronic toys, batteries
- Health and beauty items, including electronic toothbrushes, pregnancy test kits
- Over-the-counter medication, including allergy medication, weight loss pills, diabetic testing strips, pain medication

The goal of ORC groups is to steal items that can be easily resold by fences. Popular venues used to resell stolen items are

- Flea markets
- Swap meets
- Yard sales
- Retail storefront locations (typically in disreputable locations)
- Internet auction websites

The popularity of using these resale venues is so the sellers can be lost in a world of people selling similar material. Flea markets, swap meets, and yard sales are popular locations for anyone to sell items they no longer want. Popular items for fences to sell at these venues are clothing, household and electronic items, home goods, etc.—items that any individual might purchase. Since many individuals at flea markets and swap meets are selling similar items, the fences can blend into the marketplace.

Another popular venue to sell stolen merchandise is open-air types of storefronts. In many cities across the country there are vendor markets or what are referred to as wholesale markets. Many of these venues are not located in the best part of town, but are popular because products can be purchased below market pricing. With many of these wholesale markets, the operations are not illegal: Many of the merchants are licensed to sell merchandise by the respective cities and purchase material from licensed wholesales.

What these wholesale markets provide is an area where fences can blend into the landscape as authorized retailers. A very large majority of individuals visiting these wholesale markets are looking to purchase merchandise at below market prices and are not concerned about a retail license tacked to the back wall.

Growing in popularity for fences is the use of the Internet. Anyone looking to make a product purchase can conduct an Internet search and locate several Internet auction websites. The purposes of these auction websites are to

- Allow sellers to open an account for the purpose of offering items for sale.
- Allow the sellers to post pictures of the items for sale.
- Establish a bidding time frame for consumers to bid on the posted items for sale.
- Establish a starting bid price.
- Once the bidding window closes, sell the item or items to the highest bidder.
- Allow the bidder to make a payment for the product or products purchased.
- Provide an avenue for the seller to receive the payment.
- Provide a complaint arena for consumers who received poor-quality products or those who never received the items purchased.

Popular items that are sold through this venue are the ones listed previously, especially items that many consumers need on a daily basis, such as

- Allergy medication
- Weight-loss pills
- Diabetic testing strips
- Pain medication
- Infant formula

A major issue with anyone purchasing the previously mentioned items through the Internet is that these items all carry an expiration date. Another major health-related issue is that these items are consumed or come in contact with an individual's mouth. For consumers purchasing health-related items through the Internet or on secondary markets, concerns are twofold:

- They are purchasing stolen merchandise.
- They are opening up the possibility of purchasing items that are past their expiration date.

Organized retail crime groups use individuals who specialize in the repackaging of stolen material. Stolen merchandise is removed from its original packaging and repackaged to present a more professional appearance. With health-related items and infant formula, part of the repackaging process involves changing product expiration dates. With a current expiration date, consumers are led to believe they have purchased a product well within the prescribed consumption window. What they have actually purchased is product that may or may not be within the original time window.

Another computer-related avenue used by ORC groups is popup advertising. Many individuals have experienced working at their computers and being instantly interrupted by a popup advertisement. As discussed in Section V, many of these popup advertisements are used for the purpose of downloading unauthorized malicious software on individuals' computers (refer to Section V for detailed discussion).

The use of popup advertisements is to offer an individual the opportunity to purchase popular over-the-counter medication items below the market price. Consumers are enticed by the offer made as part of these popups and quickly follow the instructions provided. By clicking on any of these popup advertisements, computer users are exposing themselves and their systems to the following:

- Purchasing medication that is beyond the expiration date.
- Purchasing medication that can cause health issues.
- Exposing their computers to the unauthorized downloading of malicious software.
- Providing their credit card information to individuals involved in ORC.
- Providing their personal information to individuals involved in ORC, thus exposing them to the possibility of becoming victims of identity theft.

It is important to understand that anyone deciding to make a purchase of products through an Internet auction website via a popup advertisement is most likely getting in bed with people involved in organized retail crime. It is also important to understand that any person or group who participates in the crime of selling stolen and repackaged merchandise has no problem with using customers' personal and credit card account information.

Organized retail crime groups also work to get bulk amounts of stolen merchandise back into the retail arena. As previously discussed, they have members that repackage items for resale. Part of the repackaging process also involves changing production and expiration dates on items like infant formula and over-the-counter pills and medications. The purpose is to have customers believe the items are within the sell-before window or expiration date.

In addition to selling stolen items at the previously discussed venues, fences will also sell items in bulk to wholesale operations. Some of these operations are aboveboard and are convinced by the fences that the products for sale came from legitimate distributors. Other wholesale operations are aware they are purchasing repackaged retail items. In their eyes they have the ability to purchase items below current market prices.

No matter which type of wholesale operator is making the material purchases from dishonest fences, stolen and potentially expired merchandise is making its way back into the market. Unfortunately for consumers, the retail items that are introduced back into the market bear the same appearance as items that were previously stolen. This is especially an issue for items that are actually past their original sell-by date or expired.

Boosters looking to steal merchandise from retail operations have many methods that have proven to be successful:

- Barcode counterfeiting. Individuals can easily purchase software programs that can be used to produce barcodes (Figure 27.1). In organized retail crime the participants will create barcodes from low-dollar items obtained from specific retail locations. Using the barcode software, they can create duplicate barcodes that are printed on properly sized label paper. The counterfeit barcodes are then taken into a retail location and placed over existing barcodes of high-dollar items. At the register the item barcode is passed over a scanner. The scanner reads the item-specific barcode and displays an item description and price [8]. Boosters using this method target busy sales attendants who are not engaged in implementing loss prevention techniques. The store cashiers are more concerned with processing customers through the line than taking the time necessary to inspect the items presented for purchase. In order to prevent this type of theft, cashiers are or should have been taught to compare the item being scanned with the register LED description [9] (Figure 27.2). They should also take notice of the price of the item being purchased. Most cashiers might think it odd that a digital camera only costs $4.99.
- Barcode switching. Boosters will enter a retail location and remove barcodes from lower priced items. These barcodes are then placed over the existing barcode of high-dollar items. Once the switch is made, the booster uses the same procedure as discussed with barcode counterfeiting to purchase the item and exit the store undetected.

1234567890

Figure 27.1 Sample barcode.

Figure 27.2 Sample LED register display.

As discussed in Chapter 19, individuals will target a specific employer for the purpose of getting hired so that they can commit fraud or theft. These types of individuals have been known to be associated with organized retail crime. Having a member of an ORC group working in a specific retail location has many benefits:

- A dishonest cashier working with a booster allows the barcode counterfeiting scam to avoid detection.
- A dishonest cashier working with a booster allows the barcode switching scam to work.
- Dishonest retail store employees have been known to assist boosters with the concealment of items prior to leaving the store without paying.
- Dishonest retail store employees have been known to allow boosters to remove items directly from the store inventory (stockroom) or from the receiving area.
- Dishonest retail store employees have been known to assist boosters by providing them with store alarm codes, management and owner work schedules, and other types of security related information as well as leaving doors unlocked.
- Boosters and people working with ORC groups have been known to hide out in stores and wait for closing. Once the store has closed and all associates have left for the night, these individuals leave their hiding place. If they have been provided with the alarm codes, they can easily disarm the store alarm. Once the store alarm is disarmed, the thieves can take their time in collecting targeted items. If they do not have the alarm codes, they will quickly work to gather large amounts of targeted items and leave through emergency exits.

In addition to using the assistance of accomplices working for the targeted retail establishment, ORC groups will also use the following tactics to conceal and steal merchandise:

- Retailers use electronic article surveillance (EAS) tags placed on items for sale. At the time of purchase these tags are moved over a scanning device and deactivated. Scanning antennas are placed at all store exits and if the EAS tag has not been deactivated, an alarm will sound, alerting store employees of a potential theft. Boosters will collect store-specific shopping bags and line them with foil or another type of metal. They will then load the metal-lined shopping bag with merchandise and hope to be able to walk out the door undetected. (Refer back to Chapter 21 for examples of EAS tags.)
- The same technology that gave retailers EAS tags to help prevent shoplifting also gave criminals the ability to create jamming devices. These EAS jamming devices are used to interfere with the in-store detection equipment. Once the EAS jamming device is activated, it allows a person to exit the store undetected while carrying merchandise with EAS tags still attached.
- The use of security tags (EAS type) by retailers is a popular tool in working to prevent shoplifting. As previously discussed, criminals have discovered tactics to skirt around these detection systems. One other tool that is used by many in ORC groups is magnetic detachers that can remove various types of security tags from items and garments. Once the security tag has been removed, the item or items can be concealed and the thief can exit the store without being detected by an alarm system.
- Boosters use other tactics to remove merchandise from a retail location without making proper payment. These might include the use of a jamming device or the removal of security tags. A lot depends on the items targeted. One tactic is referred to as box or carton stuffing. Individuals or an individual will enter a retail location and locate a big box item, like a stroller. The actual retail item located in the box is removed and left in the store. Boosters will then fill the empty box with smaller items. Once the box is full, it is taken to the register for payment. Instead of paying for a $30 stroller, the booster has removed hundreds of dollars' worth of merchandise from the store. Boosters will also work in groups and, while in the store, certain members of the group will work as lookouts and will use various methods to distract store employees while others steal targeted items. With the booster lookout scenario, many of the previously discussed shoplifting methods will be used to steal merchandise.
- At times those looking to steal merchandise from a retail location will be more blatant in their tactics:
  - Boosters will use what is referred to as a walkout: simply filling a shopping cart with merchandise and exiting the store to a waiting vehicle.

- Boosters will use several individuals to quickly rush a retail location, grab as many targeted items as possible, and then run out of the store to a waiting vehicle.
- Boosters will also participate in smash-and-grab types of operations that take place when the retail location is closed. With these operations, a person will ram a vehicle into a front store window. After the window has been rammed, several individuals will rush into the store. These individuals will quickly grab as many targeted items as possible and exit the store to a waiting vehicle.

As previously discussed, merchandise stolen from retailers is sold through Internet auction websites, at swap meets, wholesale markets, etc. for the purpose of generating cash from the stolen items. Individuals participating in ORC groups are also using other tactics to generate cash from stolen merchandise and to obtain additional merchandise:

- As discussed, technology has opened windows for criminals to commit acts of fraud and theft. A popular method of generating cash from stolen material is to return the items to the store from which they were illegally removed. Thieves can choose to return merchandise to the retailer in exchange for an in-store gift card. The gift card option is used because some retailers will not conduct a cash return without a receipt. The gift cards obtained are later sold for cash, used to purchase other items, or traded for drugs.
- Those looking to generate cash by returning previously stolen merchandise will use software to create counterfeit receipts. With a store receipt, the thieves can return the stolen merchandise for cash.
- Individual consumers can also become victims in the world of ORC. Members of these groups will use stolen or cloned credit cards of unknowing consumers to purchase store merchandise. Once purchased, the merchandise enters the system of the ORC group. With these types of theft, the retailer receives payment for the merchandise, so the victims then become the financial institutions that originally issued the credit cards. If consumers fail to report the unauthorized use of credit/debit cards in a timely manner, they themselves could suffer a financial loss.

In order to steal merchandise, some organized retail crime groups bypass the retail establishment and participate in what is referred to as cargo theft: stealing merchandise prior to its arriving at individual retail establishments. Truckers will pick up merchandise from the manufacturing center and deliver the items to a distribution center. Once in the inventory system, merchandise is loaded onto trucks and taken from the distribution center to the individual stores. Incidents of cargo theft have occurred while the merchandise has left the manufacturer and is en route to the distribution center, as well as while the merchandise has left the distribution center and is en route to the retail store.

Instead of making numerous trips to a retail location and using the varying theft tactics of stealing merchandise, cargo theft provides ORC groups with a much larger score. Additionally, the crime of cargo theft could require a violent interaction with truck drivers delivering the merchandise. Cargo theft tactics and prevention measures are discussed later in Chapter 28.

Organized retail crime has been an issue for the retail community for a number of years and there is no end in sight. Each year retailers must divert more personnel assets and money to combat the crime. According to the NRF [10], ORC costs the retail industry approximately $30 billion per year.

Organized retail crime has a strong history and roots in the retail community. As time goes by, more and more retail, investigative, loss prevention, law enforcement, and prosecution assets are employed to combat the threat. Due to the increased awareness and efforts used to combat the issue, success has been made in identifying and prosecuting offenders. The area where little success has taken place is stopping the trend. No matter how many surveys are completed or associations formed, ORC continues to be a thorn in the side of retailers across the country.

As with any fraud or theft issue, questions are always asked as to how retailers can avoid becoming victims of organized retail crime. The problem arises that there is no catchall tactic that can be employed to prevent victimization. From a prevention perspective, going forward, retailers need to

- Continue working with law enforcement on investigating retail thefts and identifying and prosecuting offenders.
- Develop a detailed organized retail theft awareness and prevention training program that is delivered to all associates. In order to maintain the effectiveness of the training program, it cannot be a one-time delivery. The program needs to be constantly updated and delivered.
- In order to have the most up-to-date information on organized retail crime trends and other related information, loss prevention and security personnel need to be active in statewide and national associations.
- The information sharing through these ORC associations has to be a two-way street. Learn what others are providing and also share with the group.
- Continue participation with the NRF and respond to the annual surveys.
- Understand the cost of doing business aspect of being in the retail market and devote assets to surveillance systems in each retail location. By knowing the tactics of many boosters, suspicious individuals can be monitored from a separate video surveillance room.
- Place surveillance cameras where they can monitor the items being scanned at the register, along with the LED register display.
- Place many of the popular items stolen by ORC groups behind counters that can only be accessed by store personnel.
- Make sure to employ the strictest of hiring standards for new employees and conduct detailed background verifications.
- Place enough theft prevention measures in place so that competitors become a more attractive target.

Endnotes

1. "A Decade Later, Organized Retail Crime Still Major Problem for Retailers." https://nrf.com/media/press-releases/decade-later-organized-retail-crime-still-major-problem-retailers (accessed August 8, 2015).
2. "2014 Organized Retail Crime Survey." https://nrf.com/resources/retail-library/2014-organized-retail-crime-survey-0 (accessed August 8, 2015).
3. US Legal.com. http://definitions.uslegal.com/s/shoplifting/ (accessed August 8, 2015).
4. The Free Dictionary. http://legal-dictionary.thefreedictionary.com/Shoplifting (accessed August 8, 2015).
5. "Organized Retail Crime: Scope, Solutions." http://www.retailsolutionsonline.com/doc/organized-retail-crime-scope-solutions-0001 (accessed August 8, 2015).
6. Congressional Research Service. "Organized Retail Crime." https://fas.org/sgp/crs/misc/R41118.pdf (accessed August 8, 2015).
7. National Retail Federation. "Organized Retail Crime Survey." https://nrf.com/media/press-releases/decade-later-organized-retail-crime-still-major-problem-retailers (accessed August 8, 2015).
8. A barcode is a machine-readable code that consists of a series of numbers and parallel lines. These codes are placed on retail items and the entire barcode is moved over a scanner. The scanner reads the code, which lets the register know the item being purchased and the price.
9. The LED display is connected to the cash register at retail locations and, once a barcode is scanned, the display will show the item price and description.
10. "Organized Retail Crime/NRF." https://www.google.com/search?q=cost+of+organized+retail+crime&ie=utf-8&oe=utf-8 (accessed August 9, 2015).

Chapter 28

Cargo Theft

According to CargoNet, a division of Verisk Crime Analytics, the crime of cargo theft has increased 11% over the past year [1]. Cargo theft allows thieves to bypass the retail establishment and steal directly from the source—that is, merchandise en route from the supplier or warehouse to the various retail operations. The goal of cargo thieves is to target shipments that contain high dollar items or merchandise that can be quickly resold. One popular item of interest to cargo thieves is food. Once stolen, truckloads of food items can be quickly passed on to unscrupulous distributors. These distributors quickly turn around the product and move it back into the supply chain.

The methods of cargo theft vary, but most involve intercepting the load between the warehouse and its destination. Many cargo thieves wait for the driver to go into a rest area or truck stop, prior to making their move. Once the driver separates from his or her truck, thieves either steal the entire truck and trailer or just the trailer loaded with merchandise. In addition to taking the time for the driver to leave the truck unattended, some drivers have been forced to give up their load at gunpoint. Thieves approach the driver, brandish a weapon, and steal the truck and trailer.

As the use of technology increases across all industries, thieves are now using the Internet as a starting off point for cargo theft. They are taking a page from the identity theft playbook and using this tactic to steal trailers full of merchandise.

There are several websites used in the trucking and hauling industry where shipping brokers advertise loads in need of delivery. This information is posted on these websites, referred to as load-boards. Thieves will use this posted information, determine the valuable loads, pose as a respectable company, and pick up the shipment. To pull off this type of scam, the tactics are as follows:

- Even though the contents of the loads in need of shipment are not provided on the load-board information, thieves use certain details that can signal a potentially valuable shipment. Some of these tactics are shipments coming out of the technology corridors, shipments coming from general locations, loads that require a team of drivers, or shipments requiring higher than normal amounts of insurance.

- Once a particular load has been identified, cargo thieves will create false credentials in the name of legitimate trucking companies. After creating the bogus credentials, the thieves will show up at the distribution center or warehouse and pick up the load. All that is needed is the bogus credentials and a truck to haul away the merchandise.
- Creating the bogus credentials is an easy process for the thieves. All they need to do is identify a legitimate trucking company and visit its website. The thieves will then use the targeted company's logo, address, and the Department of Transportation-issued interstate operating authority number [2].

In order to prevent cargo theft, there are a few tactics that can be used:

- First, the goal is to keep the cargo moving. The longer a load sits unattended in a rest area or truck stop, the more time there is available for the thieves to steal the merchandise.
- Develop an intelligence database of times, dates, and locations of past thefts. Across the country there are locations and neighborhoods where cargo thefts take place at a higher rate. Companies need to identify these areas and avoid them if a load has to be left unattended.
- Warehouse and distribution centers need to know who they are dealing with, making sure to conduct some type of due diligence on the company picking up a load prior to releasing the merchandise.

Endnotes

1. "Midwestern Theft Ring Busted amid Rising Cargo Thefts." http://www.claimsjournal.com/news/national/2015/09/04/265573.htm (accessed September 11, 2015).
2. " 'It Fell off the Back of the Internet': Freight Thieves Are Becoming Cybercriminals." http://fortune.com/2015/07/29/cargo-freight-thieves-cybercriminals/ (accessed September 11, 2015).

Chapter 29

Financial Institution Fraud

Introduction

Banks, large and small; credit unions; lenders; etc. are all known as big-pocket institutions. In an effort to dip into these big pockets, criminals will develop various types of attacks in order to gain access to that big pile of money. Causing billions of dollars of losses to financial institutions across the country, criminals looking to attack banks use various tactics to gain access to the assets. Individuals looking to commit financial institution fraud can be a lone wolf, a small group of people, or large and well organized fraud rings. The largest dollar loss threats facing financial institutions are

- Business account takeover fraud
- New account fraud
- Counterfeit and forged checks

In order to be successful at two of the major threats (new account and business takeover) facing financial institutions, those looking to commit the acts of fraud need to become someone else. John Fraudboy, opening new checking/savings accounts at a local bank branch and using his real name and identification, will have a brief career. If John Fraudboy obtains the necessary personal information of an individual or business, he can then obtain the necessary documentation to become someone else. Acting as another individual or business owner, John Fraudboy can have more success committing financial account fraud.

On face value, John Fraudboy is not the initial target of the investigation. The initial target of the investigation is the actual person or business name that was used to open the account. At the end of the investigative process, the individual or business name used for the fraud is not responsible for the loss to the financial institution. What the individual or business is responsible for is the months of time and money needed to clear up a once good name.

Over the years, those committing individual and business identity crimes have been very successful. Leading to this success is the criminal's ability to commit the crime, steal large amounts of money, and move on. The identification and conviction rates of those committing these types of crimes is low and allows for the operations to continue—leaving the various financial institutions holding the bag and responsible for the monetary loss.

Understanding Identity Theft (Individual and Business) as It Relates to Financial Institution Fraud

According to the Federal Trade Commission and its 2014 Consumer Sentinel Network Data Book, identity theft has been the number one consumer complaint for 15 consecutive years [1]. Growing along with that number is the continuing increase in businesses that are falling victim to identity theft. Criminals are now targeting businesses (especially small businesses) in an effort to take over their names. With individual identity theft, a person assumes the identity of an unsuspecting victim. With business identity theft, one or more people assume the identity of an unsuspecting business operation. No matter how the identity of an individual or business has been obtained, the end goal is to use this information for fraudulent purposes and financial gain.

In an effort to assume the identity of an individual, the following methods are used:

- An individual's personal computer is accessed through phishing techniques (discussed in detail in Section V). Once inside the personal computer system, attempts are made to locate financial information, bank account information, personal information (name, date of birth, Social Security number [SSN], etc.), etc.
- Unauthorized access is made to the mail delivery box of a neighborhood resident. Attempts are made to locate delivered mail that contains the recipient's personal information.
- Criminals will complete a change of address form on unsuspecting community residents. The purpose is to collect mailed items that contain residents' personal information.
- Information is obtained from a lost wallet or purse. In order to protect against being an identity theft victim as a result of this loss:
  - Never carry a Social Security card in a wallet or purse.
  - Only place credit/debit cards in a wallet or purse that will be used that day.
  - If it will not be necessary to write a check, leave the checkbook and individual checks at home.

It is important to understand that there are those who might find a lost wallet or purse and go through these items looking for information that can be used for fraud. The goal of the person finding the lost wallet or purse is to return the lost item to the owner intact—no missing documents, cash, or credit/debit cards. The hope is that the owner goes about his or her daily business thinking there is no threat to becoming a victim of identity theft. The owner is just thankful that the property was returned intact and believes that no further threat remains. Even if the wallet or purse is returned intact, it is important for the owner to close the associated accounts of checks and credit/debit cards that were present in the wallet or purse when it was returned—cynical but safe.

- Someone can break into a vehicle in an effort to locate information contained on personal documents. Many of these sensitive documents are located in the vehicle's glove box. In an effort to avoid being a victim of identity theft from a vehicle break-in, individuals need to ensure all paperwork containing personal information is not left in the glove box. Individuals will break into a vehicle for two reasons: One is to steal the car or items inside the car. The outright thief does not care if an actual break-in does occur. Those looking to break in to locate personal information will attempt to gain access to the vehicle without actually breaking in. They hope to locate the items needed to assume an identity without the targeted individual knowing that personal information has been compromised. The thieves will not actually remove the documentation containing the desired personal information. They will simply copy the desired personal information and place the items back into the place where they were originally located. In order to protect against being an identity theft victim from a vehicle break-in, individuals need to ensure that no documents containing personal information are inside the passenger compartment. Additionally, vehicle operators should avoid picking up their personal mail and leaving it in the vehicle throughout the day. Many items consumers receive in the mail contain sensitive personal and financial information. If this information falls into the wrong hands as a result of a vehicle break-in, the initiation of an identity theft crime begins.
- Unauthorized access can be made to an individual or business owner's laptop when the owner uses unsecured WiFi hotspots. Criminals frequently hang around popular areas where consumers sit around, drink their coffee, and access the Internet. The consumer might be sharing the network, while the criminals are sharing the information on the targeted victim's laptop. These consumers are at greater risk if they are making online purchases through a public WiFi hotspot. In order to protect against the threat of having personal information accessed by using a public WiFi hotspot, the following prevention measures are advised:
  - Ensure the computer's firewall is enabled.
  - Only use HTTPS in the website address used and not the simple version of HTTP. HTTP stands for "hypertext transfer protocol." With "S"

included on the end of HTTP, the Internet user is making sure the data transmitted back and forth are encrypted. If needed, manually type in "HTTPS" at the beginning of any website visited.
   - When accessing the Internet at public WiFi hotspots make sure all sharing devices are turned off. This can be completed by accessing the computer's network settings.
   - Consumers can also purchase secure encryption/virtual network types of software that can be downloaded onto the computer. These software programs work to provide system security when accessing the Internet, especially from public WiFi hotspots.
- Individuals will also use vishing, smishing, spoofing, and cramming techniques to gain personal information. These techniques involve the use of computer e-mail, cell phone texting, and actual phone calls. These tactics are discussed in detail in Section V.
- Individuals will conduct what is referred to as "dumpster diving" or simply going through a person's trash can that is left at the end of the driveway for pickup. No matter if the individual is looking through a dumpster or a trash can in a neighborhood, people throw away documents that contain vital personal information. Prior to any documents making their way into the trash, they need to be run through a shredder.
- Individual consumers are also vulnerable to having their personal information located via a data breach. A data breach is an unauthorized access to the computer systems of retailers, government agencies, or employers. Additional information on data breaches is discussed in detail in Section V.

In an effort to assume the identity of a business, the following methods are used:

- Many of the issues previously discussed relating to individual identity theft can also be applied to business identity theft. Those looking to gather the information necessary to commit the crime of business identity fraud will resort to dumpster diving, accessing personal and business information contained in mail delivery boxes, frequenting WiFi hotspots looking to gain access to unsecured personal and business laptops, targeting business owners and their associates via phishing, vishing, smishing, cramming, and spoofing techniques, etc. (These techniques are discussed in detail in Section V.)
- A quick search of the Internet will reveal numerous organizations that offer the service of locating employer identification numbers (EINs) [2]. The same holds true for many private investigative agencies. Basically, for a fee the process of obtaining the EIN of a targeted business is a somewhat simple process. Once obtained, the business EIN can be used like an individual SSN to open fraudulent bank accounts, credit cards, and lines of credit.

- The EIN of a targeted business can also be located through public records searches. With public companies, the EIN can be located on certain documents filed with the Securities and Exchange Commission (SEC).
- For private companies, several websites exist for the purpose of locating a targeted EIN.
- Additionally, EINs can be located through various types of uniform commercial code (UCC) filings.
- There are several other venues available for the purpose of locating a business EIN. The purpose of this discussion is to provide the reader with knowledge that EINs are easily accessible. Compared to an individual SSN, the EIN for many organizations can be easily located. Although more specific detail could be provided, the exact websites to access, which forms to locate, the various financial databases to access, etc. will not be provided. The goal of this text is to discuss the business vulnerability to fraud and not to provide an education on locating somewhat private company information.

In addition to having somewhat easy access to locating the vital EIN for a targeted organization, public records allow for access to other business information. Based on the state where a business was incorporated, a quick records search can reveal a wealth of information. Many state corporation commissions allow anyone the ability to access corporate filing documents. Once accessed, these documents contain information related to the overall business operation:

- Names of the corporate officers
- Company business addresses
- Personal addresses of the company officers
- Type of corporate filing
- Corporation filing date and dates of incorporation

Based on the previous discussion, obtaining the information necessary to assume the identity of a business is relatively easy. Once the individuals looking to commit this type of fraud have gathered all of the necessary personal and business information, additional steps can be taken to add legitimacy to the crime:

- Visiting the legitimate business to obtain copies of a company letterhead
- Creating a company letterhead using logos that were cut from the targeted organization's website and then pasting them onto stationary to create a counterfeit letterhead
- Opening an office front in the name of the targeted business
- Filing paperwork with the secretary of state's office for the purpose of changing address or company officer information
- Opening up a merchant account [3] in the name of the targeted business

Business Takeover Fraud

Based on banking laws, financial institutions are susceptible to suffering monetary losses due to varying types of fraud; one type is business takeover fraud. For this type of fraud to be successful, it is necessary to obtain vital business information and documentation in order to target the organization. Based on the previous discussion, locating the business information and documentation is a simple process.

In order for a business takeover fraud to be successful, the following steps are taken by those looking to commit the fraud:

- Use the personal information obtained on the corporate or company officers to create counterfeit identification. These identification pieces can be a state-issued identification card, driver's license, Social Security card, etc.
- Establish an office front in a business district in the name of the targeted business. Once the office front is established, paperwork is filed with the secretary of state's office to change the company address. This process is conducted to ensure there is no discrepancy between the company address provided to the financial institution and the address on file with the state's corporation commission.
- Open checking accounts in the name of the targeted business. Once the accounts are opened, countless checks can be written in the name of the targeted business. Those committing the fraud are gaining access to the items purchased with the checks. Based on the activities in the fraudulent bank account opened, the entity suffering the monetary loss can vary:
  - If there is a low balance in the checking account, the checks will be returned to the merchant marked "insufficient funds." If those committing the fraud visited office supply stores in the name of the targeted business and purchased computers, printers, etc., those locations will suffer a financial loss. Based on the size of the loss, the office store's loss prevention department can make recovery attempts. Once this investigative process begins, those who committed the fraud will be long gone. At the end of the day, the trail will eventually lead to the front door of the legitimate business. It is now up to the legitimate business to prove it was the victim of business takeover fraud.
  - Once the checking account is open, those committing the fraud can deposit stolen and forged checks [4] or counterfeit checks [5] into the account. Once these checks clear the bank where they were drawn, there is money available in the account opened in the name of the unsuspecting business. These funds generated by the bogus deposit items are quickly depleted from the account. As discussed in endnotes 4 and 5, the financial institution where the forged and counterfeit checks were drawn is out the monetary amount of the items. The institution (Bank A) can elect to contact the bank where the checks were deposited (Bank B) as part of

its fraud investigation. At the end of the day it will become apparent to both Bank A and Bank B that the account opened at Bank B was part of a business takeover fraud.

- Once the checking account is open, those committing the fraud can deposit checks that will be returned from the bank on which they were drawn marked "closed account," "NSF" (nonsufficient funds), "counterfeit," etc. The goal with depositing these types of checks is that there will be little or no hold placed on the deposited items [6]. As discussed in endnote 6, financial institutions are limited on the deposit hold time for government checks, money orders, treasury checks, and cashier's checks. Once accounts are opened in the name of an unsuspecting business, those conducting the fraud will deposit counterfeit items as previously discussed. After the counterfeit items are deposited and the funds are made available, those committing the fraud will quickly withdraw assets from the account or conduct wire transfers. These withdrawals and transfers are made prior to the deposit items being returned as "counterfeit." Based on the institution where the bank account is opened and those committing the fraud using the name of a respectable business, it is possible the fraud account owners can work with the individual bank branch manager to allow fewer restrictions on deposit hold times. Many of the individuals committing business takeover fraud will inform the branch manager of the financial institution where the new accounts are opened that the company is in the process of changing banks and needs quick access to funds. The hope is that the branch manager is eager to obtain new business account customers and will relax the hold restrictions. If the individuals who opened the bank account in the name of an unsuspecting business are successful in gaining quick access to the deposit item amounts, the money will be withdrawn prior to the bank realizing that it is now the victim of business takeover fraud. During the investigative process, the financial institution suffering the monetary loss will eventually contact the legitimate business whose name was used to open the bogus account. It is now up to the targeted business to prove it has been a victim of business takeover fraud.

As far as the crime of business takeover fraud goes, there are other avenues that can be used by those committing the crime. These avenues will be discussed further later in this section, following the discussion on financial institution fraud.

New Account Fraud

As discussed with business takeover fraud and the process used to steal the identity of an individual, financial institutions can also become victims of new account fraud. Individuals looking to commit new account fraud will go through many of the steps previously discussed as they relate to identity theft. The goal is to gather enough personal information from an unsuspecting target and use this data to create identification in the name of the pending victim.

Once the bogus identification has been created, individuals will enter various financial institutions and open bank accounts in the names of the targeted victims. In an effort to gain the most "bang for the buck," the goal is to open bank accounts at several different financial institutions [7].

In order to avoid alerting the targeted individuals that their identity has been compromised, those committing the fraud will use addresses other than the legitimate one of the pending victim:

- Many groups committing identity theft/new account fraud will rent a drop house or apartment for the purpose of receiving mail—unfortunately, in the victim's name. When the rent comes due and the signed lease is in default, the location owners will initially look for the person whose name was used. It is now up to the targeted victim to convince others he or she is a victim of identity theft.
- Other groups will use what is referred to as a mail drop location. These mail drops are legitimate business operations that are established to rent post office types of mail rental boxes. They also conduct other post office activities, such as receiving mail, collecting and sending outgoing mail, etc. For those wishing to receive their mail at one of these locations, the address used is the actual building address of the mail drop—a street address and the use of the mail box number rented. In an attempt to add legitimacy to the mail drop location, individuals will use the address and, instead of using a box number, will use terms like Unit #, Apt #, 1234 A Fraud Street, Unit 123.

After gathering the information necessary to assume the identity of another and creating a counterfeit piece of identification, the process now shifts to the financial institution. As discussed with business takeover fraud, individuals will attempt to open numerous bank accounts in the names of the unsuspecting victims. In order to get as much money as possible out of the fraudulent bank accounts, the deposit items are the same as discussed with business takeover fraud, including using:

- Stolen and forged checks
- Counterfeit business checks
- Counterfeit US Treasury checks
- Counterfeit US Postal Service money orders
- Counterfeit cashier's checks
- Counterfeit state government checks

New account fraud follows along the lines of the situations discussed with business takeover fraud:

- If actual forged checks are used as deposit items, the funds generated will be withdrawn. The financial institution suffering the monetary loss is the bank on which the forged checks were drawn. The actual account holders will approach their financial institution and complete the necessary affidavits of forgery. Once this process takes place, the forged check amounts will be placed back into the account of the forgery victim and the financial institution suffers a loss.
- The same scenario holds true if counterfeit business checks are used as deposit items. The eventual victim of a monetary loss is the bank on which the business checks were drawn. Affidavits are filed and money is returned to the targeted business.
- If counterfeit cashier's checks, counterfeit US money orders, counterfeit US Treasury checks, or counterfeit state government checks are used as deposit items and the funds are made available, the eventual victim will be the financial institution where the fraudulent bank account was opened.

With many individual new account frauds, those committing the crime will have checks printed and sent to the address desired. These checks are then used by the criminals to make purchases at various retail locations. Unfortunately for the businesses accepting these personal checks, they will be returned marked "NSF." These retail locations will become a victim of a monetary loss.

Based on the size of the loss suffered by the retail establishment, its loss prevention department will attempt to locate the account holder. This path will lead them to a person who is a victim of identity theft.

Online Financial Institution Fraud

With increasing technology comes simplicity for the everyday consumer. This technology allows for easy access to financial accounts. Consumers can now track their personal and business account activity from their cell phones, tablets, and laptops. They can also transfer funds from one bank account to another, update the available balance of their college student's account, make payments online, etc. They are basically banking without leaving home—not seeing the inside of the brick and mortar financial institution and having no teller interaction.

From the consumer perspective, the ease and simplicity cannot be more welcoming. From the financial institution perspective, technology allows the institution to provide time-saving avenues to the consumer for money management. The main issue in the backs of the minds of the various financial institutions is the threat of fraud.

As discussed in detail in Section V, criminals are increasing their efforts to gather personal and business-related information through online phishing [8] and conducting data breaches [9]. Included in the information obtained as the result of a successful phishing attempt is

- Individual name and address
- Individual date of birth
- Individual SSN
- Business employer identification number
- Individual and business bank account numbers
- Individual and business bank account user names and passwords
- Individual and business credit/debit card account numbers
- Individual and business debit card account PINs

Included in the information obtained as a result of a successful data breach is

- Individual name and address
- Individual date of birth
- Individual SSN
- Individual credit/debit card account numbers

The main goal is to collect personal and business information for the purpose of committing all types of fraudulent activity.

From the perspective of financial institutions, this information is used to

- Open fraudulent bank accounts online
- Gain unauthorized access to the accounts of legitimate customers
- Gain unauthorized access to the accounts of legitimate business customers

As previously discussed with new account fraud, the goals and results of those opening fraudulent bank accounts online remain the same. One or more financial institutions suffer a financial loss and unsuspecting consumers realize they have become a victim of identity theft.

By gaining unauthorized access to the bank accounts of consumers and businesses, the goals of those committing the fraud are

- To drain the account balances through unauthorized money transfers
- To drain the account balances through unauthorized online retail purchases

After fraudulent activities like those previously discussed take place, the true account holder (individual or business) will contact the financial institution and claim to be a victim of fraud. After checking various account balances, the individual or business bank customer discovers the following fraudulent activity:

- Thousands of dollars were extracted from their account to make numerous online purchases.
- Thousands of dollars were extracted from their account and transferred to an unknown person at a financial institution hundreds of miles away.
- Thousands of dollars were extracted from their account and transferred to another financial institution. With this type of transfer it is possible the personal or business information of the victim was used to open a new account at the other financial institution. Stolen money was transferred into a bank account opened using the tactic of identity theft and fraud.

With the types of losses previously discussed, the individual or business account holder will eventually approach the financial institution and make a claim of fraud. Based on banking regulations and customer service, unauthorized account withdrawals and expenditures will be replaced by the financial institution. The account holder is made whole and the financial institution suffers a fraud-related monetary loss.

In an effort to protect against the types of fraud-related losses that take place as part of a data breach or e-mail phishing, it is imperative that financial institutions educate their individual and business customers as part of an awareness campaign. Previous discussion took place on the types of information that can be gained as a result of a data breach or phishing.

In Section V, discussion takes place on how to spot a phishing e-mail and the potential avenues used to conduct data breaches. As part of a consumer education program, this information needs to be shared with both individual and business account holders.

As referenced, financial institutions are required by various regulations to make customers whole when they suffer a fraud loss. Unless the financial institution can prove the individual or business customer provided personal and bank account information to those committing the fraud, the institution is on the hook for the monetary loss.

Financial institutions are not going to require customer fraud victims to bring their personal or business computer in for examination prior to restitution being made. Although extreme sounding in nature, a detailed examination of a fraud victim's personal or business computer could reveal the catalyst for the overall fraudulent activity.

With successful phishing e-mails, malware/spyware software is unknowingly installed on a targeted victim's computer. This software is used for many purposes, including:

- Gathering personal and business information for a personal or work computer or network
- Gathering individual or business financial account information, including account login and password information

- Acting as a Trojan horse to be uploaded into the main computer system of a franchisor network, large retail business operation, or any business for the purpose of gaining access to employee (past and present) information in order for a successful data breach to take place

As discussed in detail in Section V, the goal of any phishing attempt is to gain unauthorized access to a computer system. Once inside, the person unknowingly allowing the unauthorized access has no clue that the system has been breached and goes about normal day-to-day business.

On the part of those committing fraud associated with e-mail phishing, once they have gained successful access to a computer system, their goal is not to announce success from the rooftops. They will go about their activities of gathering the desired information and committing the related fraud. A typical fraud victim whose journey began as part of an unsolicited phishing e-mail will have no clue as to how his or her personal and financial information was compromised. For those committing the fraudulent activity, anonymity is their desire.

If those involved in the fraud world constantly bragged of their successes, they would have fewer avenues to pursue. Their main goal is to rely on consumer ignorance.

From a fraud prevention perspective, an educated bank customer is a barrier along the path of least resistance in preventing financial institution fraud. Part of this education process has to include a discussion on e-mail phishing, since it is a major gateway into the computer systems of individual and business customers. As discussed in detail in Section V, e-mail phishing is one of the five avenues used to gain access to information. The other four avenues include:

- Smishing is the use of short messaging service (SMS) technology to phish for individuals' sensitive personal information, such as Social Security numbers or user names and passwords for online banking. Smishing can also be used to infect users' phones and related networks with destructive viruses or eavesdropping software. Smishing, like phishing, is a criminal activity [10].
- Vishing (voice or Voice Over Internet Protocol [VoIP] phishing) is an electronic fraud tactic in which individuals are tricked into revealing critical financial or personal information to unauthorized entities. Vishing works like phishing but does not always occur over the Internet and is carried out using voice technology. A vishing attack can be conducted by voice e-mail, VoIP, or landline or cellular telephone [11].
- Spoofing is a technique used to gain unauthorized access to computers whereby the intruder sends messages to a computer with an IP address indicating that the message is coming from a trusted host. To engage in IP spoofing, a hacker must first use a variety of techniques to find an IP address of a trusted host and then modify the packet headers so that it appears that the packets are coming from that host [12]. If those conducting a spoofing attempt are successful, the recipient will believe that he or she recognizes the

sender of an e-mail. The e-mail recipient is asked to view a link or attachment provided. Once the link or attachment is clicked on, the recipient is opening the computer to unauthorized downloading of malicious software.

- Cramming is delivered via text message and alerts recipients that they have won a prize. In order to receive the prize, the recipient has to click on the link provided. Contained within the link is a request for personal and financial information. The recipient is advised the information is necessary to process the award. In actuality, the personal and financial information provided is used for identity theft and other types of fraud. The link could also be used for the purpose of downloading unauthorized malware/spyware software.

The five avenues used to gain access to personal and business information are a very important topic of discussion for the prevention of financial institution fraud. The relevance of the five avenues and their being a catalyst for financial institution fraud are as follows:

- Individuals, business owners, and employees store large amounts of personal and business information that can be used to commit fraud on their laptops, tablets, and cell phones.
- As discussed in Section V, technology-reliant individuals can be unwitting participants in successful fraud attempts. As each day goes by, more and more individuals grow up only knowing how to communicate via text messages, e-mail, and social media. All three of these communication options are a popular target for the five avenues used to gain access to information. With a reliance on technology to communicate comes a need to educate financial institution customers on the threats of providing information through phishing, smishing, vishing, spoofing, and cramming.
- The unauthorized downloading of malware/spyware onto a computer system is a major step in the process for a successful data breach. The steps taken by a consumer, business owner, or associate when responding to any one of the five avenues provide a starting point in the data breach process. All that is needed by those initiating the fraud attempt is an avenue into a system where an unauthorized software download can take place. Each of the five avenues has its own unique method of introduction to the target, with the hope of the eventual click on a provided link or an opening of a provided attachment. From a financial institution fraud perspective, information obtained from a data breach can be used to commit various types of fraud. With a detailed customer education program on the threats related to the cyber world, a long-term net gain could be the prevention of the steps needed for a successful data breach.

As long as financial institutions have customers who rely on technology as part of their everyday life, the fraud threat will remain. It is imperative that those working on fraud prevention programs for various financial institutions across the country take the following under advisement as part of a fraud awareness and prevention program:

- Maintain strong "Know Your Customer" programs for both current customers and potential new account holders. Just because a person opening a new account is wearing a lab coat and claims to be Dr. Smith does not make him or her an actual doctor.
- Stay away from waiving hold times on deposit items. Based on the deposit item type and amount, place an item hold for as long as regulations allow.
- Do an Internet search on each personal and business address provided. The results will show if the address is in a business or residential location. It will also show if the address is a mail drop location. Another key point for the address search is to determine if the location is in close proximity to the actual bank branch. If the applicant does not live or work in close proximity to the bank branch, ask why the applicant is traveling a distance to open a new bank account.
- Do an Internet search for all new business accounts being opened. Almost all businesses have company-related websites containing contact information, primary operating location, principal's names, etc. In addition to the company website, secondary sites (state offices of corporate commissions, state contractors offices, etc.) exist that contain business-related information. This information is vital in verifying the actual business address and contact information. Bank personnel need to ensure the address provided by those opening the new account is the same as the address verified by the Internet search. The same verification process needs to take place for all contact information provided.
- Prior to opening any new business account, make sure to conduct a records check with the state's corporation commission. New accounts personnel need to look at the status dates on the records provided. When changes are made to the corporate/business status, documentation is provided to the corporate commissions office. Once any of the requested changes are updated (records, corporate officers, managers, members, statutory agent, etc.), the date of the information change is noted as part of the official records. Caution needs to be utilized if a records search reveals newly updated information. Many times, the changes are legitimate, but for the purpose of committing business takeover fraud, bogus records and updates are made through the various state records offices. Bank personnel should never use a phone number provided by the individuals opening the new accounts. Business contact information should be obtained through a directory service operation.
- Most if not all financial institutions offer some type of account tracking fraud prevention program. These programs are based on known customer banking habits, deposits, withdrawals, monetary transfer amounts, etc. Any variations

from these known banking patterns will trigger some type of alert to the customer for verification of the questionable activity. These programs offer a great opportunity to catch fraud attempts at the inception and should be used and encouraged for all accounts.
- Initiate some type of customer education program on how to recognize phishing, smishing, vishing, cramming, and spoofing attempts. These education programs need to inform the customer on how these five avenues are used to gain personal/business information and unauthorized access to their various accounts. Customers also need to be educated on the long-term ramifications on how any of the five avenues can eventually lead to a successful data breach.
- Initiate some type of customer education program on the dangers of using WiFi hotspots for the purpose of conducting any financially related activity (i.e., making purchases online, accessing the financial institution accounts, viewing credit card accounts, etc.).

Business Takeover Fraud

Previous discussion took place on the tactics used to commit business takeover fraud. In addition to using this information to open new bank accounts in the name of the targeted business, criminals use the data to

- Open lines of credit
- Open new credit card accounts
- Obtain business loans

Based on how the business is established (partnership or some type of corporation), a key identification factor is the SSN or the EIN. These numbers are used as part of the loan process and for the tracking of the related credit score [13].

An individual has his or her own individual credit score and report, and the same holds true for a business. A large majority of these business-related credit scores and reports are driven by the employer identification number.

As previously discussed, it is a much easier process to locate the EIN of a business versus an individual SSN. Once this number has been compromised, those looking to commit business-related fraud will attempt to open loan-based accounts.

No matter whether the unsuspecting business has a line of credit, credit card, or loan opened in the company's good name, the end result is a negative impact on both the lending agency and the targeted organization.

If those looking to commit a loan-based form of business fraud are successful, they will quickly work to

- Use every dime of the line of credit amount in the quickest manner possible.
- Max out the credit card amounts in the quickest manner possible.

No matter how the amount of the approved loan is paid, the goal is to separate the money from the phony business operation.

After using the name of a business to commit fraud, the goal is to obtain the maximum amount of money possible for each operation compromised. Once those committing the fraud achieve success, they move on to new targets. What they leave in their wake is a lending agency looking to recover the stolen money and a business working to recover its once good business name:

- After depleting the assets from a fraudulent business loan, credit card, or line of credit, those committing the fraud have no intention of giving back the stolen assets. Additionally, the lending agency will quickly begin looking for repayment. Eventually, the lending agency will realize the loaned money is part of a fraudulent operation and it will need to begin the investigative process in an attempt to identity those committing the fraud to recover the stolen assets. At the end of the day, the lending agency is out the amount of money stolen as part of the bogus loan, credit card, or line of credit.
- After realizing the loaned amount is not being repaid as agreed upon, the lending agency will contact the business whose name was used as part of the loan process. Once contacted, the business has to work to convince the lending agency that it is the victim of fraud and had no role in obtaining any type of loan. After clearing its name with the lending agency, the targeted business now has to work to clear its name with the various credit reporting agencies. Just like a victim of individual identity theft, it can take from six months to over a year to repair the damage created. Even though the targeted business is not responsible for the assets stolen, once the fraud is realized its name is associated with varying amounts of negative information. In order to clear its good business name, it becomes necessary to spend time and money during the process.

In order to prevent the various types of business-related fraud, businesses and lending agencies need to do the following:

- Business operations need to
  - Employ an identity theft protection company that can alert the unsuspecting business anytime an attempt is made to open a bank account or establish some type of business-related credit.
  - Routinely conduct an Internet search of its business name. Search for websites in the name of the business that are not legitimate. Businesses also need to look for their business name associated with a different address location or a different contact number.
  - Routinely conduct a search of the state's corporation commission to ensure that records and officers' names on file are accurate.

- Lending agencies need to
  - Conduct due diligence as part of a business verification process. Work to make sure the individuals applying for credit are actual members of the applying business.
  - Conduct an Internet search of the business name applying for credit. Look for inconsistencies in the information provided by those seeking the loan and information on the company website.
  - Conduct an Internet search for company-related websites using the same business name.
  - Conduct a search of the state's corporation commission for recently updated business information.
  - Conduct a physical visit to the business address provided. Make sure there is an actual business operation at the location address.

It is imperative that both businesses and lending agencies work to protect their good names and assets prior to a loss taking place. The time and money spent up front make up a much smaller amount than that expended after a successful takeover fraud and the related losses.

Endnotes

1. Federal Trade Commission. "2014 Consumer Sentinel Network Data Book." https://www.google.com/search?q=increase+in+identity+theft&ie=utf-8&oe=utf-8 (accessed August 11, 2015).
2. According to the IRS.gov website: "An employer identification number (EIN) is also known as a federal tax identification number, and is used to identify a business entity." http://www.irs.gov/Businesses/Small-Businesses-&-Self-Employed/Employer-ID-Numbers-EINs (accessed August 19, 2015). An EIN is for a business what an SSN is for an individual.
3. A merchant account is opened for the purpose of processing credit/debit card transactions. Merchant accounts are established through a third-party processing organization that eventually deposits the funds into a selected business bank account. For simplicity, merchant accounts can be opened online.
4. Checks can be stolen from an individual or business, authored for a certain dollar amount, and deposited. Once deposited, the check goes through the system to the bank on which the check was drawn. If there are sufficient funds in the account, the check amount is then forwarded to the bank account where the check was deposited. Weeks later, the true account holder can file an affidavit with his or her bank claiming forgery. If the claim is determined to be valid, the bank returns the forged check amount to the customer. The bank of the customer who made the forgery claim is now out the amount of the check.

5. An individual can obtain a legitimate check from a business. Once the check has been obtained, counterfeit checks are created using the true business account number and the true bank routing number. These counterfeit checks are then deposited into fraudulent accounts. Like the forged check previously discussed, the funds will become available for the account into which they were deposited. The amount of the counterfeit checks is eventually deducted from the balance of the legitimate business. It is up to the legitimate business to make a claim with its bank by filing an affidavit of counterfeit checks. The legitimate business will eventually be credited for the money deducted as a result of the counterfeit checks. The financial institution on which the counterfeit checks were drawn is out the amount of the checks.
6. Based on the type of item deposited into an account, the financial institution where the deposits were made is mandated by regulations as to the length of time the funds will be made available. According to Regulation CC, financial institutions are mandated on how long a deposit item amount can be held. These hold times are based on the institution where the deposit items are drawn, the geographical area of the issuing financial institution, and the dollar amount. For simplicity's sake, financial institutions have to make the funds available on the next business day for US Treasury checks, US Postal Service money orders, cashier's checks, and state government checks.
7. This is based on the fact of not wanting to waste effort. It takes time and effort to gather the information necessary to assume the identity of another. The process also involves creating counterfeit state-issued driver's licenses/identification cards.
8. From a technical standpoint, Dictionary.com defines phishing as "to try to obtain financial or other confidential information from Internet users, typically by sending an e-mail that looks as if it is from a legitimate organization, usually a financial institution, but contains a link to a fake website that replicates the real one."
9. A data breach takes place when individuals outside an organization gain unauthorized access to internal computer systems. The purpose of these breaches is to gather personal and business-related information on past and current customers. Individuals will also attack a business or government operation for the purpose of obtaining personal information for previous and current employees. Once the desired information is obtained, criminals will use it to commit all types of financial institution fraud, individual fraud, business-related fraud, etc.
10. "Smishing." http://www.investopedia.com/terms/s/smishing.asp (accessed August 24, 2015).
11. Vishing (voice or VoIP phishing) definition. http://searchunifiedcommunications.techtarget.com/definition/vishing (accessed August 24, 2015).
12. IP spoofing. http://www.webopedia.com/TERM/I/IP_spoofing.html (accessed August 24, 2015).
13. A number indicating whether a company is a good candidate to lend money to or do business with. Business credit scores, also called commercial credit scores, are based on a company's credit obligations and repayment histories with lenders and suppliers; any legal filings such as tax liens, judgments, or bankruptcies; how long the company has operated; business type and size; and repayment performance relative to that of similar companies. http://www.investopedia.com/terms/b/business-credit-score.asp (accessed August 31, 2015).

Chapter 30

Medical Identity Theft

The Office of Inspector General, US Department of Health and Human Services, defines medical identity theft:

> Medical identity theft occurs when someone steals your personal information (like your name, Social Security number, or Medicare number) to obtain medical care, buy drugs, or submit fake billings to Medicare in your name. Medical identity theft can disrupt your life, damage your credit rating, and waste taxpayer dollars. The damage can be life-threatening to you if wrong information ends up in your personal medical records [1].

As previously discussed throughout this section and the book, personal information obtained from successful data breaches is growing. The tactics used to conduct the data breaches vary; many rely on an uneducated consumer as a possible window into the information source (see Section V).

No matter the exact manner as to how more and more data breaches become successful, the discussion needs to be placed at the door of concern—concern on how the information obtained from a successful data breach can be used to commit the following fraudulent activity:

- Identity theft
- Business identity theft
- New personal account fraud
- New business account fraud
- Personal loan or credit card fraud
- Business loan, credit card, and line of credit fraud
- Medical identity theft

In order for medical identity theft to be successful, those committing the fraud look to obtain the following personal information:

- Individual names and address information
- Individual Social Security numbers
- Individual Medicare numbers
- Individual medical insurance account information

Once obtained, the individual and medical account information is used to

- Receive unauthorized medical services in the name of the unsuspecting policy holder
- Obtain prescription drugs in the name of the targeted individual
- Commit unauthorized medical billing schemes

Individuals committing medical identity theft are not limited to those wanting to use the personal and account information of everyday citizens. Other parties involved in the scam are as follows:

- Doctors, medical office staff, and individuals working in the insurance industry have a detailed knowledge of how the insurance billing systems work. Individuals working in the medical field will submit bogus medical claims against the insurance policies of targeted future victims. Fraudulent claims are also made against Medicare accounts of unsuspecting victims.
- Organized theft rings, as previously discussed in this chapter, are involved in activities other than the theft of retail merchandise. Individuals operating in these groups are also heavily involved in unlawfully obtaining prescription medication. Medication prescriptions are obtained in the name of unsuspecting medical patients and the items are paid for by using the targeted individual's insurance information. Additionally, bogus medication prescriptions are created and presented at pharmacies in the name of unsuspecting victims. Along with using the name of targeted individuals, those involved with the crime will use the person's medical insurance information. No matter the technique used to obtain the medication, the drugs are later sold for cash.

From an individual perspective, the short and long term ramifications of medical identity theft victimization are as follows:

- With unknown individuals obtaining medical services in their name, victims can go unaware of the expenses created. Unpaid medical bills can work to have a negative effect on their individual credit report.

- Unauthorized individuals using the health insurance policy of an unsuspecting victim can result in the cancellation of coverage.
- Individuals using the name of an unsuspecting person can work to create inaccurate medical records.
- Unauthorized usage of an unsuspecting individual's health insurance policy can lead to the victim having to pay higher premiums [2].

Medical identity theft can lead to the previously discussed negative situations for the targeted victims. Additionally, it can result in monetary losses for medical offices, health care providers, health insurance providers, pharmacies, etc. As with individual and business identity theft, the victims have an opportunity to prove they were not directly involved with the resulting crimes. This leaves the affected medical businesses on the hook for any financial loss [3].

In order to avoid medical identity theft, it is imperative that various types of businesses become involved in educating their patients and the general public on medical identity theft.

Individual consumers, clients, and medical patients need to be made aware of the following:

- Medical identity theft is a crime that is growing larger each year.
- Victimization of medical identity theft can result in a financial loss.
- Victimization of medical identity theft can result in individual medical records containing inaccurate information.
- Victimization of medical identity theft can result in having a poor credit report.
- Individuals need to be encouraged to review their individual explanation of benefits (EOB) reports that are supplied by their health insurers. Consumers need to examine these reports for services and treatments they never approved or received.
- Individuals need to be encouraged to review their individual credit report on a routine basis. Credit reports need to be examined for claims filed by medical offices for nonpayment.
- Individuals need to monitor the benefits paid out by their health insurance provider. The policy holders need to ensure they were the recipient of benefits paid.
- If possible, patients need to examine their individual medical records for inaccuracies. Patients need to be assured that they are the only person receiving treatment under their name [2].

A major deterrent in the rising crime of medical identity theft is consumer and patient awareness programs. These programs need to be initiated by any and all companies involved in the medical services industry.

Endnotes

1. Office of Inspector General. http://oig.hhs.gov/fraud/medical-id-theft/ (accessed August 31, 2015).
2. "Medical Identity Theft." http://www.insurancefraud.org/scam-alerts-medical-id-theft.htm#.VeUYrZdKDF1 (accessed August 31, 2015).
3. "Medical Identity Theft Victims Are More Likely to Suffer a Financial Loss Than Those of Identity Fraud. According to the Fifth Annual Study on Medical Identity Theft, These Victims Can Suffer Losses of over $10,000." medidfraud.org/wp-content/.../02/2014_Medical_ID_Theft_Study1.pdf (accessed August 31, 2015).

Chapter 31

Vendor Fraud

As discussed in Section I, there are opportunities that can lead to business-related losses. Internal business operating procedures and policies can be used to open windows of theft/fraud opportunities. As discussed throughout this section, businesses are also faced with external theft/fraud threats. Unscrupulous individuals are constantly looking for opportunities to commit theft/fraud crimes against an unsuspecting business.

One area of a business operation where there is a threat from both the inside and outside pertains to vendor activities. As discussed in Section I, it is necessary for all business operations to establish an approved vendor list. This list contains only suppliers/vendors approved to do business with the organization.

The creation of an approved supplier/vendor list is based on an investigated performance history of the organization, industry reputation, and records with business-tracking companies like the Better Business Bureau.

The main reason the supplier/vendor hiring organization needs to conduct due diligence is to prevent many types of theft/fraud. Vendors and associates working together can create havoc on a business's bottom line. The many types of vendor-related theft/fraud are detailed as follows:

- **Substandard products.** Based on the type of business, there is a need to purchase merchandise and material that meets some type of industry standard. Within the construction industry, there are regulations that dictate the strength of types of bolts. In the airline industry, safety standards require particular adherence to the purchasing and use of approved material. The same can also be stated when it comes to food-related products and meat quality. For the health of consumers, food industry organizations need to follow product purchasing and use guidelines. Without sufficient quality control standards at the purchasing level, suppliers/vendors can bill a business for industry standard quality material while actually providing a substandard product. If the supplier/vendor is working with a dishonest associate, this individual could easily approve the material being provided.

- **Bid rigging [1] or bidding assistance**. A business associate working with a supplier/vendor can ensure a selected operation is awarded a contract. This same associate can also work to provide the supplier/vendor with insider information as to the bidding contract proposals of competitors.
- **Kickback schemes**. In an effort to ensure the supplier/vendor is awarded certain and sometimes continuous contracts, the dishonest employee will demand some type of payment. For every contract awarded to a specific supplier/vendor, the employee is provided some type of payment. The unauthorized and illegal payment is provided by the supplier/vendor and is referred to as a kickback. There are several areas of concern for suppliers/vendors and employees involved in a kickback scheme.
  - Once the vendor has the employee on the hook as part of an illegal activity, he or she can demand higher dollar amount payments for services. In order to prevent his or her employer from finding out about the kickback activity, the employee becomes a victim of extortion. Additionally, the business is subject to paying above-market prices for material and services.
  - As discussed with substandard material being provided by suppliers/vendors, a kickback scheme can work to ensure this activity takes place. Again, once the vendor has the employee on the hook he or she can force the acceptance of substandard material.
  - The participating supplier/vendor can also demand to be provided with company-known information on its industry competitors. Having an internal employee on the hook for participating in a kickback scheme, vendors can make demands to obtain types of insider information. The offending employee can also be forced to ask business-related and client information questions. These questions are to be asked of other industry-specific vendors of the business where the kickback activity is taking place. This information can be used by the offending vendor to achieve an industry advantage for future bids and also work to steal existing clients.
  - Once the offending employee is working with the vendor and, in order to keep the activity silent, has become part of an extortion scheme, the benefits to the supplier can go beyond material and contract approval. Based on the monetary needs of the vendor, the employee can be forced into providing specific company-related information. This is to include company-related financial account information, personal information on other associates and the business owners, and an easy path into the computer network of the organization. As discussed in Section V, phishing scams are used in an effort to gain unauthorized access to an organization's computer network. The goal of these individuals is to use the

access to download malware/spyware software that is used for the purpose of spying and collecting financial information. A vendor having an employee on the hook for participating in a kickback scheme can force the employee to openly respond to a phishing e-mail. Once the employee actively responds to the phishing e-mail, the unauthorized malware/spyware software will be downloaded onto the business system.

- Once an employee and a vendor are involved in a kickback scheme, the associate can also reverse the tables. At times the reputation of the vendor carries a greater weight than the offending employee losing his or her job. In this scenario the associate can demand payment and favors from the vendor—items like money, sports tickets, dinners, luxury items, etc.

In an effort to prevent becoming a victim of vendor fraud, the following prevention measures need to be followed:

- As referenced in Section I, an approved supplier/vendor list needs to be created and used as part of the purchasing process. Vendors on this list have been vetted and have a solid reputation within the community.
- Business operations need to have more than one supplier/vendor for the services or products needed. A limited number of supplier/vendor options works against competition. Business operations need to establish some type of competitive vendor bidding process to ensure quality pricing. Competitive bidding also works to ensure that only one specific vendor is not constantly being used, which is a warning sign of a kickback scheme.
- It is also necessary to establish a supplier/vendor rotation program. By having several suppliers and vendors that provide the same types of services and products, purchasing decisions can be rotated. Establishing a forced vendor rotation policy can work to uncover kickback schemes.
- As discussed, with many positions in an organization, it is necessary to establish job rotation programs. With a job rotation policy, associates work in a departmental position for six months and then rotate to another position. Job rotation provides a diverse workforce and can be used to prevent supplier/vendor theft/fraud issues.

Endnote

1. Bid rigging is a scheme in which businesses collude so that a competing business can secure a contract for goods or services at a predetermined price. http://www.investopedia.com/terms/b/bid-rigging.asp (accessed September 14, 2015).

CYBER SECURITY AND CYBER FRAUD

V

Chapter 32

Understanding Cyber Security and Cyber Fraud

Introduction

In what is referred to as the "good ol' days of fraud," contact with the intended targets was made through personal introductions, telephone calls, or the US mail. A once popular fraud scam that was used for the purpose of obtaining credit card information from unsuspecting consumers involved the simple use of a mailed postcard. Random recipients were mailed a postcard-sized document. The information on the postcard informed the recipient he or she could easily protect his or her credit cards.

The postcard contained the name and address of the recipient and claimed to be an official fraud prevention tool. In an effort to add legitimacy to the fraud prevention tool, a professional sounding business name was also provided. Many of these mailed documents used a business name that revolved around the category of fraud and credit card protection, such as Credit Fraud Awareness or Credit Card Protection Service, or used the name of an actual credit-card-issuing organization.

The recipient of the mailed postcard was advised the mailing organization represented professionals in the credit card industry. The goal of this organization was to provide the consumer with protection against unauthorized usage of various credit cards. The recipients were advised the protection covered bank-issued cards, retail-store-issued cards, service-station-issued cards, etc. No matter the issuing organization of a credit card, the goal was to provide protection against unauthorized usage.

Recipients were asked to provide the following information:

- Credit card issuing agency (Visa, Sinclair, Macy's, etc.)
- Credit card number
- Expiration information

Individuals receiving these mailed credit card protection postcards were asked to provide the requested information on the mailed document. On the reverse side of the postcard (Figure 32.1), lines were available for the consumer to write in the requested information.

Although the credit card scam postcards were crude in nature, many recipients provided the requested information. Instead of placing a barrier in the path of becoming a victim of fraud, complying recipients were actually opening the door toward victimization.

This story is provided to offer a comparison between the thought process of yesterday and that of today. In a world not so long ago, information sent through the US mail was believed to be from a trusted source. Many held the opinion that "if it was sent through the mail it has to be official."

Forward a few decades: the new adage is, "If it is on the Internet, it has to be true." Those involved in defrauding businesses and organizations rely on the trust and belief in security within the cyber world. As technology advances, more and more information is transmitted through computer systems. Many individuals and businesses conduct all of their banking online. Their bank statements are viewed online, while cancelled checks are no longer mailed to a residence or business. This information can also be viewed online.

In order to receive complete fraud protection against the unauthorized usage of your personal Credit Cards, please provided the requested information below:

Card Issuing Agency	Card Number	Expiration Date
______________	____________________	___/___
______________	____________________	___/___
______________	____________________	___/___

Figure 32.1 Credit card protection postcard example.

Additionally, fewer and fewer people are writing checks for the purpose of paying bills. A majority of personal and business payments are conducted through prearranged online account deductions. These payments include the monthly mortgage payment, personal or business water bills, phone bills, insurance payments, etc. From a business perspective, many no longer issue their employees a weekly paycheck and rely on a direct deposit. Companies have an in-house employee payment system or outsource the process to a third-party payroll management organization.

Looking back again at the "good ol' days," many large-ticket items purchased by the consumer came with some type of instruction manual. These manuals were like small books and provided the consumer with all of the information needed to operate the product correctly. Many can remember purchasing a new vehicle or personal computer and relying on the owner's manual if questions arose during the operating process. In most cases, these books or paperbound manuals have been replaced with an easy-access version available online. All a consumer has to do is visit the website of the organization that sold the purchased product and, a few clicks later, he or she has full access to the owner's manual.

As the economic machine of this country and those of the world go forward, gone are the days of visiting the brick and mortar buildings to cash a check, thumbing through a cumbersome owner's manual, or relying solely on the advice received from a customer service representative contacted via a telephone call. A majority of the information and services required by the individual consumer and business owner can be obtained through some type of online process. Consumers rely on the Internet and the cyber world to purchase products and conduct commerce, while businesses use these systems to make product sales and grow their operation.

The title for Section V of this book is "Cyber Security and Cyber Fraud." As the purchasing public and business operations evolve from the trust-based level created from information received through the US mail system to transfer to a greater level of trust into the cyber world, many nameless and faceless individuals are relying on the individual belief that the overall system is trustworthy and secure.

The Future of the Threat

Recently a major international security organization (ASIS International) and a large American university (University of Phoenix) worked together and issued a research report [1]. The focus of this report was on the future threat of cyber security; it basically stated that cyber security would be the top national security risk for the next five years. With the movement of almost all personal and business activity taking place through the Internet and cyber world, there is a question to be asked: "Can the threat be diminished within a five-year time frame?"

Barring a major electromagnetic pulse (EMP) [2] or a king's decree, businesses and commerce will go forward using computers and computer-based systems to operate.

Knowing that all future business activity and commerce will take place in the cyber world, one must develop an understanding of the future of the threat. To understand the future, one must look back at the past of fraudulent activity that occurred as a result of commerce, social media, and transactions that took place via technology:

- Over the past few years major business operations were the victims of cyber attacks or data breaches. Individuals from outside the organization managed to access the internal computer systems of large business operations. A majority of the targeted data revolved around customer information. Within the customer information was personal data such as names, addresses, credit/debit card account numbers, etc. The intent of those looking to commit a data breach is to obtain previous customer information for the purpose of participating in identity theft.
- In activity referred to as "hacking," other countries have targeted large government operations for the purpose of accessing internal computer systems. Recent targets within the US federal government were the Office of Personnel Management, the State Department, the White House, the National Weather Service, the National Oceanic and Atmospheric Administration, etc. The intent of the hackers could have been to obtain personal information on current and former employees or to obtain national secrets.
- According to a report issued by the Federal Trade Commission [3], identity theft has been the number one consumer complaint for the 15th consecutive year. The crime of identity theft is not only the number one consumer complaint, but the number of cases also has risen and it has been identified by the FBI as the crime of the twenty-first century. Individual consumers can be targeted, as well as associates within the workplace. Many individuals are targeted through phishing scams (discussed later in Section V), and associates in the workplace are targeted via hacking-related data breaches.
- A quick search of the Internet will reveal numerous organizations that provide identity theft protection services. Initially, these services were offered by the three major credit reporting agencies. Over the past 15 years, however, there has been a growth in number of identity theft protection services companies. Individuals starting a new identity theft protection company see an arena to turn a profit and offer a level of consumer protection. However, the main focus of any entrepreneur is opportunity—basically seeing an opportunity for growth and success, coupled with a need from the consumer to purchase the service.

The information previously discussed on past fraudulent activity is information that is known by members of society. When a large retail organization is the victim of a data breach or a government agency has had its computer systems breached, this becomes headline news. Reporters inform people that if they recently shopped at a location of retailer X, their debit/credit card information could have been compromised. Consumers are advised to obtain some type of identity theft protection service and to check their individual credit report for signs of unauthorized activity.

When an attack takes place at a large government agency, former and current employees are informed of the breach and the potential for fraud. These individuals are provided information on the possible threat of identity theft and offered free access to an identity theft protection service.

The overall goal in both of these incidents is to limit the amount of information obtained via the data breach and to provide as much calm to the customer base and current and former employees. What is not provided to the employee base and consumers is the HOW: How did the data breach occur?

Looking back at the victims of identity theft, all they know is they are victims and their personal and financial information has been compromised. Sure they lost their wallet, but it was returned intact—no need for suspicion. Again, when was the moment their information was obtained? The consumer has no clue, while the identity thief knows the exact moment but does not shout this information from the roof top.

The same holds true for the large retailer or government agency. They know there was a breach, but who or what opened the window into their computer systems?

Looking forward, society and businesses are going to become more and more reliant on technology. A major EMP is not likely to take place and, thankfully, we are not a nation ruled by a king that can issue a decree. We are not going back to a time before the personal computer and technology-based business operations.

So what is the future of the threat? The answer is that the future is coming and the threat is real. The goal of all business owners and operators is to work to limit the threat and to develop an education program on the access routes used to enter the computer systems of the business. Owners and operators also need to ensure they educate all employees on the threat potential and the *do*s and *don't*s of the activity that can take place when accessing company computer systems.

The Importance of Full Disclosure on Fraud Threats to the Employee Base

The goal of any business operation is to identify avenues, internally and externally, where it is susceptible for fraud to take place. A quick review of the business operation could reveal the following:

- Ms. Mable, a 20-year employee, has recently been handed the duties of overseeing both accounts receivable and accounts payable.
- The antivirus software on all office laptops has not been updated in six months.
- Employees can freely access their social media accounts on company computers.

These few examples are areas within any business operation that should immediately raise a red flag. Once identified, changes should be put in place at the earliest possible moment in order to lower the threat potential.

When a threat assessment is conducted within any business operation, many internal and external threats are unique to that particular operation. During the process it is quite possible to locate "no-brainer" issues like lack of dual control in the accounting department. Other issues could be more complex, such as outside individuals using phishing techniques (discussed later in Section V) to obtain access to company computer systems and financial information. Many within an organization have no clue what a phishing attempt would look like or the possible delivery mechanisms.

In order to have a successful fraud/theft threat identification and prevention program, company owners, managers, and security and loss prevention personnel have to ensure their associate education process is detailed. As discussed throughout the following chapters, business managers, owners, and security and loss prevention personnel need to develop an understanding of the threats present and why it is important to convey this information to all company associates.

As discussed later in Section V, all associates need to be included in the threat discussion. Additionally they need to be made part of the awareness and prevention process from a personal perspective. This will basically show that management is equally concerned about the protection of individual information as well as that of the business—developing a team-first approach: "I would rather take time and concern to protect something we all own versus something you own."

An employee cannot be accused of doing something wrong if he or she did not know it was wrong. With the ever changing world of fraudulent activity, all associates need to be continuously updated on the threats and the identification measures.

The Necessity of Learning the Aspects of Cyber Fraud for All Loss Prevention/Security/Law Enforcement Professionals

The necessity of having company-related loss prevention and security personnel up to date on all the aspects of cyber fraud activity is to ensure they have the knowledge base to identify and prevent fraudulent attacks. From a law enforcement perspective, this individual need is twofold.

One concerns the investigative aspect of law enforcement. As the incidents of cyber crimes increase, as well as those of identity theft and financial fraud, law enforcement personnel need to have a knowledge base of what to look for. As police departments have a special investigative department dealing with homicides, they also have a financial crimes division. A lot of information can be gained from the postmortem investigation of a murder victim. The same holds true for the cyber crime; there is a postmortem investigation.

The other aspect of the need-to-know for law enforcement is in the identification and prevention of data breaches. As discussed later in Section V, the victims of data breaches range from the small mom and pop business to the large retail operation. Individuals looking to commit a data breach for information-gathering purposes have attacked local hospitals, municipal offices, medical clinics, dental offices, etc. Within the computer systems of local law enforcement agencies is a database of information that could be used to commit all types of financially related crimes, including identity theft, account takeover fraud, and credit/debit card fraud.

The avenues used by those outside the municipal buildings and medical offices are also the ones that can be used to infiltrate the computer systems of the local sheriff's office. Within the world of cyber fraud, the target is database information. The personal information of Officer Smith is just as valuable as that of Doctor Smith.

Endnotes

1. Fickes, M. End User Correspondent. SourceSecurity.com US edition. http://us.sourcesecurity.com/news/articles/co-177-ga.16414.html#.VND1_4a0_Dk.linkedin (accessed July 13, 2015).
2. An EMP is a blast of electromagnetic energy that can cripple or destroy electronic devices—basically, any computer system or anything that operates using a computer. The major threat today is from a nuclear explosion. However, there are enemies believed to be working on a device that sends out an EMP without the use of a nuclear weapon.
3. Federal Trade Commission. 2014 Consumer Sentinel Network Data Book.

Chapter 33

Keeping Malware/ Spyware Off Office Computers

Introduction

According to Dictionary.com, malware is defined as "software intended to damage a computer, mobile device, computer system, or computer network, or to take partial control over its operation." Dictionary.com defines spyware as "software that is installed surreptitiously and gathers information about an Internet user's browsing habits, intercepts the user's personal data, etc., transmitting this information to a third party."

Anyone reading these definitions about malware and spyware software would work to ensure it is never installed on a personal or office computer. Business owners would ensure that office computers had the most up-to-date antivirus software and they would ensure that employees were thoroughly educated on how these programs make their way onto computers and computer systems. Some business owners place effort into associate education on computer threats, while others use the "I hope it does not happen to me" theory. Computer attacks are something that happens to someone else.

Malware/spyware types of programs that are unknowingly installed onto computer systems can complete the following functions:

- Shut down the system or network.
- Obtain individual or business-related information.

- Obtain individual or business-related financial information, to include bank account and credit card account information.
- Obtain bank account PINs.
- Obtain website login information for the user—a dangerous prospect for those who like to shop online.
- Identify an individual's Internet activity.
- Track keystrokes of the computer user.
- Obtain password information.
- Direct the user to counterfeit websites, while having the user believe the browser took him or her to the legitimate company website.
- Steal address book information.
- Flood the system with unwanted pop-up advertising and spam e-mail.

In addition to the computer system being a target for malware/spyware, other electronic devices that are connected to the Internet can also have this unwanted software installed. These devices include:

- Cell phones
- Tablets
- Smart TVs

As with a personal or business computer system or a single laptop, individuals store a lot of personal and business information. Once installed, malware/spyware software can also gather the intelligence information of the user who connects through a laptop to a bank, credit card accounts, other lenders, etc. The purpose of this type of unwanted software is to gather the information sought by the software designer or those who use malware/spyware for malicious purposes. Once the desired information is obtained, it is sent back to those who initiated the scam for the purpose of committing fraudulent activity.

As the use of technology increases and more and more people spend time online, malicious software is also unknowingly installed onto other electronic devices. Cell phones and tablets are also targeted. Basically, any device that contains personal and business information and connects to the Internet is a gold mine for those looking to commit fraud.

In addition to the increasing use of technology by all, the amount of information stored on other devices creates a greater chance of becoming a fraud victim. With an increase in technology, users also obtain the benefit of mobility. Many would not carry a laptop down the street while checking e-mail. With access to a tablet or cell phone, users are now connected no matter where they go.

With the benefits of mobility comes the need to store information onto these other Internet-friendly devices. Personal, business, and financial information that was once stored on the home or business computer is now copied and retained on mobile devices. Additionally, since these devices can be used to access the same business and financial websites they are ideal candidates for malware/spyware. The goal of the business owner or associate is an ease of connectivity and mobility, while those looking to commit fraud are overjoyed by the aspect of connectivity and mobility basically increasing the target base.

Is Scareware the First Threat?

No one in his or her right mind would download or insert a disk or thumb drive into a computer that contained malware/spyware. Knowing this fact, the question remains as to how this malicious software makes its way onto the computers and systems of individuals, small business operations, and large corporations.

Those looking to use malware/spyware for the purpose of committing fraud have to develop a delivery system where the target allows the unauthorized downloading. Discussed later in this section is the use of phishing, vishing (voice or VoIP phishing), smishing, and spoofing—all tools used by criminal elements to gain unauthorized access to personal and business computers and systems.

In addition to these tools, many targeted individuals are contacted via what is referred to as scareware. Scareware is a program or tool that convinces the target that his or her computer is in danger and that the program or tool can provide the needed assistance. The computer user receives a pop-up message stating the system is in danger and requires a stronger firewall, cleansing, or some type of anti-spyware/-virus software.

Going by the name of the technique, the user is scared into believing there is an issue with the system or computer and clicks on the pop-up advertisement. Believing he or she has been directed to a legitimate website, the user purchases what appears to be the software necessary to protect the system or computer. What the user has actually purchased is a program that downloads malicious software such as malware and spyware. Instead of protecting the system or computer, the user has caused additional harm and also wasted whatever money was paid for the product. Additionally, the user has provided those selling the bogus software with personal or business credit/debit card information.

In order to protect against unauthorized downloading of malicious software, users need to stay away from answering pop-up advertisements. Hopefully recipients of pop-up advertisements will think twice and go about their business, not falling for the bait. Unfortunately there are those who only think once and click on the link provided. Prior to making the purchase and providing personal or business-related financial information, they have that second thought. A decision is made to click on the cancel tab or X out of the website.

Hopefully by exiting the website and not making the purchase, the user has taken the steps necessary to protect against becoming a victim of scareware. Unfortunately, there could be hidden directions in the actual pop-up advertisement or within the visited website that lead to what is referred to as clickjacking.

The computer user might try to click on the cancel option or X out of the website visited as a result of clicking on the link in the pop-up advertisement. Instead of having the pop-up advertisement simply go away, the user is taken to an unauthorized website where unauthorized software is downloaded. Or instead of leaving the website visited, the X-out option actually directs the user to an unauthorized website where malicious software is downloaded.

In order to avoid the temptation of responding to a scareware advertisement or that of clickjacking, users need to ensure their browser is set to block all incoming pop-up advertisements. With most browser systems, users do have the option of adjusting the settings and only allowing pop-up advertisements from trusted organizations.

For a business owner, manager, or security/loss prevention professional it is important to ensure all office computers are configured to block pop-up advertisements. As previously discussed, they are a main source of delivering malicious software to personal and business computer systems. In an effort to ensure complete protection against the dangers of malicious pop-up advertisements, it is important that all employees be educated on the overall threat potential.

It is not enough to configure browser settings to prevent these pop-ups from appearing on the computer screens of employees. From a business theft/fraud prevention standpoint, there has to be an assumption that one or more unsolicited advertisements might slip through the system.

An employee sitting at a desk has a pop-up advertisement appear on the computer screen. The advertisement pertains to the many computer-related threats present and the need to protect all systems from receiving malicious software. An educated employee who understands the threats related to pop-up advertisements will not be intrigued. An uneducated employee might formulate a plan to protect the office computer systems. Thinking he or she is acting in the best interest of the organization, the employee elects to purchase the protection software offered in the advertisement.

After clicking on the link provided in the pop-up advertisement, the unknowing employee believes he or she has acted in the best interest of the company. What the employee has actually done is turned the concept of a good deed into a major threat area for the employer and the related computer network.

In an effort to ensure employees do not take the bait and purchase virus protection software offered through a pop-up advertisement, a threat-related education program is necessary.

Understanding Phishing, Spoofing, Smishing, and Vishing

Phishing

One issue I have always had with fishing is the need to get up before dawn, because it is easier to catch fish while they are swimming around looking for their breakfast.

Knowing the patterns of many fish species, anglers look for the ideal spot on the lake or one where they have had previous success. With almost any body of water, the desired targets (fish) are present. All that the individual fishing has to know is the types of fish that are in that particular body of water. Knowing this, the individual fishing has to select the correct bait and make a decision to either fish from the top or bottom of the water line.

With the sport of fishing, those looking to catch their limit on the day in question must target a captive audience. As referenced, most bodies of water contain some types of fish. Most individuals looking to catch their limit have gathered their intelligence information, which is based around the types of fish in the lake, the proper bait to use, and whether to use a bobber or drag the line across the top of the water.

With the sport of fishing, success is based on selecting the proper location and knowing the target audience (types of fish in the lake), as well as what it eats and how to attract its attention. This same practice can also be used by other types of individuals, who go "phishing."

From a technical standpoint, Dictionary.com defines phishing as "to try to obtain financial or other confidential information from Internet users, typically by sending an e-mail that looks as if it is from a legitimate organization, usually a financial institution, but contains a link to a fake website that replicates the real one." Merriam-Webster.com defines phishing as "a scam by which an e-mail user is duped into revealing personal or confidential information which the scammer can use illicitly."

Many looking to go fishing choose to fish so they can catch their dinner. Those who look to go phishing have a goal of committing fraud against an individual or business. Although spelled differently, both activities are similar in nature. See Figure 33.1.

A large majority of phishing e-mails are unsolicited. Basically, the e-mail randomly pops up in someone's inbox. Once it is delivered, the receiver is attracted by the subject line in the e-mail. The sender hopes to gain the attention of the receiver and that he or she opens the e-mail and reads further.

	Location	**Bait**	**The Hook**
Fishing	Target is located in a set body of water.	Anything the fish eats.	Line placed in the water to attract the type of fish in the lake.
Phishing	Anyone using a computer who receives email.	An attractive offer sent via email.	An offer too good to be true or a belief there is an issue with one of their accounts.

Figure 33.1 "Fishing" to "phishing" example.

With phishing e-mails, the receiver or target is attracted to the subject line for various reasons, based on whom the sender is believed to be. Individuals crafting phishing e-mails will use the names of financial institutions, credit card companies, investment offers, etc. to attract attention. Some successful subject lines are as follows:

- Your XXXXXXX Bank Account Information Requires Updating
- Your XXXXXXX Bank Debit Card May Have Been Compromised
- Your Cable Bill Is Late, Make Your Payment Online Here
- You Are the Lucky Winner of an International Lottery
- A Special Investment Offer for YOU

When it comes to the "sport" of phishing, those looking to make their catch for the day have a computer-using audience and the bait information is up to the imaginations of those creating the fraud attempts. Their desire is to create a level of concern (bank account, cable, etc.) or interest (won the lottery or a get-rich-quick possibility). As discussed with the unauthorized downloading of malware/spyware, phishing e-mails are used to have the recipient click on a link or attachment contained within the e-mail.

Using the phishing bait attempt of supposed issues with an individual's financial account, the sender is hoping the recipient clicks on the link provided in the e-mail. By taking the bait, the e-mail recipient believes he or she will be taken to the legitimate website of the financial institution. In reality the recipient is transferred to a bogus website where unauthorized software is downloaded onto the computer.

In an effort to have the phishing e-mail recipient believe he or she is correcting the issue with the financial institution, the target is taken to a professional-looking website. While at the website, the e-mail recipient is asked to provide varying types of personal and financial information. The recipient is led to believe the information request is necessary so that the financial institution can verify that the e-mail recipient is the true customer. Once the requested information is provided, the recipient is informed that the account issue has been corrected. The individual then goes about his or her daily business believing he or she has dodged a bullet.

Those initiating the phishing e-mail have been successful in downloading unauthorized malicious software onto the target's computer. They have also collected the target's personal and financial information that can later be used for identity theft and identity fraud purposes.

As previously referenced, the subject matter of the phishing e-mail is open to the imagination of the sender and can vary. What makes the "sport" of phishing a successful fraud is that the unsolicited e-mails are distributed on a large scale. That secret investment opportunity is not sent to the one individual who received the e-mail. It is received by thousands. All the senders are doing is looking for one or more people to take the bait.

Figures 33.2 through 33.5 show a few examples of phishing attempts where the target could be an individual or a business. Additional phishing examples are detailed in Appendix B—Examples of Phishing E-mails.

From: SunTrust service@suntrust.com

To: Recipients service@suntrust.com

Subject: Dear SunTrust Customer

Note:This is a service message with information related to your SunTrust account(s). It may include specific details about transactions, products or online services. If you recently cancelled your account, please disregard this message.

Dear Suntrust customer:

Thank you for maintaining your **Everyday** account with outstanding features tailored to help you reach your financial goals.

We're writing to let you know that we upgraded our servers.

You are hereby required to log on to www.suntrust.com and confirm your email address and your contact information.

Failure to do so may lead to the suspension of your account.

Sincerely,

Online Banking Team

SunTrust Bank, Member FDIC. © 2015 SunTrust Banks, Inc.

Please don't reply directly to this automatically-generated e-mail message.

If you aren't enrolled in Online Banking and think you've received this message in error, please disregard this message.

This email was sent on behalf of SunTrust Customer Care, 1575 Lemon Farris Road, Cookeville, TN 38506.

Figure 33.2 Bank-related phishing example.

From:	Chase Online (SM) vzesi2hv@verizon.net
To:	Undisclosed recipients:;
Subject:	New Message From Chase Online(SM)

CHASE

Dear Chase Online℠ Customer:

Thank you for using Chase Online℠. We have upgraded our online service to the new Secure Socket Layer (SSL). You are required to click the link below to validate your account information.

Click Here Now To Validate Your Account Online

This update will be available in your Secure Message Center until 08/08/2015
Thank you for being a valued customer. You can view this Policy Update by logging in to your account.
To log in to your account.Once you are logged in,look at the Notifications section on the top right side of the page for the latest Policy updates.

Sincerely,

Figure 33.3 Financial institution phishing example.

Phishing e-mails can take many forms and, as previously referenced, the information contained and the purported sending individual or organization are open to the minds of the creators. As shown in the figures, some e-mails are crudely composed, while others have a more professional appearance. Unfortunately, many phishing attempts achieve success no matter the format in which the e-mail was sent or the professional appearance.

Many are fooled into believing they have received an e-mail from their financial institution, credit card company, or cable provider, based on the appearance of the message. The thinking goes along the lines of, "The e-mail looked like the company website I recently visited." Those looking to commit phishing types of frauds will actually copy and paste sections from the legitimate website of many organizations. It is up to the receiver to do his or her due diligence and inspect the e-mail, make sure the company address provided is legitimate, and answer the questions why no

From: Mr.Urbanski<info@helloaccessories.com.tr>

Subject: Re:Private Investor!

Hello,

I apologize for sending you this sensitive information via e-mail, Instead of a Certified mail/Post-mail. This is due to the urgency and importance of this information. I am a private business consultant based in Dublin (Ireland) I have the mandate of a highly placed Iraqi top government official in the Oil and Gas sector to source a trustworthy and reliable individual whom he can place a huge sum for management, either in an existing establishment or other venture to be undertaken at your discretion.

This amount is an over-invoiced contract bills awarded to some foreign firm by The Iraq National Oil Company (INOC). The actual contract bill has been paid out already leaving the aforementioned sum. I'm seeking your honest and sincere participation in this venture. Hence; all legal documents will be prepared in your name as the last contractor whose fund is yet to be claimed. You will not be breaching any law or see yourself at any risk if you accept this proposal and willing to work with TRUST. All that we require is your TRUST and ability to receive the funds and invest it in profitable ventures.

This project is based on Trust, confidentiality and sincerity of purpose in order to have an acceptable meeting of the minds. Details of this will be made clear as you respond to this letter. In line with this I crave your indulgence to treat this letter with utmost seriousness and confidentiality trusting that this will be the beginning of a long lasting business relationship between us.

Thanks

Mr. K. Urbanski

Figure 33.4 Investment-related phishing example.

return phone number was provided and why he or she was not directly referenced by name in the salutation. Other warning signs are as follows:

- Why does the "To" line on the e-mail not have my actual name and e-mail address?
- If I hold my cursor over the link provided (but do not click on it) why does it show it being redirected and the information does not contain the name of the supposed sending organization?
- Does the receiver actually have an account with the sending organization?
- Why is the e-mail crudely composed?

A good tactic for all to use upon the receipt of an unsolicited e-mail is to type the information into the search section of their browsers.

From:	Thai Lottery Draw dcollin1@tcd.ie
To:	Undisclosed recipients:
Subject:	Hearty Congratulation

WINNING NOTIFICATION:

We wish to congratulate and inform you on the selection of cash prize $1,400,000.00 (United State Dollars) held on the 30th June 2015 in Bangkok,Thailand.

You have therefore been approvad to claim a total sum of 1.4 Million Dollars,(One Million and Four Hundred Thousand United State Dollars) in cash.

For due processing of your winning claim,please contact the Fiduciary Agent Information Officer Mr. Charn Luchai who has been assigned to assist you. You are to contact him with the following details for the release of your winnings.

Agent Name: Mr. Charn Luchai
Email: mrcharn.luchai@yandex.com

Contact her, please provide him with the following Requirements below

Claims Requirements:
1.Name in full---------------------
2.Address--------------------------
3.Nationality----------------------
4.Age-----------------------------
5.Occupation-----------------------
6.Sex ----------------------------
7.Phone/Fax------------------------
8.Present Country------------------

Accept my hearty congratulations once again!

Regards

Mr. Vanvilai Chong.

Figure 33.5 Lottery-related phishing example

An e-mail was received from what the receiver believed to be the company used to make certain payments. The main focus of the e-mail informs the receiver the sending company needs to verify the recipient's e-mail and personal information for Pay Buddy. Upon receipt, the e-mail is professional looking in nature and the coloring looks like that used on the official website of Pay Buddy.

By typing "Pay Buddy information update scam" into the search line, results will be returned from several professional scam tracking organizations warning of a potential fraud. Additionally, one of the results will be from the actual organization detailing how its name has been used to defraud its customers. Internet searches are a great tool when suspicion is raised on e-mail phishing attempts.

From a business standpoint, managers and owners need to be aware of the threats present as a result of phishing. They themselves can respond to one of the many phishing expeditions used by those looking to commit fraud. Additionally, associates working within the organization can be the target of a phishing attempt and expose office computers to an unauthorized invasion and the downloading of malware/spyware.

Spoofing

Spoofing is a fraud in which the recipient receives an unsolicited e-mail from a trusted source. This source can be an individual the recipient has traded e-mails with on a few occasions or one where there is routine contact. The goal of those sending a spoofing e-mail is to have the recipient believe it was sent from a trusted source so that he or she will not think twice about complying with the request. Many spoofing e-mails ask the recipient to visit a certain website or click on the link provided to watch an "amazing" video.

If the recipient does as desired and clicks on the link provided, the recipient is opening up a computer and network to unauthorized downloading of malicious software. The goal is to get the target to unknowingly download malware/spyware software onto the computer or system.

The trick that makes spoofing successful is that it appears the recipient has received an e-mail from someone he or she has exchanged e-mails with previously. The sender hopes the recipient recognizes the name of the proposed sender and does not look at the entire directory information.

The secret to recognizing a possible spoofing e-mail is in the "From" line. A legitimate e-mail will contain the name of the sender, followed by the actual return e-mail address. With a spoofed e-mail, the "From" line does have the name of the sender, but what follows the sender's name is not the actual return e-mail address. For example, a typical normal e-mail received from a trusted friend will look as follows:

From: John Doe <johndoe21@gmail.com>

With a spoofed e-mail, the "From" line could look as follows:

From: John Doe <nickowen.latent@btconnect.com>

At first glance, the receiver recognizes the name of the sender. In order to protect themselves from becoming victims of a spoofing scam, e-mail recipients need to look at the entire "From" line information. Is the e-mail address that follows the sender's name the true address of a known individual? If not, the requests of the e-mail should not be followed.

Another clue to look for in a suspected spoofed e-mail is the content. When corresponding with a known individual via e-mail, some type of written conversation takes place. With many spoofing e-mails, the recipient is directed to check out the link provided. In order to add legitimacy to the request, the subject line of the spoofing attempt also provides a clue. Some examples of subject line spoofing attempts are as follows:

- A Perfect Site for You
- A Perfect Site for (the receiver's name is inserted here)
- Check Out This Video
- If You Love Dogs, Watch This
- The Perfect Football Catch

The goal of those sending a spoofing e-mail is to have the receiver believe it was received from a trusted source and follow the instructions. If the receiver clicks on the link provided, he or she is opening the computer or office network to unauthorized downloading of malicious software.

From a system security standpoint, business owners and managers need to be aware of how spoofing takes place and make this information part of their associate fraud awareness program.

Smishing

Smishing is a fraud attempt that is like phishing, but takes place via a cell phone. Smishing is a combination of a phishing attempt while using short message service (SMS) or what is referred to as texting. As the popularity of text messaging increases along with the growth of a younger generation in the workforce, smishing is a serious threat to individuals and business operations.

The goal of those looking to commit fraud through smishing is to gain access to the cell phone of the receiver. The hope is that personal and business-related financial information is stored in the many phone apps. Additionally, individuals gaining access to the internal information of a victim's cell phone can also obtain the directory contact list. This information is used for future smishing attempts. The contact information can also be used as part of vishing fraud, which is discussed later in this chapter.

With smishing, the cell phone user receives a text message from what appears to be a known and trusted party. Popular subjects of smishing attempts use the names of large financial institutions, credit card companies, cable providers, etc. The goal of the text message is to have the receiver believe there could be an issue with one of his or her accounts and follow the instructions provided. The text messages received as part of a smishing attempt can range from a request to call back a certain number or to click on a link provided.

With the callback process, a text message is receive that attracts attention:

4807970000@verizon.net
(Contact Card Services at Bank of America) Call (xxx) xxx-xxx

With the smishing text message referenced, the first line contains the actual phone number of the receiver along with carrier information. The second line is the bait used to attract the recipient's attention. Because the receiver is a customer of the financial institution referenced, he or she could actually believe there is an issue with an account. Once the hook is set, the text receiver calls the number provided. Typically, the callback number goes to an automated answering machine where the caller is walked through a series of information requesting prompts.

The caller is informed that a bank debit card has been deactivated and that, by providing the requested information, the issue can be quickly resolved. Callers are prompted to enter their full name, card number, PIN, security code, and card expiration date. Once the requested information has been provided, the caller is advised that personal and account information has been verified and the card is now active. The caller goes about the day believing that a technical issue has been resolved, while the initiators of the smishing scam now have the information necessary to commit credit/debit card fraud. From a business perspective, associates falling victim to smishing scams can have a negative effect on business-related financial instruments. If the smishing target is led to believe there is an issue with a business-related credit/debit card, a possible response to the scam would be to provide vital financial information to the criminals initiating the fraud—basically placing business-related financial information in the hands of unscrupulous individuals.

Those committing smishing scams are not limited to using the bank credit/debit card scenario. Other successful smishing frauds have used the names of phone service providers, cable providers, local workout facilities, etc. As with many frauds, the bait information is open to the imagination of the sender. The end goal is to have the text message recipient or future smishing victim provide the requested information.

Smishing attempts also involve the bait text message that informs the receiver of an issue with financial accounts, credit card accounts, a cable provider, etc. Instead of providing a callback number, the target is provided with a link to click on. Once the target clicks on the link provided, he or she is taken to a prompt screen that requests the same type of personal and business information as with the callback number aspect.

An additional bonus for those committing a link-provided smishing scam is that they have the ability to download malicious software onto the cell phone of the targeted individual. Once installed, malware/spyware is used in the same manner and for the same purpose as the previously discussed computer-targeted scams.

In order for business managers and owners to avoid their financial and business-related information falling into the wrong hands, associates need to be educated on smishing frauds. If the associate believes there could be an issue with an account, he or she needs to use a directory assistance service and obtain a contact number for the bank, credit card provider, cable provider, etc. After obtaining a legitimate callback number, the associate can verify if there is an issue with the account in question.

Vishing

Vishing is like phishing and involves the use of the cell phone. Instead of sending a smishing text message informing the target of an issue with an account, the person answering the phone is spoken to directly. Like a smishing attempt, the caller is informed of an issue with a financial account (possible fraud detected, with a temporary hold placed for protection) and is asked to provide account-verifying information such as name, address, Social Security number, date of birth, etc. Once this personal information is provided, the target is informed he or she is the correct individual to resolve the problem.

Once the information is verified, the target is asked to provide account holder information for the issue in question. Typically, the issue revolves around a credit/debit card (personal or business). In order for the target to have the temporary hold removed from the credit/debit card, the target has to provide the correct account holder information. The target has no idea the person on the phone has no clue of the actual account holder information. On the other hand, the caller is hoping to receive true and accurate account holder information.

The target is asked to provide the complete name on the card in question, account number, expiration date, PIN if a debit card, and card security code. Once this information is provided and the target has been verified as the actual card holder, the target is informed the account hold has been lifted. To add legitimacy to the overall process and decrease suspicion, the target is advised that unauthorized transactions were prevented as a result of his or her providing the proper account holder information.

From a business perspective, vishing can be an issue if the target believes there is a problem with a company-provided credit/debit card. All associates have to be made aware of vishing frauds and the need to protect company-sensitive financial information.

Spear Phishing

In the business world, owners, managers, and security/loss prevention personnel need to be aware of what is referred to as spear phishing. Like phishing and using characteristics of spoofing, a specific organization is the target. Recipients of spear phishing unsolicited e-mails work for the targeted business. The spear phishing target receives an e-mail that he or she believes is from a known individual or organization. To add credibility to the attempt, the e-mail receiver is addressed by name, work title, and organization of employment.

Based on the nature of the business operation, the e-mail will be tailored specifically to a potential operational need. If Sally Target works as a payroll processing manager for a third-party payroll service, the sender of the spear phishing e-mail will offer new and improved data processing software. Sally Target, payroll processing manager for Pay Me Corporation, will receive an e-mail from the Super Software Company. The e-mail is professional looking in nature and will contain company-related pictures and wording so that the recipient will believe she is working with a legitimate organization. Spear phishing senders will also hijack the name and e-mail background of a legitimate organization Sally has worked with in the past. If Sally Target has worked with Super Software Company in the past, she will be led to believe she has been contacted by Super Software.

Once convinced she is being offered the ability to review a new version of payroll processing software, Sally clicks on the link provided. Instead of going to the legitimate website of a known organization, Sally is redirected to a bogus site. The bogus website has the appearance of the legitimate organization and allows Sally to view the many services offered to Pay Me Corporation. The goal is not to add Sally as a new customer, but to download unauthorized and malicious software onto her computer and office system.

Once inside the computer system of the targeted organization, the e-mailers have access to the personal information of company officers, trade secrets, and financial information. Additionally, the breach will allow those initiating the fraud to continue with a tactic known as whaling.

Whaling

Instead of Sally Target at the lower level of the organization, upper level individuals can become the victim of what is referred to as whaling. Whaling follows the same format as spear phishing, with the intent to target individuals at the upper end of the organization.

Using the spear phishing tactic of contacting Sally Target, the goal is to gain access to the internal databases of a specific organization. Once unauthorized access has been gained, the goal is to obtain the names and contact information of company executives—the large phish or whales of the organization.

Once the desired contact information of the company whales is obtained, one or more of these individuals are contacted through a spear phishing type of scam: The targeted whale receives an e-mail from a source believed to be trustworthy (the same trusted source scam as used with Sally Target and the Super Software Company).

If the whaling scam is successful and the company executive takes the bait, those initiating the fraud will attempt to gain access to the organization's internal computer system. If successful, the whaling victim is exposing the organization's internal data to untrustworthy outside sources. The sought after data could be the following:

- Detailed personal information on the company executive and his or her family members (ideal information for those looking to commit identity theft and identity fraud)
- Personal financial information of the company executive
- Business-related financial information of the company (Many con artists figure those at the top levels of the organization could have information on company-related financial accounts and credit data they could not access at the lower employee levels of the business.)
- Company-related trade secrets, research and development information, etc.

In order for an organization to avoid becoming a victim of spear phishing or whaling, it is vital that companies initiate some type of fraud/security awareness training. No matter the level of the individual in the organization, all need to attend regular fraud awareness identification and prevention training. From a spear phishing and whaling standpoint, all levels of employees need to be sure to conduct proper due diligence on e-mails received from sources believed to be trustworthy:

- Do not take an unsolicited e-mail from a vendor source at face value.
- Use caution for e-mails sent from vendor sources that do not contain a contact number of the sender.
- Does the e-mail address on the sender line contain the necessary wording? A typical e-mail sent from the Pay Me Corporation will contain some version of the company name in the sender address: BillyBudget@Paymecorp.com—not BillyBudget@thisisasccam.com.
- After receiving an e-mail from a vendor source, research the actual company name used prior to complying with the requests of the initial message. Conduct an independent Internet search on the company name. Look up the website of Pay Me Corporation.
- Ensure that Pay Me Corporation provides the services offered through the initial e-mail.
- Use extreme caution prior to clicking on links or attachments contained in any unsolicited e-mail.

Raising Awareness of Unsolicited E-Mails and Texts

As the world of technology increases and becomes a larger part of our daily lives and business operations, it is vital that an education process takes place on how simplicity can lead to fraud. As the experts at Microsoft, Google, Verizon, etc. sit around and develop the next big item in technology, criminal elements are also sitting around because they have the luxury of time and targeting people at their leisure. They also have time to sit around and use technology to target the largest number of people and businesses possible—for example, with old-fashioned advanced-fee fraud letters:

> Dear Friend,
> I am Mr. Ma Guang Lu the Head of Accounting Audit Department of BANK OF CHINA in Hong Kong. In my department, I discovered a sum of $17.5 Million In an account that belongs to one of our foreign deceased customers, a billionaire Business Mogul Late Mr. Moises Saba Masri, a Jew from Mexico who was a victim of a helicopter crash since 2006 resulting to his death and his family members.
>
> And nobody has come forth to our bank for the funds claims since 2006. My Good friend I want to let you know that I have the entire legal document for us to win this transaction if you provide me the following information below to
>
> 1. Full Name:
> 2. Your Telephone Number:
> 3. Your Contact Address:
> 4. Age:
> 5. Core Job/Occupation:
>
> I will furnish you with more information on this business transaction, once I get fill back from you.
> Regards
> Mr. Lu

Before technology gave us the ability to send mass e-mails, people looking to commit fraud were restricted to contacting targets via the US Postal Service. Advanced-fee fraud letters, as the one previously detailed, were placed in an envelope and individually mailed. It took time to hand-address each letter and the related envelopes, as well as gather the names and addresses of intended targets.

With the current ability to obtain large amounts of mass marketing e-mail addresses, those looking to commit advanced-fee frauds and other types of frauds can target a large audience with minimal effort. Various programs allow senders to e-mail the same information to thousands of recipients, while having each target receive the contact message in a more personal manner. An unsolicited e-mail addressed to Mr. John Doe will attract greater attention than one addressed to "Recipient."

Associates working in any business, large or small, need to be made aware of the delivery methods used to initiate contact for fraudulent purposes. This education process has to include protecting an employee's personal computer and cell phone, as well as work phones and computers. Even though an employee is contacted through an unsolicited e-mail received in a personal account, work-related information and computer systems could be at risk generated from a cross-contamination effect between a personal and business computer. In an effort to identity the potential threat for cross contamination, these questions need to be asked:

- Is the employee checking personal e-mail from an office computer?
- Is the employee accessing personal social media accounts from an office computer?
- Is the employee checking a business e-mail account from a personal computer?
- If the employee is checking personal e-mail from a personal computer, has any work-related business been conducted with this personal computer?
- Is the employee receiving unsolicited text messages on a personal cell phone?
- Is the employee receiving unsolicited text messages on a business cell phone?
- What business-related information is contained on an employee's personal cell phone?
- What text messages are employees responding to from their work-related cell phones?

When looking at these questions, it is an easy process to see where a cross-contamination effect could take place. All an unsuspecting employee needs to do is respond to a phishing e-mail on a personal computer. If the phishing e-mail is successful, the personal computer is infected with malicious software. Once the personal computer is infected, all the employee has to do is access a work-related e-mail account or other company databases from the personal computer. Like a flu virus, the contamination is spread.

No matter the nature of the device used to respond to unsolicited e-mails and text messages, caution needs to take place on protecting work-related information and financial data. In order to avoid a business operation falling victim to phishing, spoofing, smishing, and vishing frauds, associate education and awareness are vital for future protection and success.

If It Sounds Too Good to Be True, IT IS

In addition to the account-related phishing scams previously discussed, recipients are enticed by being provided the unique opportunity to get something for nothing. The success of many phishing types of e-mails and texting scams is based on the prospect of getting something for nothing or being presented with an offer that is unique to the targeted individual. One issue many recipients of unsolicited e-mails fail to understand is that the "unique" offer has been made to thousands of others. Their individual solicitation is not unique to them. When presented with a promising offer of something for nothing, past fraud victims did not look beyond the obvious to answer the question, "Why was I selected out of millions of individuals?"

Random individuals do not win lotteries and contests they never entered. People with a vast amount of wealth do not simply collect random e-mail addresses, place this information into a database, and randomly select a winner to receive large amounts of cash or other expensive prizes.

For many, the concept of others being taken in by successful computer-based frauds is beyond their level of belief. A large percentage of society will look at the offer presented and immediately go about other business—basically not taking the bait and exposing personal and work computer systems to unauthorized access from those looking to commit fraud.

Unfortunately, 100% of the population cannot see a potential scam as a fraud attempt. The issue for business owners and managers is to accept the fact of naïve associates within their workforce. Accepting this fact, it is imperative that fraud awareness education and training programs be presented in the simplest terms. What might seem common knowledge to many is an open fraud window for some.

Mobile App Fraud

More and more people are using their mobile phones for recreational purposes—gaming, making reservations, placing orders, etc. With the growing popularity of mobile devices also comes the use of apps. Apps are typically downloaded from various company websites and can be used for many purposes:

- Having a flashlight on your phone
- Preordering a meal from a local restaurant
- Making a dinner reservation
- Scheduling a pickup from a ride-sharing company
- Ordering a taxi pickup
- Playing a game
- Finding directions
- Checking the local weather

As time goes by there will be more and more apps available for the mobile device users. Additionally, a majority of the apps available are free to the consumer and can be downloaded from various locations. Unfortunately, as with any type of service provided, there is an avenue for fraud with mobile device apps.

For those looking to commit various types of the fraud discussed in this text, there is a need to gain access to electronic devices for the purpose of gathering information. The information can be both personal and business related. Based on the information gathered, it can be used to commit identity fraud, financial crimes, business-related fraud, etc.

A popular avenue that can be used to collect the desired information is to gain unauthorized access to an unsuspecting individual's mobile device. As discussed with successful smishing attempts, the potential for cross-contamination between personal and business devices is a given. A personal cell phone breach can lead to the unauthorized access of the victim's business-related computer network. Once inside the business network, those looking to commit fraudulent activity have access to a wealth of information.

Before, those looking to take this path into the target's business network had to rely on successful smishing attempts. Due to the growing popularity of mobile device apps, criminals now have another avenue. Instead of sending a smishing e-mail, those looking to commit fraud can wait for the mobile device user to initiate the process, which begins with the mobile device user downloading an infected app.

When the target downloads an infected app, it is not necessary to wait for the target to click on the attached link in a smishing e-mail. Once the infected app is installed in the mobile device, outside individuals now have access to the inner workings of the device. Whatever is possible with the downloading of malicious software through smishing is now possible with an infected app. The app is bringing the malicious software to the mobile device.

Prior to the downloading of any mobile device app, it is up to the user to conduct some type of due diligence, making sure the app is coming from a trusted source. The mobile device user also needs to conduct an Internet search for any negative information available on a specific app.

From a business perspective, it is necessary to include mobile device app fraud in theft/fraud awareness and prevention training. Associates need to be aware of app fraud in order to protect their personal and business mobile devices.

Chapter 34

Technology-Based Fraud

Introduction

Computers, the Internet, e-mail messaging, text messaging, etc. are all technology-based tools that are vital to success in the workplace. The increase in technology has allowed for business to be conducted faster across the country and around the world. Communication with associates in the next cubicle or in a foreign land is almost instantaneous. Retailers are no longer restricted to making sales to customers visiting their brick and mortar establishments. Online shopping has become the preferred method for many consumers, saving retailers money in renting retail space and paying additional sales associates.

In the business environment of today, technology drives the train. It is a process accepted by many and is well known by the younger generation of workers. Employees hired today were born into a world of Internet access, carrying a phone in a pocket or purse, and a wealth of information at their fingertips. Advanced technology is all that is understood by the younger generation of today and for the future of all people born into this world.

In the business environment, owners, managers, and security personnel have to use technology for job and organizational success and growth. These same individuals also have to look at technology as a major avenue for fraud. As previously referenced, fraud attempts no longer arrive through the US mail service. Targets are approached via technology, which can expose business information and financial data to those looking to commit fraud. It is vital for all to understand the threat avenues and close these routes of approach.

Unauthorized Access to Company E-Mail Databases

Numerous organizations maintain countless databases of information that contain employee information, client information, sales data, consumer financial transaction history, etc. As long as this information remains within the walls of the business, as stated in the movie, *A Christmas Story*, "All is right with the world." If, for some reason, there is a breach into the systems where this information is stored, the targeted company has opened the door to all types of potential issues:

- Having personal employee information placed in the hands of those looking to commit identity fraud
- Allowing unauthorized individuals access to company financial information
- Having personal financial information of past customers fall into the hands of those looking to commit identity fraud (This same consumer information can also be used to commit credit/debit card fraud.)
- Having private vendor information fall into the hands of those looking to commit fraud using the names and information of trusted vendors
- Having this vendor information used against the targeted organization for fraudulent purposes (discussed later in this chapter)
- Exposing company trade secrets
- Exposing information about projects in the research and development phase that can be used by rival organizations

Once unauthorized individuals gain access to the internal information retained within the walls of a targeted business, the threat potential is extremely broad. The aforementioned potential issues that can result from allowing unauthorized access into the databases of any organization are unlimited. What is listed are popular reasons why organizational database information is desired, but additional reasons can be based on the specific operational aspects of a company in question.

From a fraud perspective, the goal is to protect the personal information of employees, customers, vendors, etc. It is also vital to ensure that all company-related financial information is protected.

If a data breach takes place at a targeted organization, the negative outcomes are numerous. The information desired and how it is used are based on the imaginations of those looking to commit fraud. Some of the potential outcomes and ramifications are as follows:

- A data breach can result in unauthorized access to customer financial information. Unsuspecting consumers can become victims of identity theft and fraud. From a company perspective, there is a potential for future lawsuits from individuals who had their personal information accessed by unauthorized individuals. Also, the targeted company has created additional expenses in identifying and closing the breach. These expenses are related to assuring past and previous customers that their information will be protected, investing in restoring the good name of the business operation, and offering former customers free access to identity theft protection services.

- The same threat level holds true if internal company records are the target. If unauthorized access is made to the employee database, current and past associates are now potential targets for identity theft and other financial fraud. From a public relations perspective, the internal path that led to the breach can be retained in house. However, exposure still exists from potential lawsuits and the expense of providing identity theft protection services.
- Individuals looking to obtain the personal information of company associates can also find a gold mine of information in the databases of current and past vendors. Most internal vendor accounts contain detailed personal and business information, as well as electronic payment data. This information refers to the specific bank accounts that are related to a specific vendor and the account numbers required for electronic financial transactions to take place. Additionally, the vendor account information can be used to commit business identity theft [1].
- Business identity theft is defined as taking over the name of a good business operation for the purpose of opening unauthorized credit accounts and then draining the assets from these accounts. Once the account is overdrawn, the creditors come looking to the legitimate business for payment [2]. Within the computer systems of most business operations is a wealth of information on the business, its officers, financial information, etc. Once unauthorized access is obtained, the business's associates, corporate officers, and name become potential identity theft victims.
- For some in the business community, it is a cutthroat world. With the sometimes high costs associated with research and development of new product lines, it is possible competitors are looking for shortcuts. As with the names and account information located within the systems of business operations, data on new product development are also available. This information in the hands of competitors can lay waste to years of research and cost-related development if the initiating business operation is beaten to the open market.

The goal of those looking to gain unauthorized access to the computer systems of a targeted business will vary based on the type of operation and the intent of the criminal elements. The information previously discussed is based on known breaches of victim businesses over the years. As time goes forward, other business operations will be the victims of a data breach and the information sought will be based on the fraud-related needs of those attempting to gain unauthorized access.

In order to put as many barriers in place to prevent a future data breach, it is vital that security and loss prevention personnel and business owners and managers develop detailed fraud awareness and prevention training programs. These educational programs need to be based on the years of knowledge of in-house industry (security) personnel and the fraud-related discussion throughout Section V of this text.

Need to Protect Vendor History Transactions and Vendor Identities (Payment Redirect Fraud)

As previously discussed, many businesses have been the target of those looking to gain access to internal computer systems. A treasure trove of information resides in the company's internal records system:

- Internal employee roster and related e-mail addresses
- Internal roster for vendor names and contact information
- Past vendor payment history and methods of paying for services rendered

Individuals successfully hacking into the internal computer system of a targeted organization have used the internal records information to commit various types of vendor-related fraud. All that is needed is the current vendor names, accounts payable information, and company employee e-mail data and the related job functions within the organization. With this information, individuals outside the organization can commit payment redirect fraud.

In one scenario, an associate working in the Accounts Payable Department of the targeted organization receives an e-mail from his or her boss or someone higher up in the company. In the e-mail the associate is instructed to change the manner in which a specific vendor payment is made. Instead of making the upcoming payment through a mailed check or direct deposit, the Accounts Payable associate is instructed to conduct the transaction via a wire transfer. The wire transfer instructions are included within the e-mail.

The employee in the Accounts Payable Department is asked to make a one-time change in policy for making the payment due to a specific vendor/supplier. In order to avoid some suspicion of the request, the employee is the associate who manages the monetary account for the vendor/supplier in question.

The payment e-mail request from a supervisor or high-level company executive contains exact payment instructions. These instructions include the payment amount, the person to receive the wire transfer and the location to send the money. An employee who believes the e-mail request on face value will most likely comply with it. Complying with the payment request results in money sent via a wire transfer falling into the hands of those committing what is referred to as payment redirect fraud.

As a result of the Accounts Payable employee conducting the wire transfer, the organization and vendor become victims of fraud. The organization suffers a loss of the payment sent via the wire transfer and the vendor/supplier does not receive money. From an employee perspective, the e-mail appeared to come from a supervisor or company executive. The only thing suspicious was an e-mail request for a one-time change in policy.

In another variation of a payment redirect fraud the associate in Accounts Payable is contacted by the actual vendor/supplier that is due payment. As with the first version, the employee in question is the account manager for the vendor/supplier. Typical correspondence between the employee and vendor/supplier takes place via e-mail.

The Accounts Payable associate is informed, via e-mail, not to make the upcoming payment to a specific vendor/supplier as in previous transactions. The employee is asked to wire-transfer the funds to a third party. The e-mail from the vendor/supplier also provides the employee with the name of the receiving individual.

Once the wire transfer is completed, the associate believes he or she has followed the vendor's instructions. Unfortunately, the funds sent as part of the wire transfer did not go to the specific vendor. Waiting to receive the wire transfer is the individual committing the payment redirect fraud.

As part of an ongoing fraud awareness and prevention program, associates need to be educated on the types of frauds related to a data breach and the suspicious activity to look out for. From a theft/fraud prevention perspective, Accounts Payable associates need to add a verbal verification step to any e-mail requests for changes in vendor/supplier payment procedures.

As previously referenced, those looking to commit fraud are not going to announce success once they have obtained the desired internal company information. These individuals will use one of the various tools available to successfully breach the internal systems of a targeted organization. Once inside, they will collect the desired information and then select the date and time to initiate the payment redirect fraud. Once the fraud has been discovered, company executives and security personnel will realize their organization has suffered a data breach. Now the process begins to identify the path of the breach and shut it down.

Hijacking Legitimate Websites

With many e-mail fraud scams, individuals will cut and paste pictures and other information from the legitimate website of an organization. This is conducted to add validity to the scam and have the targeted individual believe he or she is working with associates of the organization they are purporting to represent.

In an effort to add more validity to certain scams, individuals are creating new websites for existing organizations. A majority of the pictures and discussion used in the counterfeit website comes from cutting and pasting from the actual website. Once this process is complete, the fraud of website hijacking has begun. The purpose is to use a variation of the services offered by the targeted organization to defraud others. Many of the individuals who become victims of the frauds are contacted through unsolicited phishing e-mails.

A very popular phishing scam is to offer individuals the opportunity to make money by becoming mystery shoppers [3]. The targeted individuals are contacted through an unsolicited e-mail, with the sender claiming to represent an actual organization, which is one of many companies that provide mystery shopping services for retailers across the country.

Within the initial and subsequent e-mails are wording and pictures from the actual website of the legitimate mystery shopping company. Attached to the e-mails is also a link to the website of the mystery shopping company; any recipient clicking on the link will be redirected to a website containing all of the bells and whistles of the legitimate website of the legitimate organization. The two websites, at times, look exactly the same in terms of wording, services provided, coloring, background pictures, etc.

On face value, the unsolicited e-mail recipient believes representatives of the actual organization have offering him or her a job. The only differences are the following:

- Mystery shoppers hired by legitimate organizations actually go through a training process.
- There is also an actual job application process, as well as applicant interviews.
- With legitimate mystery shopping organizations, their websites will advertise they are always looking to hire shoppers. Individuals visiting the mystery shopping companies' websites are encouraged to click on the applicant link to begin the application, interview, hiring, and training processes.
- With those looking to commit fraud as part of a mystery shopping scam, contacted individuals are asked to provide some personal information. This information is usually name, address, contact phone numbers, e-mail address, etc. Once the basic personal information is provided, they are then "hired" as "official" mystery shoppers.

Individuals hired as mystery shoppers by the counterfeit operators place belief in a process that is not typical to a normal job application, interview, and training procedure for almost any new job. Another bright red flag is randomly being offered a job through an unsolicited e-mail and being immediately hired once the necessary personal information has been provided. For the success of frauds of this nature, those sending the initial contact e-mails are banking on gullibility.

A popular scenario with the phony mystery shopping scam is to have the newly hired shoppers conduct a transaction at a money wiring service location. The shopper is given the name and address of a legitimate money wiring location and is sent a professional looking evaluation survey that is to be completed after the money wiring transaction has been completed. The shopper is mailed a professional looking cashier's check that is made out in the name of the mystery shopper. He or she is asked to deposit the check into a personal bank account and immediately withdraw a large portion of the check amount to be sent via a wire transfer. Usually, the check is around $2,000. The shopper is asked to wire-transfer $1,700 and keep the remaining

$300. (Check and payment amounts vary based on who is conducting the scam.) After the wire transfer is complete, the shopper completes the evaluation survey and mails it to an address provided. The shopper thinks he or she made an easy $300, until the cashier's check is returned a few days later as being counterfeit. Instead of making a $300 profit, the mystery shopper is out the $1,700 sent via a wire transfer.

The only monetary victim of the mystery shopping scam is the individual who removed money from a personal bank account and sent it via wire transfer to an unknown third party. Individuals initiating this type of fraud will contact numerous targets, using the legitimate company name and website of the legitimate mystery shopping company. As time goes by, more and more individuals are duped into becoming mystery shoppers.

Individuals who were victimized and are out a large amount of money will eventually contact the legitimate mystery shopping organization for restitution. Outside of having its website and company information used as part of a scam, the legitimate organization has committed no crime. However, its operation and reputation have now become victims.

The details of the mystery shopping scam are provided to show the reader the complexity of website hijacking for fraudulent purposes. When discussing the potential for organizations to become the victim of website hijacking, it is one example of many. Based on the needs and imagination of those looking to commit this type of fraud, the variations can be many. Basically stated: no legitimate business operation is immune.

Organizations looking to prevent their good name from being used for fraudulent purposes have to be proactive in ensuring there is no copycat information on the Internet. Routine checks need to be made via Internet searches on the company name, names of company officers, services offered, etc. These searches are vital to ensure a company name is not being used for fraudulent purposes and that website search results lead only to the website of the legitimate organization.

Endnotes

1. Business identity theft works in the same manner as with the individual. Instead of opening up bank and credit accounts in the name of an unsuspecting person, lines of credit and other financial accounts are opened in the name of the unsuspecting business (vendor).
2. As with individual identity theft, the victim is not responsible for the money lost due to fraudulent activity. However, the individual or business is burdened with a large cost and time commitment attempting to prove they did not open the accounts in question.
3. Mystery shoppers are hired by third-party organizations for the purpose of conducting transactions at the retail locations for the parent company. In order to test customer service standards, store cleanliness, associate professionalism, etc., shoppers are paid to conduct transactions for the parent company. The shoppers are not employed by the parent company, but by those organizations specializing in mystery shopping. Once the transactions are complete, a report is sent back to the parent organization detailing the customer service aspect it wanted evaluated by a third party.

Chapter 35

Understanding and Preventing Data Breaches

Introduction

Question: How does an organization prevent a data breach?
Answer: Stop using computers as part of the daily operation and records-storing processes.

This question is one that is on the minds of many individuals. The answer, although effective, is not possible. We are a society that is technology driven and one that relies on the process more and more each day.

It is becoming commonplace to report in newspapers and on the news that another organization has been the victim of a data breach. The first question on everyone's mind is, "How did this happen?"

- What technology and tools were used to gain access to a large corporate or government organization?
- Should they not have had the necessary firewalls in place to prevent such a breach or cyber attack?
- If so, are there activities conducted within the daily operations of the business or government office that are opening a window of opportunity?

Unfortunately, many people only hear of the data breach incidents that make national news—for example, the large retail organization or a government agency that houses thousands of employee records. What is not commonly known among the smaller business operators and consumers is the data breaches that take place, but are not reported on the national or local news. According to the latest report from the Identity Theft Resource Center, there were 700 reported data breach incidents in 2015 [1]. These 400 known incidents discuss breaches that occurred at the small business operation, up to the large cases that gain media attention. According to this report the number of internal records exposed, as a result of the breaches, range from a few hundred up to millions. Exposure of a record relates to individual information that was in the database. Obtaining the name, address, Social Security number, date of birth, etc. of one person counts as an exposure.

Another point to consider is how many incidents were not reported. Companies might choose to keep a breach into their computer systems private, hoping to avoid damage to their reputation. Incidents might also go unreported because those working within the business operation simply do not know a breach took place.

With many successful data breaches, a lot of the information concerning the cause is retained within the company walls. No one wants to tell others that someone or some procedural policy messed up. From a specific standpoint, this text was not written to discuss detailed computer security. Those looking for the data breach answer of "why" need to locate the end investigative results of past victim organizations that were developed by individuals with a unique understanding of the organization and the subsequent computer operations analysis.

When discussing the crime of data breaches for the purposes of this text, the goal is to provide an understanding of what the end results of a data breach could be and to shine a light on what could cause an "open window."

One of the main goals of those looking to gain access to the internal customer records of government and retail organizations is to commit various types of fraud—basically, to use the personal and financial information of current and past employees and previous customers to commit identity theft and other types of financial fraud. When a major retailer is attacked, there is a wealth of information on customer names, along with credit/debit card data. When the files of a large government office are attacked, there is a wealth of information on previous and current employees. This information includes names, addresses, dates of birth, Social Security numbers, etc. This is all information that can be used to assume the identity of another.

Based on the unique operation of some specific organizations, internal customer information can also be used for extortion purposes. For married and seriously dating individuals, there are companies that offer confidential services where clients can meet others online for the purpose of infidelity. Consumers using these types of services pay a fee and create a profile for other clients to view. What happens after that, only the clients know.

From a data breach perspective, these internal client databases of information not only provide an avenue for possible identity theft. The internal information can also be used to extort money from the parent organization or the client base. A website infidelity operation that promises confidentiality does not want its customer base to know outside sources have gained access to private internal records.

Additionally, the clients of one of these operations do not want their names associated with a company specializing in infidelity. If a data breach takes place [2] at one of these operations, current clients can be contacted by outside individuals for the purpose of extorting money from the potentially cheating customer. Many people will go through extreme measures to keep incidents of infidelity from their spouses.

No matter what services are provided by the organization, large or small, they all contain some type of internal database of consumer information. This information can be both personal and financial in nature. This is information no one wants in the hands of those looking to commit fraud.

Outside Hackers versus Internal Ignorance (Both a Threat to Internal Company Information and Data)

Individuals looking to gain access to the employee and customer databases of information, within any sized business operation, understand that certain internal operations and controls of associate actions can open windows to fraudulent activity. Hackers understand that a large majority of companies have to access the Internet in order to conduct business. This business activity includes:

- Making product purchases online
- Conducting product searches online
- Making vendor payments online
- Conducting competition searches
- Creating and maintaining a company website
- Selling products through the company website
- Conducting new-associate hiring activities via the company website
- Receiving and sending e-mails

These online activities are just a few of the many legitimate reasons company associates need to access the Internet to complete their daily job functions. Out of all of the legitimate reasons listed for online activity for a business operation, one that provides open windows is the need to receive and send e-mails. As previously discussed, the receipt of and then acting on unsolicited e-mails provides an open window for many phishing and other fraud-related activities.

In addition to associates having to go online for normal business activity, there are other areas where access to the Internet can be a catalyst for fraud:

- Associates accessing e-mail through their personal computers, where company-related information and business account data are stored
- Associates sending and receiving text messages on personal cell phones, where company-related information and business account data are stored

- Associates accessing social media websites while at work and using a company computer
- Associates accessing social media websites and using a business-related cell phone
- Associates accessing social media websites from a personal computer or cell phone where company-related information and business account information are stored

With all of the legitimate reasons for company associates to conduct business activity online and those listed as a possible catalyst for fraud, people looking to gain access to organizational databases are targeting the many open windows provided as a result of the need to go online. What the hackers are relying on is a certain level of associate-based ignorance of how daily online activities can lead to fraud. The main group of company associates that can provide the open windows for unauthorized access to the organization's databases are the younger technology users. These millennial individuals, coupled with their level of impatience, are two categories that provide a catalyst for fraud.

Younger Technology Users and Impatience as a Catalyst for Fraud

As previously discussed, many remember the "good old days," where computers were those rare tools located only in certain businesses, most communication took place over a landline telephone, and information came and went through the US Mail Service. Most company-retained customer records were retained as paper documents and stored in boxes somewhere on the property. Anyone looking to conduct an old-fashioned data breach had to actually gain unauthorized access to the company property, locate the storage area, and conduct a hand search of all of the paper documents. These old-fashioned data breaches could produce fruit, but were time consuming and risky. Most people who gained unauthorized access onto company property in those days were looking to steal valuable property, not personal customer information.

Fast forward to today: Very few business operations still retain customer data in boxes in the storage room. Prior to the use of the ever present credit card swiping machines, (Figure 35.1), all credit-based transactions took place using a sales slip (Figure 35.2) and a manual credit card impression machine (Figure 35.3). The customer name was handwritten onto the sales slip and then placed onto the manual credit card impression machine over the customer's credit card. The impression machine handle was moved from right to left and back to the right where an impression of the credit card number, expiration date, and customer name was imprinted onto the sales slip. At the end of the business day the store

Figure 35.1 Credit card swiping machine.

owner had to physically contact the financial institution related merchant provider [3] and provide the customer name, credit card information, and purchase amount. The store owner was then provided with an approval code that was written on the sales slip. After a few business days, the charged amount was deducted from the customer's credit account and deposited into the business owner's bank account. For records retention purposes, these credit card sales slips were retained in the storage room.

Today almost all credit/debit transaction activity takes place through register-based card swiping machines. The transactions are all processed electronically from the swiping machine, to the business merchant account, to the customer's credit card account, and back to the retailer's bank account. Instead of having to store all

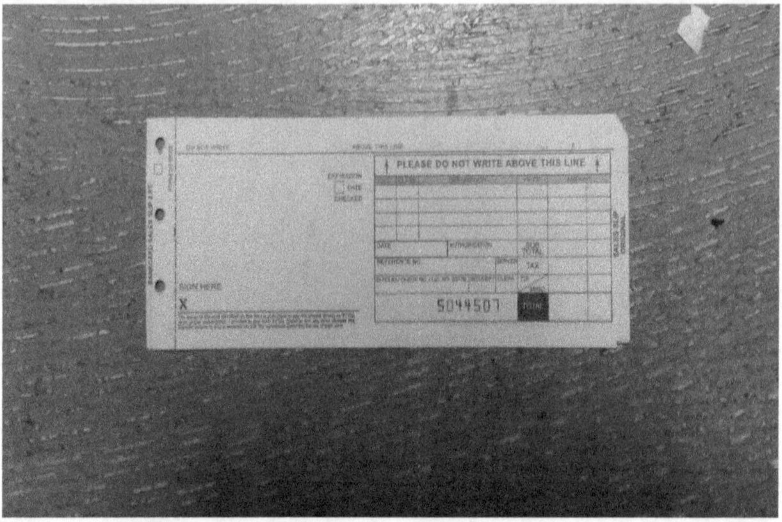

Figure 35.2 Credit card sales slip.

Figure 35.3 Manual credit card impression machine.

of the processed sales slips in the company basement, all transaction information is stored electronically within the databases of the specific organization.

The same holds true for employee personal information. Back in the good old days, all associate information was originally provided on paper documents and this information was stored in boxes in the storage room. With the reliance on technology and computers, all employee information is now retained in electronic databases.

Having customer data and financial information, as well as employee personal information, retained electronically in databases provides a target for those looking to commit all types of fraud. Many individuals looking to gain unauthorized access to organizational databases rely on the computer habits and sometimes the impatience of the younger generation.

The younger workers of today, or what many refer to as Millennials, only know a world of instant access. These individuals grew up online, communicate with their friends through social media, and have developed a trust in the Internet. This is not to say that all of these younger individuals believe the adage, "If it is on the Internet it has to be true." But what is true is that people tend to place a large amount of faith into a process they grew up with and use throughout their daily personal and business interactions.

One negative of growing up only knowing life transacting through the Internet and electronic communication is the speed at which this process takes place. Again, back in the good old days, a person would either make a phone call hoping the person they wanted to speak with was home or actually sit down and create a handwritten letter. If the individual he or she was calling was not at home to answer, the caller only hoped there was an answering machine present so a callback message could be left. If the person called did not have an answering machine, the caller had no choice but to call back later. With the process of actually mailing a handwritten letter, days and weeks could go by before a response was received. People communicating in that era understood the aspect of not having instantaneous contact with others.

From the perspective of Millennials, all they know is that all communication is instant—e-mail, texting, and social media communication. They ask the question: "What, exactly, is a handwritten letter?"

As discussed previously with phishing, spoofing, smishing, and vishing, targeted individuals are contacted via some type of electronic device and informed of an issue with some type of credit-related account. The goal of the person sending the unsolicited e-mail or text message is to have the recipient click on the link provided and supply the information requested electronically or directly after answering a vishing phone call.

Those used to a world of instant contact and feedback would rather fix the problem quickly and go about their day. If all a person knows is communicating, purchasing products, and setting up services electronically, why not respond to a request for information that was delivered through a system he or she has used and grown up to trust?

For many individuals who grew up outside the millennial age group, more caution might be raised after being contacted through a phishing, spoofing, smishing, or vishing attempt. Instead of clicking on the link provided or answering the caller's question by providing personal financial information, the proper choice would be to contact the legitimate questioning organization directly. Ideally, a targeted individual who receives a text message claiming an individual or a business debit card has been suspended will make a customer service phone call to resolve the issue. In order to ensure the integrity of the accounts and personal information in question, many will choose to wait for the next available operator. For those growing up and living in a world of instant communication and results, there is no time to wait for the next available operator.

This is where the resulting level of impatience comes into play. Living in a world of instant access, communication, and results creates an impatient individual who does not have time to wait for the next available operator. This level of impatience does provide a catalyst for fraud.

Millennials Quitting over Not Being Able to Access Social Media While at Work

A Philadelphia "Three on Your Side" news report [4] recently discussed an issue that was shocking for some and understandable for others. A survey of Millennials took place where they were asked about using social media in the workplace. A whopping 60% of those aged 18 to 34 stated they would quit their job if not allowed to use social media while at work.

The younger workers of today believe their employers should allow them to access social media accounts and conduct other private activities while on the job. This includes texting friends, checking their private e-mail accounts, using picture-sharing websites, etc. Millennials are so used to being connected 24/7 that many share a belief there should not be a separation between their contact with friends at home or in the office.

One positive aspect for the younger generation and having a desire to conduct personal communication activities in the office is their knowledge of technology. Being raised on technology, Millennials can easily access new technology and programs that might drive older office workers, managers, and owners crazy. Their individual knowledge of and ease working with technology-driven systems makes them an asset to the workforce. This asset will most likely be a factor in allowing younger workers the ability to access social media accounts from the workplace.

From a productivity perspective, happy workers are effective workers. By having their bosses show concern for their need to stay connected while at the office, the work efforts of Millennials could be paid back in a very productive manner—a type of quid pro quo.

From a fraud perspective, business managers and owners could be opening their systems up for potential fraud and outside data breaches. By allowing younger workers the ability to access social media accounts while in the office, a decision needs to be made on what system(s) can be used:

- Is it acceptable to allow younger workers to use office computers to check social media accounts, as well as checking private e-mail?
- Should people who want to access social media accounts and private e-mail while at work be forced to bring their personal computers to the office?

- Should office managers set up a separate office computer that is not connected to the main network? This separate computer needs to be free of company-related information, as well as business financial data.

Based on the need of younger workers to stay connected, should it

- Should staying connected, be allowed in the office?
- Be assumed that workers are going to access social media websites from their office workstations?
- Be assumed that workers are going to access private e-mail accounts from their office workstation?

Because accessing social media websites and personal e-mail accounts is accepted in the workplace or conducted behind the backs of managers and owners, it is imperative that the proper fraud awareness and prevention measures are implemented.

Social Media Website Hijacking

For various reasons, as discussed previously in Section V, individuals looking to commit fraud are hijacking the information from existing company websites. This information is then used to create look-alike websites that are similar to or exactly the same as the official site of the targeted organization.

Taking this process a step further, individuals are now falling victim to having their personal social media website hijacked. Unsuspecting social media website account holders are having their legitimate site recreated. Once those looking to commit this type of fraud have established the counterfeit social media site, the friends and contact lists of the true account holders are contacted. These current friends and contacts are prompted to reconnect. Once reconnected to the counterfeit social media website, these friends and contacts are opening a door to potential fraudulent activity.

Just short of creating a counterfeit social media website, many accounts are being compromised for the purposes of conducting fraudulent activity. Due to a successful breach of a social media user's personal computer, information about login information could have been obtained. Once this login information has been obtained, those committing the fraud will change the user login name and password. These individuals now have the ability to post unauthorized information to the victim's social media account. Once an account has been compromised, current friends and contacts are probed for the purpose of fraudulent activity.

The ramifications associated with having a social media account counterfeited or compromised are as follows:

- Once reconnected, current friends and contacts will most likely interact with their known friends as they normally do. If the trust factor remains constant, reconnected friends and contacts will visit websites recommended and click

on links provided. The danger of clicking on the links posted on a counterfeit social media website can lead to the unauthorized downloading of malicious software.
- Individuals reconnecting to their perceived friend or colleague are exposing their current contacts to potential fraud. The individual reconnecting is now in danger of having his or her social media account hijacked or counterfeited. If this takes place, the list of individuals being exposed to the potential of downloading malicious software increases.
- If a social media account is compromised, individuals will post must-see links for the unsuspecting friends to click on. These links could be presented as cute videos, classic cartoons, or heart-tugging appeals to look at the request of a terminally ill individual. The goal is to have the friend or contact click on the link provided. By clicking on the requested link, the friend is opening up his or her computer to the unauthorized downloading of malicious software.

The previously discussed ramifications of accessing counterfeit or compromised social media accounts are many. Those committing these acts do want to have their malicious software downloaded onto the target's individual computer. Additionally, many committing this type of fraud hope that it occurs in the workplace. Ideally, someone at his or her workstation checks his or her social media account and visits a link provided by the perceived friend or contact. If this action takes place, the social media accessing associate is opening up the business computer and systems to the unauthorized downloading of malicious software.

How Is the Internal Business (Customer Information) Accessed?

The question for this section title can have multiple answers. One of the forerunners does come from the use of phishing, spoofing, smishing, and vishing tactics. It is unknown how many data breaches have taken place due to the aforementioned tactics, but an argument can be made that they are effective.

Looking at the overall scope of those looking to conduct data breaches, there are many topics to consider:

- Foreign governments are using the best and brightest computer hackers to gain military and business intelligence.
- Individuals, groups, and countries are looking to do harm to varying government offices and this nation. Based on the funding aspect and intent, the best and the brightest of computer hackers can be employed.
- Anticapitalist hackers are looking to do harm to big business. Many of these individuals are well versed in computer technology. They have the time,

funding, and patience to carry out their attacks. (These individuals are looking at harming business operations from a public relations perspective.)

- Well-funded individuals and countries are looking to access the databases of business operations for the purpose of committing identity theft and financial fraud.
- Some organized criminal groups or gangs have the funding and knowledge to carry out their crimes. The intent of these groups or gangs is now mostly financial in nature. Lillian Ablon of the RAND Corporation states that "ten to fifteen years ago, these were ad hoc networks of individuals motivated by ego. Now it's almost all financial gain" [5].

No matter the motivation factor for those looking to access the information databases of companies large and small, there resides a necessity to develop a thorough understanding of the threats. There is also a necessity to develop an understanding on the avenues of ingress into the computer networks of all businesses.

Based on the size of the business or governmental agency, some of the larger operations employ very knowledgeable computer technicians with the hope of placing the proper barriers in place to prevent such attacks. At times these prevention measures are effective, while at other times they are not.

When discussing data breaches in the national media, the reporting revolves around the incidents where a large corporation or governmental agency was attacked. Very little information is ever reported on the smaller business operations where a breach took place. According to the annual Data Breach Report from the Identity Theft Resource Center, smaller types of business operations are just as likely to fall victim to an attack as the larger organizations reported in the media. Outside the extremely large retail operation, victims also include:

- Small 100-employee business operation
- The corner dental office
- The local independent hotel
- Small-town government office
- A local medical clinic
- Community hospital
- Local community college
- Small chain franchise operation

No matter what the size of the operation is, all businesses where employee and consumer information is housed are potential targets. Unfortunately for those smaller types of operations, budgeting allows for fewer internal controls to prevent such attacks.

As previously referenced it is unsure how all data breaches take place. This is due to pure ignorance of the process, an inability to accurately analyze what took place, and nondiscussion due to potential embarrassment and potentially negative public relations issues. Based on the business or government agency that was breached, there is a reluctance to allow outside individuals to investigate the incident. There is also a reluctance to openly discuss the internal failures that led to the breach.

What is known as to how many successful data breaches have taken place is in the area of phishing e-mails. According to the 2015 Data Breach Investigative Report:

- A large percentage of breaches are coming through unsolicited phishing e-mails. These contain either an infected attachment or a link that leads to the unauthorized downloading of malicious software.
- With regard to phishing e-mails, infected attachments accounted for 40% of the breaches, while an attacked link represented 35%.
- Roughly 23% of those individuals receiving phishing e-mails open the message and about 11% click on the link or open the attachment.
- The study found the median time from opening the e-mail to clicking on the link or opening the attachment was one minute and 22 seconds. After the phishing attempt gained success, about 75% of the attacks were spread to another victim within one day.
- A majority of these phishing types of attacks were preventable [6].

Although phishing (spoofing) attacks do not account for all of the data breaches that take place, the statistics are cause for alarm. They are also cause for the development of a detailed and effective employee awareness and prevention program.

As the use of mobile types of devices increases, so will the smishing and vishing attacks. Educational and employee training programs should be developed to recognize and shut down these types of attacks. As referenced in the Data Breach Investigative Report, a majority of the known attacks could have been prevented.

Separation of Business Computers for Personal and Work-Related Activities

Based on the previous discussion of how a large percentage of younger workers would quit their jobs if they were not able to access social media while at work, it is imperative that proactive prevention measures are employed to protect the business databases. Since a large majority of all known data breaches take place through some type of unauthorized access to the company computers, this is ground zero for proactivity.

- If company policy dictates there will be no accessing of social media accounts while at work, business owners need to ensure they still maintain the most up-to-date antivirus protection software on their computers and systems.

Firewalls need to be put in place to block employee access to social media websites.

- If company policy allows the accessing of social media accounts while at work, there needs to be a separation of computers where access can take place. If an employee needs to access a social media account, employers need to set up a separate computer for this purpose. This computer should not contain any company-related information or data storage. It should not be connected in any way to the actual organization's network.
- If company policy allows the accessing of social media websites while at work and there is no stand-alone computer designated for this purpose, employers need to ensure their antivirus software is up to date and constantly updated. A detailed employee education process has to take place on the threats that can take place through social media access (associate education takes place later in this section).
- If company policy allows the accessing of social media websites while at work and there is no stand-alone computer designated for this purpose, then associates need to be allowed to bring their own computers to the office. Associates can log in through an established secure Wi-Fi connection.

As the use of accessing the Internet increases from a cell phone perspective, employers need to establish policies on using company-designated cell phones for personal use:

- If company policy allows for associates to stay connected to their friends and personal social media accounts while at work, regulations should dictate this activity takes place via a personal cell phone.
- If company policy allows for associates to stay connected to their friends and social media accounts while at work and associates are allowed to use their business-designated cell phones, employees need to be educated on the associated threats (associate education takes place later in this chapter).

Even though there are company policies present against accessing private e-mail and social media accounts while at work, an assumption has to be made that some or many associates will violate the regulations. In order to protect the computer system of any organization, it is vital that prevention measures are put in place:

- Establish strong firewalls within the network to block access to social media websites.
- Ensure the company employs the most up-to-date and effective antivirus software programs.
- Establish a zero tolerance policy for those associates who violate the rules against accessing social media websites while at work.

No matter how an employer wishes to handle the potential of associates accessing social media websites from their office computers, an effort needs to take place to protect the computer systems from unauthorized access. This can be conducted by developing and delivering fraud awareness and prevention programs to all individuals working within the organization. This is to include the entry associate up to the person in charge.

Educating Employees on Computer-Related Fraud (Deliver as Concerned about Individual Victimization)

Business managers, company owners, information technology personnel, and security and loss prevention professionals need to work together to develop the most up-to-date computer-based fraud awareness and prevention program for the organization in question. In an effort to ensure buy-in from all associates, especially the Millennials, the focus of the fraud awareness and prevention program has to be developed and delivered in a manner that shows the company is concerned about protection of the individual associate.

Instead of having a program that consists of *do*s and *don't*s, the information delivered should be explained in detail and include the negative outcomes. These outcomes should also be discussed as they relate to potential negative outcomes for the company and the associate as well. If the training discussion involves a section on what an unsolicited phishing e-mail looks like and the potential ramifications, the trainer should also provide the potential negative ramifications on how this type of attack could hurt the individual associate and his or her personal computer and financial information.

Employers need to show a level of concern about the personal well-being of all associates receiving the training. Computer-related threats can have negative results for a business operation, as well as an individual. The benefits of tailoring a fraud awareness and prevention program in this manner are the following:

- Associates will become more interested in the training if a concern is shown that management actually cares about their individual well-being.
- Associates will practice computer security at home that will carry over into the workplace.
- Associates will develop an understanding of the need of separating work and personal devices and how cross contamination can take place.
- A total team effort in combating fraud will be established.

In addition to developing a fraud awareness and prevention program that includes interest in associate well-being, the following factors should also be part of the organization's fraud awareness and prevention process.

Avoid Using a Personal Cell Phone to Check Company E-Mail

Company policy should dictate against associates checking their company e-mail with their personal cell phones. It is unknown as to how the individual associate uses this personal device and the associate's actual concern for fraud awareness and prevention. The friend base is also unknown, as well as how many friends have an awareness of fraud potential and threats. The unknowing employee could have friends whom they interact with via text messaging and link sharing. If the associate's friends have a low understanding of phishing types of attempts and activity, their potential of downloading malicious software is dangerously high. As discussed in the 2015 Data Breach Investigative Report [6], after a phishing attempt succeeds, about 75% of the attacks are spread to another victim within one day.

Warn against Placing Company Information on Personal Computers and Cell Phones

As previously discussed, how associates use their personal computers and cell phones is unknown. The fraud knowledge and activity of their friends is also unknown.

The more active an individual is on social media websites and sharing links between friends, the greater the risk is for fraudulent activity to take place. Phishing attempts are made through the delivery of unsolicited e-mails. Phishing is becoming more popular with social media websites and there is a history of social media accounts being hijacked, counterfeited, and compromised.

With this information in hand, it is vital that all associates be educated on the negative aspects of placing company-related data and financial information on their personal devices.

Remove the Hyperlink

An effective training tool is the use of visual material. A trainer can discuss what a phishing e-mail would look like or show a copied example. Providing an actual example would have a greater learning effect.

Based on how the training is delivered, caution has to take place. An actual phishing e-mail that contains an attachment or link should never be forwarded via e-mail. If forwarded as a training tool, the links and attachments are still active.

Caution should also be used with the cut/copy and paste method. A trainer could choose to use an actual phishing e-mail and cut/copy and paste the data to a word document. If the document is printed and provided as a visual tool, there is little room for concern. However, if the word document is sent via internal e-mail there is a potential for fraud.

After the information is cut or copied, it needs to be pasted using the text only option. One issue with using the text only option for pasting is that the data does not come across as the original. If pasted as original, there is a potential for fraud. The associated hyperlinks are still active and can be easily accessed.

Even though the information was copied from the original e-mail into a word document and sent via e-mail, the receiver can still access the link or attachment. If a Word document is attached to an e-mail, the receiver can choose to download the document. Once downloaded, all associated training hyperlinks are active. The receiver can place a cursor over the link or attachment and use the control/click option. A browser is opened by the computer and the user is taken to the link or the attachment is opened—basically serving the purpose as intended by the sender.

If a phishing e-mail is copied and pasted as original, the trainer needs to take an extra step prior to forwarding. With an attachment or site link, the trainer needs to place the cursor on the link, right-click the link, and select the "remove hyperlink" option. The actual link wording remains the same, but the link is no longer active.

This leaves the information as delivered, but the receiver cannot use the control/click option to inadvertently access the link or attachment.

Do Not Remember Me

When websites that require the user to enter login information are accessed, there is a potential for fraud. Many browsers allow the user an option of having the computer remember their user name and password to access the site. For simplicity's sake, this is a time-saving tool. From a fraud perspective, it is an option that is not recommended. Computer users need to understand that the browser recognizes the computer and not the user. All the computer knows is that a certain website was previously accessed that required login information. If the site is visited again and the "remember me" option was previously selected, anyone accessing this particular computer will be taken to the protected website.

When a user logs into a user name and password-protected website, some browsers will display a pop-up box offering the user several options:

1. Remember me next time you visit this website
2. Not now
3. Never

All computer users need to select option three. The computer remembers the website and not the user.

The potential for fraud exists if not-so-honest employee A is using the computer at employee B's workstation and the credit card associated with the "remember me" website is company issued. Employee A can gain access to the specific site and make unauthorized purchases that will be charged against the company-issued credit card.

How Can This Remote Computer Affect the National Office?

The best way to answer this question is to look at the workings of a franchise operation. There is a single-store franchisee somewhere in the Midwest. The owner employs a majority of younger workers who are active with their friends via text messaging and social media. Within the single franchise location, the owner has a single computer that is used by all. The younger associates access social media accounts and also check their personal e-mail accounts. The single computer is also used to forward the weekly transmittal of the location's sales information to the national franchisor.

Allowing the employees to visit social media accounts and to check their personal e-mail accounts makes the computer a potential source for the unauthorized downloading of malicious software. If this software is unknowingly downloaded onto the computer of the franchisee, all associated threats become an issue for the main office. The threats are related to all documents forwarded to the parent office from an infected computer.

Hopefully the parent office has the necessary antivirus software in place to prevent the uploading of an infected weekly sales report.

Always Remember to Log Out

No matter what program is used, at home or at work, once one is finished it is necessary to log out. It is not impossible to walk by the workstation or office of a co-worker and see the computer screen. By looking at the screen it is easy to determine that the co-worker has not logged out before leaving the desk. For the normal worker, the mind-set is, "I have done that." For those looking for an opportunity, this provides a perfect avenue for fraud.

This is especially true for someone who has left access open to his or her office or personal e-mail account. If allowed at work, has the worker left an open access to a social media account? Either way, unauthorized access to these types of open accounts can be potentially dangerous to the company computer systems. As referenced, not everyone in the workplace is aboveboard; some may be looking for the perfect avenue to commit fraud. This fraud-related activity is an easier process to conceal if it takes place through the computer of an unknowing co-worker. Additionally, one or more associates in the office may not be liked by everyone in the office. An open computer program at the organization provides a perfect avenue for a revenge type of attack. A vengeful co-worker can use a logged-on office computer to engage in various types of malicious activity.

In order to ensure office computer systems are protected at all times, policy should dictate that, before someone walks away from a computer and workstation, it is necessary to log out of all open programs. Ideally, when someone leaves the workstation or office, the policy should dictate a need to log out completely with a user name and password required to regain access to the computer.

Check with the Social Media Account Provider for Tips on Recognizing a Hacked Account and Necessary Correction/Prevention Measures

Social media accounts are part of the workforce today and will increase in the future. Whether it is acceptable to access these accounts while at work or not, the belief of company managers, owners, and security and loss prevention personnel has to be that company employees will visit social media accounts. In order to prevent a data breach type of attack taking place on the computers, employees need to be educated on what to look for if they suspect their accounts have been hacked, counterfeited, or compromised. The main providers of social (professional) media accounts—Facebook, LinkedIn, Twitter, and Instagram—all provide their users with safety tips, how to recognize a hacked account, prevention measures, etc. It is necessary for all associates to be brought up to date on the fraud-related threats present with social media. Additionally, all associates should be encouraged to visit the websites of their providers and conduct their own fraud awareness research.

Answer the Password Question

Many computer experts advise it is necessary to have employees change their passwords on a routine basis. Usually, the time frames range from 30 to 90 days. Additionally, these experts advise that passwords contain the following:

- At least eight characters in length
- At least one uppercase letter
- At least one lowercase letter
- At least one number
- At least one special character (those goofy looking symbols located above the numbers on the keyboard)

Additionally, there are those in the industry that advise against changing office passwords routinely. The argument is that having associates constantly changing their passwords leads to a memory loss and the need to write down the password on a piece of paper.

No matter on which side of the debate the powers-that-be in a particular organization reside, an agreement should be made that any password should have at least the minimum characteristics previously referenced.

This same level of password protection should also be conveyed to associates for password strength on their private e-mail and social media accounts. This is especially true if policy allows for access to these locations while at work.

Advising associates on the necessity of creating a strong password policy at home and at work shows that there is a concern for employees' well-being from company management. As previously referenced, associates who are shown a concern by management for their individual fraud protection will most likely carry the efforts to the workplace.

Endnotes

1. Identity Theft Resource Center. http://www.idtheftcenter.org/images/breach/ITRC BreachReport2015.pdf (accessed July 26, 2015).
2. In 2015 a large company that specializes in providing infidelity services had its internal records breached. The intent of those who conducted the breach was to have the company close down its operation. "Hackers Target Users of Infidelity Website." *Wall Street Journal*, July 21, 2015.
3. Many banks would set up business operations with a third-party company to process credit card transactions. They would take the customer name and credit card account information from the business owner and use it to receive payment from the actual credit card holder's card-issuing organization (Visa®, MasterCard®, Discover® Card, service station credit cards, etc.).
4. "Three on Your Side: Many Millennials Would Quit If Not Allowed to Do Personal Tasks at Work." http://philadelphia.cbslocal.com/2015/07/08/3-on-your-side-many-millennials-would-quit-if-not-allowed-to-do-personal-tasks-at-work/ (accessed July 26, 2015).
5. "Gangs of Hackers Cause Cyber Breaches to Spike 23%." http://www.usatoday.com/story/tech/2015/04/14/symantec-threat-report/25738203/ (accessed July 27, 2015).
6. "Phones, Phishing and Practical CyberSecurity: Lessons from 2015 Data Breach Investigation Report." http://www.industryweek.com/technology/phones-phishing-and-practical-cybersecurity-lessons-2015-data-breach-investigation-report (accessed July 28, 2015).

Chapter 36

Ransomware

According to Techopedia.com, ransomware is defined as a type of malware program that infects, locks, or takes control of a system and demands ransom to undo it. Ransomware attacks and infects a computer with the intention of extorting money from its owner.

A simple explanation of ransomware can be made with the comparison of a kidnapping. Throughout the history of man, there are those who have kidnapped others for the purpose of collecting a ransom. Once the requested ransom is paid, the kidnap victim is usually released.

When looking at a personal or a business computer, unscrupulous individuals gain unauthorized access to the system for the purpose of committing extortion. Once inside the computer system, the hacker or hackers encrypt the internal data. After the personal or business computer is encrypted, those perpetrating the fraud will demand payment to decrypt the internal files, basically holding the computer system for ransom.

With successful ransomware attacks, the computer users have been known to pay between $200 and $10,000 to have their system decrypted. After the system has been successfully encrypted, the computer user is contacted by those initiating the scam through screen pop-up notices or e-mail messages. These notifications inform the user his or her system is basically being held hostage until a monetary payment is made. If the computer user wishes to make the requested payment, the user is instructed on how to complete the process. Hopefully once the requested payment is made, the accessed files are decrypted.

Two of the most popular types of ransomware are known as Cryptolocker and Cryptowall. Once these types of ransomware are successfully employed, it is almost impossible for the user to access the system to recover the blocked data [1].

Once an individual or business has had a computer system successfully blocked with ransomware, there are three options available:

- Pay the ransom amount requested.
- Use the services of a computer security firm that might be able to restore the data.
- Accept the loss of the data and the computer system and start anew.

From the standpoint of the user, the decision is going to be based on what the encrypted data are worth. From a business perspective, the encrypted data or information could be vital to future success. The same holds true for the individual user and the importance of the data held hostage.

With some of the types of ransomware utilized, the user can hire the services of a computer security firm. The only issue is that these firms cannot guarantee the successful retrieval of the blocked data. Thousands of dollars can be spent up front and the desired data can remain blocked. This leaves the user in the position of having to succumb to the demands of those blocking the system by paying the requested ransom.

However, paying the ransom does not guarantee that the data will be released. Many victims of ransomware keep the attack private, so the actual success rate of paying the requested ransom is unknown. From a business-related perspective, those committing the crime of holding computer data hostage will most likely comply with their end of the reached agreement. If it becomes common knowledge that ransomware hackers are simply collecting the money demanded and not decrypting the related systems, people will eventually accept the loss and not pay. This discussion is just a theory, because it is not an easy process to understand the ethics-related thought process of those committing computer fraud.

In a recent *Wall Street Journal* article titled, "Hacker Ransoms Stir Debate," discussion takes place on the success of ransomware frauds. Experts claim some of the types of ransomware are so successful that it is almost impossible to regain access to the encrypted data. For many, the only option is to pay the requested ransom and hope the files are decrypted once the money is paid [1].

In order to avoid becoming a victim of ransomware, all computer users need to understand the necessity of protecting their systems from unauthorized access. The access is gained through successful breaches into the system. As discussed previously in Chapter 35, a majority of computer breaches are made via phishing activity. In order for ransomware activity to take place, hackers need to breach the system. By developing an understanding of phishing-related activities, the prevention process for ransomware has a beginning.

In addition to ransomware success with computer systems, the activity has graduated to various types of mobile phones. As with the computer, mobile phone ransomware operates in the same manner. Internal files and programs are encrypted and held hostage. Once a requested ransom is paid, the files and programs are decrypted.

When looking at the mobile phone ransomware access tactics, they fall in line with those used for the computer: successful breaches made through phishing type activities.

Endnote

1. "Hacker Ransoms Stir Debate." *Wall Street Journal*, November 10, 2015.

Appendix A: Organized Retail Crime Associations

As discussed in Section IV, Chapter 27, organized retail crime is an issue for retailers that has been around for a number of years and that is not going away. In an effort to combat the growing crime problem, numerous associations have been formed both nationally and within individual states. Following is a listing of the known organized-retail-crime associations in the United States.

National Associations

Coalition of Law Enforcement and Retail (CLEAR); https://www.clearusa.org/
National Anti-Organized Retail Crime Association, Inc.; http://naorca.org/

State or Regional Associations

Alaska Organized Retail Crime Alliance (AORCA); https://akorca.org/
Arizona Organized Retail Crime Association (AZORCA); https://azorca.org/?AspxAutoDetectCookieSupport=1
California Organized Retail Crimes Association (Cal-ORCA); https://cal-orca.org/default.aspx?menuitemid=574&menugroup=Public+About
Carolina's Organized Retail Crime Alliance (CORCA); https://corca.org/
Central New York Organized Retail Crime Alliance (CNYORCA); https://cnyorca.org/
Collier County Organized Retail Theft Association (CCORTA); http://www.ccorta.org/
Colorado Organized Retail Crime Alliance (CORCA); https://coorca.org/?AspxAutoDetectCookieSupport=1

Dallas/Fort Worth Organized Retail Crime Association (DFWORCA); https://dfworca.org/

Florida Organized Retail Crime Enforcement Network (FORCEN); https://www.linkedin.com/grps/Florida-Organized-Retail-Crime-Enforcement-2488473/about?

Hawaii Organized Retail Crime Alliance (HIORCA); http://www.hiorca.org/

Indiana Retail Organized Crime Coalition (IndianaROCC); http://www.indianaroc.org/?AspxAutoDetectCookieSupport=1

Missouri Organized Retail Crimes Association (MORCA); https://miacx.org/default.aspx?menuitemid=504&menugroup=_Home

New England Organized Retail Crime Alliance (NEORCA); https://neorca.org/

New York Metro Organized Retail Crime Alliance (NYMORCA); https://nymorca.org/

Northern California Organized Retail Crime Association (NCORCA); http://www.roseville.ca.us/police/ncorca.asp

Northern Nevada Organized Retail Crime Association (NNORCA); https://nnorca.org/

Northwest Organized Retail Crime Alliance (NWORCA); https://www.linkedin.com/grps/Northwest-Organized-Retail-Crime-Alliance-6641988/about?

Ohio Regional Organized Crime Coalition (OROCC); https://orocc.org/

Organized Retail Crime Association of Idaho (ORCAID); https://orcaid.org/

Philadelphia Organized Retail Crime Alliance (PORCA); https://www.facebook.com/Philadelphia-Organized-Retail-Crime-Alliance-776373382473502/

Pittsburgh Organized Retail Crime Coalition (PORCC); https://www.linkedin.com/grps?gid=4118944

San Diego Organized Retail Crime Association (SDORCA); https://sdorca.org/?AspxAutoDetectCookieSupport=1

Southern Nevada Organized Retail Crime Association (SNORCA); https://snorca.org/?AspxAutoDetectCookieSupport=1

Twin Cities Organized Retail Crime Association (TCORCA); https://www.tcorca.org/

Utah Organized Retail Crime Association (UORCA); https://utorca.org/?AspxAutoDetectCookieSupport=1

Virginia Retail Merchants Association (VRMA); http://www.virginiaretail.org/

Washington State Organized Retail Crime Alliance (WSORCA); https://wsorca.org/?AspxAutoDetectCookieSupport=1

Appendix B: Examples of Phishing E-Mails

EXAMPLE 1
From: Peter Dargle ppddydargle@email.com
To:
Subject: Investment
Hello,
My name is Peter Dargle and i want to confirm to you my interest to invest good money with trust,I know this message will definitely come to you as a huge surprise but i implore you to consider it for mutual benefit,i have a business proposition involving a huge sum of money 12.5 million If you will be kind enough to grant me the permission,I'll be glad to give further details.kindly reply me via my private-email: ptdgle@gmail.com
Thank You,
Peter

In this example the hope of the sender is for the recipient to click on the e-mail link provided. With these types of phishing e-mails, the "phisherman" is looking for someone to "bite" on the link provided. Also notice the poor punctuation, use of lowercase i, and poor grammar. No information is provided in the "To" line of the e-mail.

EXAMPLE 2
From: American Express ama@send.com
To: jyoungblood5@cox.net
Subject: Account Verification

Security Notice

�

You are receiving this e-mail because we noticed an attempt to sign in to your account from an unrecognised device. Our system has blocked this sign in attempt as a security measure.

In order to safeguard your account information we have temporarily restricted your access to certain features within our online system. To restore full access please click the link below to validate your account information.

Restore Access ↣

Please note: Failure to restore full access can lead to permanent suspension of access.

�

Best Regards
American Express Customer Services

�

Security Notice

�

You are receiving this email because we noticed an attempt to sign in to your account from an unrecognised device. Our system has blocked this sign in attempt as a security measure.

In order to safeguard your account information we have temporarily restricted your access to certain features within our online system. To restore full access please click the link below to validate your account information.

Restore Access ↣

Please note: Failure to restore full access can lead to permanent suspension of access.

�

Best Regards
American Express Customer Services

The intent of those sending this phishing e-mail is to have the recipient believe there is an issue with his or her American Express account. Some recipients might take the bait and click on the "Restore Access" link provided. However, I do not have an American Express account.

Anyone clicking on the link provided will most likely be taken to a professional looking website where the individual is asked to provide personal verifying information. If the information is provided, it will most likely be used for identity theft. Additionally, clicking on the link provided will allow the unauthorized downloading of malicious software.

The end goal of those sending the e-mail is to have the recipient click on the link provided, provide the requested information, and believe issues with his or her account have been corrected.

EXAMPLE 3
From: Chase Notification onlinesecure@customerservice.com
To: jyoungblood5@cox.net
Subject: Confirm your identification!

CHASE

Dear Chase Online℠ Customer:

There were multiple attempt to access your online banking from an UNRECOGNIZED computer other than yours.

And as out latest security, we screen all our customers account to make sure you are safe from online theft.

For your security and safety, we have placed a temporary inactive notice on this account. To confirm this was done in error or was not authorized by you. Click on www.Chase.com and verify to us your online banking session.

Thank you.

Sincerely,

Online Banking Team

In this example, the receiver is led to believe an unauthorized individual was attempting to access his or her bank account online. The goal is to have the receiver click on the Chase.com link, which will open the receiver's system to the unauthorized downloading of malware/spyware. The user may be asked to provide verifying information, such as a Social Security number, date of birth, account number, etc. If provided, the verifying information can be used to commit identity fraud.

EXAMPLE 4

From: FedEx International Economy jesus.mercer@ip-23-229-226-98.ip.secureserver.net
To:
Subject: Shipment delivery problem #0000796785
Dear Customer,
Your parcel has arrived at September 05. Courier was unable to deliver the parcel to you.
Please, download Delivery Label attached to this email.
Thanks and best regards,
Jesus Mercer,
FedEx Operation Manager.
Open Attachment FedEx_ID_0000796785.zip

In this example the recipient is led to believe that a package delivery from a well known organziation was missed. Many people might not know who could have sent them a package. This unknown works to create a level of curiosity, which can lead to the recipient clicking on the attachment.

As with any phishing e-mail, the goal is to have the recipient click on the attachment link for the purpose of downloading unauthorized malware/spyware.

EXAMPLE 5

From: County Court tom.mullins@bacma.co.uk
To:
Subject: Notice to appear in Court #00898179
Notice to Appear,
This is to inform you to appear in the Court on the October 07 for your case hearing. Please, do not forget to bring all the documents related to the case.
Note: If you do not come, the case will be heard in your absence.
The copy of Court Notice is attached to this email.
Kind regards,
Tom Mullins,
Clerk of Court.
Open Attachment Notice_to_Appear_00898179.zip

In this example the recipient is led to believe that he or she has an upcoming court apperance. The goal of the sender is to have the recipient believe that he or she might have missed a mailed summons and the e-mail is another attempt at notification. As with all phishing e-mails, the hope is that the recipient clicks on the attachment link.

EXAMPLE 6
From:
To: Recipients
Subject: RE
BRITISH SAMSUNG COMPENSATION
1000 SURREY KT16 0PS,
HILLS WOOD DRIVE CHERTSEY,
LONDON UNITED KINGDOM
TEL: +448712370371

We the staff and member of British Samsung Award Compensation wishes to congratulate you as the first among our Ten (10) Star Lucky Winners of the Email Lottery draw, held on Monday 12th of October 2015, in London United Kingdom.

This makes you a proud owner of Two Hundred and Fifty Thousand United State Dollar ($250,000.00USD) with Advanced version of 52 Inches Plasma TV and Latest version of Samsung S6 Edge Smart Phone, Attached with Ticket Number (BSEP6904523).

And for you to begin your claim urgently provide the below details to: prizeclaimunit@live.co.uk for immediate commencement

1. Full Names.
2. Mobile Number.
3. Complete address/State/Country.
4. Age/Sex/Marital Status
5. Occupation.
6. And Scanned Copy of Any Valid ID Proof Recognized by the Government of your Country for Proof of Ownership.

Please be informed that all Winners must claim their Prize without further delay as to avoid disqualification of Award Prize.
Yours Sincerely,
Mr. Patrick John (OVERSEAS CLAIM MANAGER)

The goal of this phishing e-mail is to have the recipient believe he or she has won a prize in a contest the recipient did not enter. If the recipient takes the bait and clicks on the link provided, the system could be opened up to the downloading of unauthorized software. By providing the personal information requested, the recipient could be a future victim of identity fraud.

EXAMPLE 7
From: WhatsApp Service drgoalkeeper@bergware.net
To:
Subject: [Spam] New voice mail - 1:03PM

WhatsApp

Missed voicemail.

Description

Oct 25 1:03 PM
09 seconds

Play

© Whats App

The purpose of this phishing e-mail is to have the WhatsApp user believe a new service was added to use to check voicemail. What is actually taking place is the hope the recipient clicks on the "Play" button.

Thinking that this might be a new feature that WhatsApp developed, chances are the recipient might want to click on the "Play" button, which will lead to a malicious website that will download and install a file called "Browser 6.5" on an android phone. If users then click the "Agree" button in the "browser," text messages will be sent to premium-rate phone numbers. The scammers will also try to convince users to download another malicious app [1].

EXAMPLE 8
From: Janice Allen barbara.riekert@lvbprint.de
To:
Subject: [Spam] Fwd: permanent weight secret of success
it's just my recommendation to you
http://thermokingindia.com/start/?42
this amazing fat loss supplement worked for me and i'm sure it can work for you!
take care,
Janice

The intent of this poorly constructed, unsolicited e-mail is to have the recipient believe he or she can access a weight loss supplement. By clicking on the link provided, the recipient is taken to a website where unauthorized malicious software is downloaded.

EXAMPLE 9
From: ian@higginsonequip.com ian@higginsonequip.com
To: XXXXXXX@cox.net
Subject: billing_conf.doc (368.8 KB)
Hi.I have made an order from [$DOMAIN] one week ago.
I have received the billing confirmation but nothing else.
You can find it attached, please let me know what is going on.
David Haggard
CMIT Solutions of Newport Beach
4000 Barranca, Suite 250, Irvine, CA 92604
Work Phone - 949.653.1393 x1015
Fax Number - 949.612.0831
Open Attachment billing_conf.doc

The sender of this phishing e-mail is using the name of an actual IT Services Company located in California, as well as the company address and a close variation of the contact number. For the numbers listed in the e-mail, both are non-working numbers.

The sender hopes the recipient recognizes the company name or believes there is an issue with the domain provider. If the bait is taken, the recipient clicks on the attachment link and can then be asked for personal information in order to clear up a billing issue with a perceived account. What is most likely to take place is the unauthorized downloading of malicious software.

EXAMPLE 10
From: Margred Cooper foste@jclc.com
To: XXXXXXX@usa.net
From: [Spam] You have 1 unread private message from Margred Cooper

---

LinkedIn

Margred Cooper sent you private message

Date: 10/25/2015

http://www.linkedin.com/do?action=viewMessage&q=member&id=6819713

View/reply to this message

Don't want to receive e-mail notifications? Adjust your message settings.

© 2015, LinkedIn Corporation

The sender of this unsolicited phishing e-mail uses the name of the professional organization of LinkedIn. LinkedIn members do actually receive e-mail alerts if one of their contacts has sent them a message. However, legitimate LinkedIn alerts are formatted differently and provide the name and photo of the sender.

With this particular notification message, the name used was not a contact of the recipient. With many LinkedIn members having over 500 contacts, it is quite possible the recipient will assume the name used is one of his or her contacts.

The overall goal is to have the recipient click on the link provided so that malicious software can be downloaded onto the computer.

EXAMPLE 11
From: "Investments Portal" info@investments-portal.info
To: XXXXXXX@usa.net
From: Energy Company Cash flowing, Selling @ $18/mcf, Commences drilling
China is going to great lengths to satisfy its growing hunger for energy to fuel its expanding car fleet and electrify its swelling cities. The country has an insatiable appetite for Energy and it's only getting bigger. The long term government policy led support for gas means pricing and other dynamics make it one of the best end markets in the world

One of Asia's wealthiest families thinks so and is placing its bet on one undiscovered company to supply the massive demand.

Asia is unaffected by North American gas prices. Primeline Energy receives $18/mcf. That's 5X the price that is paid in North America!

The company has $50m in cash and is about to spud an exploration well which it is very optimistic about. McDaniel says that its COS is as high as 78% which is extremely positive. If it should come in, any gas could very quickly be tied in as there is spare capacity in the pipeline. With one well to drill and probably two more behind it the shares are looking incredibly attractive.

INVESTMENT HIGHLIGHTS:

- Mergers with Primeline Petroleum Corporation and Loyz Energy to create a leading Pan-Asia/Pacific E&P company.
- Enlarged company has production in China and Thailand and exploration upside in both countries, Australia, the Philippines and New Zealand.
- Leverage their access to their $700m+ regional production infrastructure hub in East China Sea.
- Production and cashflow from LS36-1 gasfield and fully funded 2015 2 well exploration programme in China.
- Depressed natural gas prices in Canada are locked into the supply/demand reality of North America. The supply/demand situation for oil and gas is very different in China. Primeline has a price of $18/mcf guaranteed in long-term contracts.
- Significant gap between share price and intrinsic value makes way for exceptional returns.

CATALYSTS:

Drilling to commence imminently. http://www.stockwatch.com/News/Item.aspx?bid=Z-C:PEH-2311593&symbol=PEH˙ion=C

The East China Sea is a very significant gas resource. Primeline has identified excellent locations for exploratory wells. Its drilling partner is a Chinese national oil company, China National Offshore Oil Corp. (CNOOC - CEO:NYSE]

VALUATION:

178M outstanding *.20 = $35.6M mkt cap.

MAJOR SHAREHOLDERS:

Victor Hwang – 70%
Fidelity – 7%

GEMS finances a US $20m convertible bond (exercisable @.75 CDN) to provide funds for the forthcoming interesting exploration program in Block 33/07;

General Enterprise Management Services (GEMS) is an Asian private equity group with a core focus in the natural resources sector. Since 1998 GEMS has managed over $850 million of capital commitments GEMS concentrates on identifying companies with strong ties to Asia that we consider to have well defined assets or projects, excellent growth potential, and qualified management teams.

We are sorry if we sent you this email by accident. Please unsubscribe here: Unsubscribe me from this list

The purpose of this unsolicited e-mail is to get the recipient to believe in the opportunity to get involved in an investment opportunity. The goal of the sender is to have the recipient click on either of the two links provided to gain additional information on the opportunity. If either link is clicked on, the individual could be taken to a website with investment-related information. What is also taking place is the unauthorized downloading of malicious software.

It is also important that unsolicited e-mail recipients use caution if selecting the "unsubscribe" link. If a person clicks on this option, he or she will most likely receive a confirmation e-mail that the recipient will no longer receive additional messages. What actually takes place is that the computer user is opening his or her system to the downloading of malicious software.

EXAMPLE 12

From: jyoungblood5@cox.net bfleming@nantucket.net
To: jyoungblood5@cox.net
Subject: Erection Meds
Buy it
http://luckypillsquality.ru

This unsolicited phishing e-mail also goes along the lines of a spoofing e-mail. The only problem is that I am led to believe I sent myself this message.

With this type of unsolicited phishing e-mail, the goal is to have the recipient click on the link to purchase the advertised product in the subject line. The computer user might be taken to a website with a medication discussion, but through the back door he is becoming a victim of malicious software downloading.

EXAMPLE 13
From: Automation YouTube Reminder comercialn@elviramatilde.com.br
To:
Subject: Caution, You have missed notifications publicizing

YouTube

You have missed notification.

View notifications.

Regards
YouTube support

© 2015 YouTube, LLC 901 Cherry Ave, San Bruno, CA 94066. This notification was sent to XXXXXXXXXXX@usa.net because you indicated that you are willing to receive occasional YouTube product-related notifications. If you do not wish to receive such notifications in the future, please unsubscribe. You can also change your preferences by visiting your Email Options in your YouTube account.

The senders of this phishing e-mail use the name of a popular social media site. When creating the e-mail they used the actual address for the YouTube Corporation in California. The intent of this e-mail is to get the recipient to believe he or she has received a notification from YouTube. By clicking on the "View notifications" link, the recipient is subjecting the computer to the unauthorized downloading of malicious software.

EXAMPLE 14

From: Google Reminder fabien.prevost@hraccess.com
To:
Subject: Hey missed notifications bicycles

Google

Missed notification.

View notifications.

Regards
Google service

This notification was sent to timreddick@usa.net; don't want occasional updates about Google activity and friend suggestions? Change what notification Google sends you. Google Inc., 1600 Amphitheatre Pkwy, Mountain View, CA 94043 USA

This unsolicited phishing e-mail follows in line with the previous example that used the name of a well known company. Like YouTube, Google is also popular among computer users. The recipient could be led to believe he or she has received a notification from Google and click on the link provided. By clicking on the "View notifications" link, the recipient is opening the computer up to the downloading of malicious software.

EXAMPLE 15

From: Google Corporation [mailto:zheweifei@xinhuamed.com.cn]
Sent: Tuesday, 3 November 2015 11:11 PM
Subject: CONGRATULATIONS!
Dear Winner,
Click on the attached to View your Winning notification letter.
Congratulations!
MD. Matt Brittin
Chairman of Board and Managing Director
Google United Kingdom
Open Attachment GOOGLE ANNIVERSARY WINNING NOTIFICATION.pdf Open Attachment GOOGLE ANNIVERSARY WINNING NOTIFICATION.pdf

In this phishing example the recipient is led to believe that Google conducted a contest in which the recipient is a winner. It is important for anyone receiving an e-mail referencing winning a contest to think back to determine if he or she recently entered a contest.

By using the name of an organization known throughout the world, it is hoped the recipient clicks on the notification attachment.

There are two different scenarios that can result from clicking on the attachment link. The recipient is asked to provide detailed personal information in order to claim the prize. Instead of receiving the promised prize, this personal information is used to commit identity fraud.

The other scenario is that the attachment allows the unauthorized downloading of malicious software.

EXAMPLE 16

From: dhl International express [mailto:dhlnternationalexpress@mail.com]
To: undisclosed-recipients:
Subject: Your Shipping Document Delivery Date
Attachments: DHL Line Express tracking.html (4.3 KB)

Dear Sir/Madam,

Please find your newly posted invoice(s) and BL for your shipments and services through DHL Express. Before your package gets to you, see the attachment file to track your package to know it's current location, and exactly when it will get to you, and view your package current status.

Kindly keep the viewed information safe, we will need you to provide them for confirmation before delivering your parcel.

We would like to thank you for accepting the services of DHL Express.

With kind regards,

DHL Team

DHL

The purpose of this phishing e-mail is to get the recipient to believe that a package is being shipped to him or her. Not knowing the sender or the purpose of the shipment, it is likely the e-mail recipient will be curious and click on the tracking attachment. By clicking on the attachment, the recipient is exposing a personal or business computer to the downloading of malicious software.

EXAMPLE 17
Subject: Update Your XXXXXXXX University Webmail
Date: November 16, 2015
We temporarily locked your **XXXXXXXX University** webmail account from sending messages, Our system has detected unusual virus in your Inbox and trash folder, We advice you to empty your trash folder and update your email account for Security maintenance and protection of your email from virus attacks. We recommend that you update your account to avoid termination.
UPDATE
Thanks,
The System Administrator Management Team

This phishing e-mail example is basically a template for those looking to have current and former college students believe there is an issue with their university-based webmail account. Numerous variations have been used with the difference being the university name used. The goal is to have the recipient click on the UPDATE link to correct issues with the account. After clicking on the link the recipient is most likely taken to a legitimate looking website that asks the user to provide verification information. Once the recipient's personal information is provided, he or she is advised the issue has been corrected.

The e-mail recipient believes the issue has been resolved and goes about his or her business. Those sending the phishing e-mail were most likely able to download malicious software and collect personal information that can be used for identity theft.

EXAMPLE 18
From: Verizon Notification
To:
Subject: Important Notice: Please verify your Email Address
Dear Valued Verizon Customer,
Security settings updated, please verify your email and help us provide a safe envioremeent for all our users. To verify this email address, please select the 'Verify Email Address' link below and enter your credentials.
Verify Email Address
Verifying your email address improves the security of your Verizon account. Once you've verified your email address, you will be able to:

- Get important updates about your account and services
- Receive a code for your online account if you forget your password or get locked out
- Protect your identity and help keep your account secure

Thank you for choosing Verizon.
Sincerely,
Your Verizon Team

The purpose of this phishing e-mail is to have the recipient believe Verizon cares about the quality of service provided to its customers by providing additional account security. The goal is to have the recipient click on the "Verify Email Address" link and provide the information requested. As with a majority of e-mails of this nature, the recipient is providing personal information that can be used for identity theft, as well as exposing the system to unauthorized downloading of malicious software. It is important to notice the misspelling of the word "environment" and the absence of a contact phone number.

Endnote

1. WhatsAPP Scams. http://scam-detector.com/online-auction-scams/whatsapp-voice mail-scam (accessed October 26, 2015).

Index

This index includes the foreword, endnotes, and appendices. Page numbers in italics refer to figures.

F

G

H

R

S

U

V

W

Y

For Product Safety Concerns and Information please contact our EU
representative GPSR@taylorandfrancis.com
Taylor & Francis Verlag GmbH, Kaufingerstraße 24, 80331 München, Germany

www.ingramcontent.com/pod-product-compliance
Lightning Source LLC
LaVergne TN
LVHW011110300926
849160LV00008B/337
9781498742436